# RE-WRITE YOUR LIFE

## *A Transformational Guide to Writing and Healing the Stories of Our Lives*

by June D.Swadron

Order this book online at www.trafford.com
or email orders@trafford.com

Most Trafford titles are also available at major online book retailers.

Cover painting by Nikki Menard
Sketches by Josée Hart
Excerpt from *Journey to Personal Freedom* with permission from Heart Solutions, publisher.

Printed in Victoria, BC, Canada.

ISBN: 978-1-4251-0294-4 (sc)

*Our mission is to efficiently provide the world's finest, most comprehensive book publishing
service, enabling every author to experience success. To find out how to publish your book,
your way, and have it available worldwide, visit us online at www.trafford.com*

Trafford rev. 11/4/2009

 www.trafford.com

North America & international
toll-free: 1 888 232 4444 (USA & Canada)
phone: 250 383 6864 ♦ fax: 812 355 4082

# Further Praise for Re-Write Your Life

"This book is wonderful, amazing and wise. I was inspired to write from the very first pages. But it does more than simply inspire – it is a map. It guides its readers, with signposts and specific details, in how to write their life stories. As a hospice counsellor, I lead journaling groups to help people express and work through their grief, but for many it is hard to continue this process when alone. *Re-write Your Life* provides the encouragement and support needed for anyone to begin and continue on their own. I would recommend it to any of my grieving clients, and to anyone at all who wants to examine their life to find healing and joy and discover the sheer pleasure of writing their life story."

Steve Silvers, MA, MFT, Hospice Counsellor, Licensed Marriage and Family Therapist

"June guides us through a gentle process that is both healing and empowering. ...my past no longer haunts me but enriches and enlightens me to a new aliveness. ...a true gift to myself."

Rev. Doris Trinh Lewis, Unity Church, Victoria, BC

"June's raw honesty with her personal stories sets the tone for an inspirational book that will nudge all readers to open up to writing their own experiences. The stories here are moving, some heart wrenching, and truly awaken more appreciation for life; they speak to the ability of the human spirit to transcend circumstances, accidents, dysfunctional families and all challenges, and most definitely remind us that by writing our own stories, we can gain a deeper insight into our lives. Anyone reading these stories will be lifted up!"

Melba Burns, Ph.D. writer, writing coach, author of *Woo Your Writing Within & You'll Write with Wonder.*

# Workshop testimonials in Appendix B

# TABLE OF CONTENTS

Dedications .................................................................................. v

Acknowledgements ..................................................................... ix

Foreword ...................................................................................... xi

Introduction ................................................................................ xv

Getting Ready ............................................................................. xix

Part A ............................................................................................. 1

  Chapter 1.   Beginnings: Looking Back To Step Forward .................. 3

  Chapter 2.   Opening To Grace A Personal Story ............................... 9

  Chapter 3.   Finding The Gift ................................................................. 13

Part B............................................................................................. 17

  Guidelines How To Use This Book ...................................... 19

  Guidelines For Writing Your Life Stories .......................... 23

Part C ........................................................................................... 31

  Centering Exercise Before Writing .................................... 33

Part D ........................................................................................... 35

  Invocation – Opening To The Gifts .................................... 37

Stories........................................................................................... 39

  Chapter 1.   Gratitude ............................................................................ 41

  Chapter 2.   Teachers And Mentors..................................................... 49

  Chapter 3.   A Time In My Life When I Was Stronger Than I
                Thought .............................................................................. 57

  Chapter 4.   A Significant Relationship ............................................... 73

  Chapter 5.   A Significant Move............................................................ 79

  Chapter 6.   Occupation/Career............................................................ 91

  Chapter 7.   Spirituality/Religion ........................................................ 99

  Chapter 8.   Your Birth Story.............................................................. 111

  Chapter 9.   About My Father............................................................. 121

Chapter 10.   About My Mother ........................................................ 129

Chapter 11.   About My Sisters And Brothers ................................. 143

Chapter 12.   About Children ............................................................ 153

Chapter 13.   On Forgiveness ............................................................ 159

Chapter 14.   Transitions & Crossroads .......................................... 175

Chapter 15.   A Health Setback: An Illness, An Accident ............. 183

Chapter 16.   Death Of A Loved One ............................................... 193

Chapter 17.   Another Kind Of Death: The Death Of Your Spirit.... 205

Chapter 18.   Letting Go .................................................................... 217

Chapter 19.   Holidays ....................................................................... 225

Chapter 20.   Re-Write Your Life: The Highest Vision You Hold For
Yourself ...................................................................... 231

In Conclusion .................................................................................... 237

Appendix A ........................................................................................ 239

Appendix B ........................................................................................ 243

# ACKNOWLEDGEMENTS

I THANK ESTHER Hart whose invaluable skill, commitment, kindness and deep love have made the completion of this book possible.

From the day she said YES to helping me see my book to the finishing line, there has only been delight. When I have been overwhelmed by the immensity of this task, her consistent joy, ease and enthusiasm erased any doubt in me. Instead her joy was contagious enabling me to come to these pages with passion and purpose. Because of Esther I have experienced what it is to be believed in and know the glorious gift of love without conditions.

I thank Eric Hellman, Shoshana Litman, Rebecca Kennel, Darlene McKee. Nadine Drexler, Tom Little and Debbi Jones for their fine edits, comments and suggestions that helped to move this book forward.

I thank Nikki Menard for creating my beautiful soul painting. I feel blessed that her artistry graces the front cover of my book. It was when I saw her creation that it all became real for me. I could, for the first time, visualize *Re-Write Your Life* in print. What a gift!

I thank Teya Danel who, with Nikki's input, did an exceptional job of the layout and design of the book cover.

I thank Josée Hart for her creativity and skill as an artist in designing the quill and pen graphics that introduce each story and the Let's Write sections.

I thank my hundreds of students over the years who have shared their life stories with me. Week after week they sat in our sacred circles (usually in my living room) willing to write and read with open hearts their stories of both love and loss. They wrote deep into their truth thus always uniting us with their honest tears or unbridled laughter.

They taught me about the many gifts that await us when we are willing to remove our masks and open to our divine nature. They reinforced in me the unmistakable knowledge that this process works.

I thank them for gracing my home and my life with their kindest and most authentic love.

I thank each of the 33 men and women who contributed their beautiful stories *to Re-Write Your Life*. I thank them for the gift of their words and especially, their hearts. Many of them attended my workshops. They filled my heart with gratitude as they moved through the process with faith and courage. Each story in this book gives the reader beautiful, personal, heartwarming stories to read and, I am certain, inspiration to pick up their pens and begin to write their own.

There is a complete listing of contributors in Appendix A.

# FOREWORD

WHO WROTE the book of love? June Swadron; and this is it. It has been my pleasure to work with June on *Re-Write Your Life* for the last eight months. She has been working on it for a much longer time.

June was a very dear friend before we started to work together on the book. She has been a blessing to me, always quick to remind me that "You are the gift" even when it was hard for me to hear it.

I have been blessed to participate in one of the groups that June facilitated. I know first hand the love that she brings to the room. She creates a safe atmosphere that allows people to go deep into their experiences, share their writing in the group and experience transformational healing from *Re-Writing* their story.

I've come to realize that most of my experience comes from stories I tell myself. Something occurs and then I make up a story about it. I ignore what actually happened and live in the story. When I look at the story closely, I usually find that based on what actually happened there are many others stories that could be just as true. June's facilitation allows us to uncover another story so that we can be at peace with our past.

The stories that you and I are privileged to read in *Re-Write Your Life* are a testament to the love and support that June offers each individual in the group as they experience the healing that comes from Re-Writing the stories of their lives.

I am pleased that June is sharing her special talent now with a much wider audience through *Re-Write Your Life*. Now an unlimited number of people can benefit from the process that June has developed over many years of facilitating groups.

Throughout the book you will also read June's stories. What she shares with others comes from her own personal experience of healing her life stories through writing. Working with her on the book gave me an even deeper glimpse of her willingness to be completely vulnerable in order to get to the truth of her stories.

Just the other day we were commenting on how beautiful the book creation process has been for us. There has been no conflict. June listened to every edit suggestion with amazing openness even when she didn't agree. Our friendship has deepened and our life journey has been blessed by the experience. I am confident that this is because both of us have very consciously Re-Written the stories of our lives, continue to do so on a daily basis and now have a much better ability to be in relationship.

My hope is that as you go through the book, follow the suggestions and Re-Write the stories of your life, you will find peace, joy and freedom even when your external world is in chaos; that you will create a habit of looking closely at the stories that are forming your experience and see where Re-Writing a story can change a troubled experience to a more peaceful one.

Allow June to be your guide to remembering who you really are.

Esther Hart
Author of *Journey to Personal Freedom* and coming soon *The Giggle Factor*.


p.s. There is great reading in this book and you may be deeply inspired by what you read. However, the greatest benefit from this book will be when you put it down to do the writing exercises. When you have completed the process, you may wish to start over again to see what new stories wish to be written. At the very least, I encourage you to continue writing. You may even consider forming a group of trusted friends to join you in working through the book.

# Forming A Sacred Circle
## To Write Your Life Stories

WRITING AND sharing your life stories with others in a safe, non-judgmental environment is an awesome, empowering and potentially life-changing experience. (See student testimonials in Appendix B).

Safety, caring, compassion and kindness are critical for the success of this process. June calls her workshops, "Sacred Circles." It is important that they not become critique groups. If they become that, the freedom for a person to write and share their personal stories will be greatly diminished. Our souls flourish in a safe, non-judgmental environment. We grow strong in an atmosphere of kindness and respect, knowing we are being supported exactly as we are.

If you are interested in facilitating your own *Re-Write Your Life* workshops with friends or family, using June's uniquely designed programme, you can download: *Re-Write Your Life - Manual for Facilitating Workshops* on June's website. www.juneswadron.com.

# INTRODUCTION

I F YOU are holding this book and reading this page, consider it no accident. Just as your life has been no accident – nor whatever you have lived, and whomever you have known. None of it has been helter skelter. At least that is what I have come to believe.

Universal intelligence and guidance has been there with us and for us in every moment. Everything that happens to us happens for a reason even if we can't make sense of it at the time. Yet, looking back somewhere down the road, we can say "Ah, yes, this is why that happened. I was put in this direction, which led me to meet up with the man who then became my mentor." or "Who would have guessed that the woman who caused the accident where I was severely injured would soon become my dearest friend?"

When we carefully look back over some of the situations we have lived, we can begin to make sense of the pieces of the puzzle that had left us with questions over time.

The focus of this book is to write the stories of our lives in such a way that will uncover the inherent truths in every story – in every situation we've lived – even the very painful ones – or shall I say, especially those. Often the people and events that have presented the biggest burdens are our greatest teachers.

In *Writing Your Life,* author Patti Miller illustrates it this way:

"Exploring your life through the written word offers: growth in self-knowledge and understanding, the sorting through of problems, the possibility of forgiveness and the freedom to make a new start, the joy of realizing unknown strengths, the pleasure of reliving good times and the value of sharing your experiences with others, including others in the future."

The processes offered in this book ask you to be a willing and loving witness to your life while letting go of old perceptions, resentments and/or hurts. It will assist you to stop investing precious energy in past memories or in future possibilities. It will propel you to live today with full appreciation for whatever this day brings.

This process does not have to be difficult. When we take the position that everything that's happened to us has happened for a reason, we then can become the observer and witness to our stories. We are no longer the victims of circumstance. We become detectives, sleuths and anthropologists – excavating that which has been buried or hidden. We become social scientists, observing our behavior, manners, beliefs, attitudes and actions that have helped shape our lives. We see what has been effective and what hasn't. We are on an exciting journey of self-discovery.

As you move through the pages of this book, I wish to be your invisible, kind and loving witness while you revisit and embrace the milestones that have made your life rich with meaning – the challenging and painful times as well as the exciting and joyful ones. You will bring new clarity and understanding to old circumstances, put closure on unfinished business, laugh and cry at the meanderings of your life and bring to the present a new respect and reverence for the blessings of every day.

Some of my life stories are inserted throughout the pages of this book. Often these stories were not written as a narrative after the fact, but while I was deep in the throes of what was going on. This may be your experience as well. Even if you are writing about something that happened twenty years ago, it is the energy that you carry with you today that defines it and gives you an opportunity to be with it, learn from it, and if necessary, release it and let it go.

Besides my own stories, woven throughout these pages, there are many remarkable true life stories written by 33 other writers. The majority have been students of my writing life stories workshop series, *"Sacred Stories – Celebrating Your Life Journey"*. The students followed the same memory prompts you will find throughout this book. It is my hope that, in reading these true life accounts, you will know that you are not alone, and that you will pick up your pen and join us in our united journey of Re-Writing and "Re-Right-ing" the stories of our lives.

Get ready to Re-Write Your Life so you can live in the here and now with peace, acceptance and gratitude.

Namaste,

June

Having had a silent prayer
To one day become aware
I yearned for knowledge
And I sought
I asked to learn and I was taught
Truly to my own surprise
I merely looked within my eyes
And grew to know the wisdom there
And now my journey is to share.

June Swadron
1974

# *Book 1,*
## GETTING READY

# Part A

# *Chapter 1*

## BEGINNINGS: LOOKING
## BACK TO STEP FORWARD

WHEN I was eleven years old, I was given a diary for my birthday. I treasured that little red book with its tiny lock and key. It brought me into a private world where no one was allowed to enter. It sent me on a path of writing and healing that I could never have known back then. That diary became my best friend, my steady companion. I learned I could say things to it that I couldn't tell anyone else. I would write my secrets, my pain, my poetry, my just about everything. In fact my 'diary', which I have since called my 'journal', has provided me a safe refuge all through my life. It never complains or gets bored or angry. I don't have to show up with my hair brushed, make-up on, clothes all clean and pressed. I can go to it in my pajamas or bring it to my favourite café or write in it in my doctor's office while waiting to be seen. There are no rules; just show up, pen in hand and a willingness to open to whatever comes.

Sometimes what comes is quite painful and raw, yet many of these tender entries have become my best poems or songs – or turned around become my most humorous stories. But many times I deserted my journal, and in so doing, deserted myself. Those were the times I didn't write. I didn't partake of its incredible generosity to help me find my answers which would give me the stability and clarity that I needed. I called it writer's block but it really was fear. Fear of saying things I didn't want to hear – afraid to see them in print. I clearly wanted to write my life story but I was scared. I didn't want to hurt anyone. And I was afraid to reveal things that I had kept secret for years.

Then one day, I found myself sitting at my desk and starting. It came to the point that writing my life story was no longer an arbitrary choice. It was the healing vehicle that jumped out at me and I had to do it. My life was filled with so much pain from the past that I knew if I didn't address it, it would eventually destroy me. I would continue to make poor choices, stay in unhealthy relationships and be stuck in the loop of blame, shame and depression. I knew I had to write my stories in order to claim back my life.

And so I did. With determination and patience, I as the older woman, was able to go back with a brand new appreciation for all the different stages of who I – the infant, toddler, pre-teen, teenager and younger adult – had once been. Looking back I could see and feel her sadness, confusion – her shyness, defensiveness – her passion – her joy – her loves and her losses. Stepping outside and being a witness to my younger self, I got to know her in a way I had never known her before. I watched her in her unfolding and was able to bring to the younger me understanding, compassion and forgiveness. The process taught me how to love myself. On the pages I didn't have to play the roles I would sometimes play in the outside world. I didn't have to smile when I was feeling sad or be brave when I was feeling anything but courageous. I didn't have to be nice or not nice. I simply had to tell my truth.

As I did, I moved from loss and confusion into a place where things began to make sense, where clarity rose up from murky waters. Over time I could see a palpable difference in the way I walked, the way I talked and the way I viewed the world. I was becoming stronger, more confident and less afraid. I still had doubts and insecurities but I was visibly miles ahead of where I was before.

For all of us, it takes great courage and determination to walk consciously into the past, back into old pain to make sense of it – to open doors that have been locked, perhaps for decades, with an intention to let in the light – letting light in to give compassion to the younger person we were. This juncture calls for a willingness to embrace the past, let go of old anger, blame and resentments, search our hearts for forgiveness for ourselves and for others and move on.

Sometimes when life is difficult we either become complacent or race quickly into what is next, not stopping to reflect on what just occurred. The road we are taking is the opposite of denial or giving up. It is one where often there is no road map. It is outside of familiar territory; it pushes all comfort zones and boundaries and is definitely "the road less traveled." Yet paradoxically, it is also the one that leaves room for love and miracles to shine in. And there is something mystical and magical about the writing process itself. We ask inside for guidance and become a conduit. Suddenly we are no longer figuring out what we want to say and how to say it. Our remembering comes from our listening, which becomes our writing on the page. We are taking dictation from what we hear. Each word flows naturally into a sentence, which breathes into the next and the next as a living entity. And it is these words, revealing new insights and memories, that become the catalyst for healing and understanding. It is here that tired or stuck energy gets lifted and a new lightness of being takes hold. New perceptions dance into consciousness accompanied by a sense of peace and often exhilaration. Our stories are being told! The truth is setting us free! We are writing ourselves home.

## Writing Yourself Home

What does it mean to "write yourself home"? For me, it's an expression of writing that originates from deep in your heart and spirit. Your soul awaits you here. You only need to step to the side and let the words flow forth. There's a kindness here, a beckoning, a sense of wholeness. There's no need to edit from this place. Truth resonates here. Here you can go back to the difficult times of your past as well as the beautiful times with brand new awareness and consciousness. It's about embracing the adult you are today as well as the life you lived before. Here you come home to yourself. The exercises in this book are designed to guide you through this process.

Writing yourself home gives you the opportunity to impart your truth. It may not be the exact way it happened. But it's your truth as to the way it happened and that's vital. Each of us can occupy the same time and space with the same outer experience yet it will be our inner experience and our personal perceptions that will determine its meaning.

Sometimes when memories surface that are painful, you may be tempted to write around them instead of through them. You might write in a fashion that sounds good in order to gain acceptance and approval – even from people who may be long since gone from your life – or to try to look good to yourself. You might find yourself holding back or relating events in an apologetic or kind and poetic way that reads nicely, but it's not the truth and you'll know it as you write it. It's important to lovingly and compassionately acknowledge that part of you that wants to hold back. Breathe and continue writing from a genuine place. Anything less would be cheating yourself and not worth the exercise.

May Sarton describes it this way: (quoted in *Writing from the Body* by John Lee, 1994).

"I believe one has to stop holding back for fear of alienating some imaginary reader or real relative or friend and come out with personal truth. If we are to understand the human condition, and if we are to accept ourselves in all the complexity, self-doubt, extravagance of feeling guilt, joy, the slow freeing of the self to its full capacity for action and creation, both as human being and as artist, we have to know all we can about each other, and we have to be willing to go naked."

Going naked is a vulnerable place to be. As well it is an authentic place to be. It gives you back your voice. It delves into shadows and rebirths the light. It portends forgiveness. It moves you along the path of resurrection that brings about closure to life-long anger, regrets, resentments and pain. Going naked allows you to call your spirit back. It doesn't happen all at once. It's a process that calls for patience, commitment and faith.

No one – not me, not your best friend, your partner, your mother – no one knows what you lived but you. Therefore no one can go back and remember and heal these things for you. Other people may have been there but their interpretations will be different from yours. When you acknowledge that which you have lived while staying open to a greater truth, the result will be a deeper clarity and compassion for you and for others.

Some years ago, while I was writing my life story, *On Her Way Home – A Woman's Story*, it was as though an angel was sitting on my shoulder – which she probably was – and I too was an angel for myself. Instead of wallowing in my past, shaming myself, minimizing my life or embellishing it, I simply wrote from memory as it was given to me – each time asking for guidance and clarity, as I allowed my hands to move swiftly across the computer keyboard – neither editing nor judging, simply writing. It wasn't always easy. Sometimes I felt completely spent afterward and wondered what the point was in doing all of this. But I honoured my commitment to myself to do it and the writing strengthened me. I didn't know this at the time. At the time I was just writing and willing to be as honest and as gentle with myself as I could be. I ask you to do the same.

We all have the ability to heal the pain in our lives. It is our perceptions of the things that occur, our interpretations of these events and our responses to them that ultimately keep us in chains or set us free. Under all that has happened to us, under all the pain, fear, chaos and clutter is a much deeper meaning. And if we dare to look for the meaning, gifts will reveal themselves.

# Let's Write

## Self-awareness Exercise

 The following is an exercise designed to help you excavate deeper truths as to why you want to write your life stories. It will give you insights and clarity as you go toward the next step. The exercise originates from one of my teachers, Leonard Shaw, author of the book: *Love and Forgiveness*. He suggests answering 4 questions 10 times as quickly as possible. Write the questions and answers as in the example below.

Here are the four questions:

Regarding writing my life stories, what do I want?
Regarding writing my life stories, what do I need?
Regarding writing my life stories, what do I fear?
Regarding writing my life stories, what do I hope for?

Example:

1.  Regarding writing my life stories what do I want?
    *I want to have a living legacy for my children.*
2.  Regarding writing my life stories, what do I want?
    *I want to reveal the truth.*
3.  Regarding writing my life stories, what do I want?
    *I want to be free of the past and live more fully in today.*
4.  Regarding writing my life stories, what do I want?
    *I want to understand myself better.*
5.  Regarding writing my life stories, what do I want?
    *I want to learn to forgive those who have hurt me, learn to forgive myself and put closure on these past events and move on.*
6.  Regarding writing my life stories, what do I want?
    *I want to be grateful for my life and see the gifts that my stories have given me and how I am stronger for them.*
7.  Regarding writing my life stories, what do I want?
    *I want to help inspire and empower others who may have had similar experiences.*

8.    Regarding writing my life stories, what do I want?
      *I want to embrace every experience in my life – knowing that there has been a gift and lesson in each.*
9.    Regarding writing my life stories, what do I want?
      *I want to write my stories to essentially let go of them and be free from old wounds.*
10.   Regarding writing my life stories, what do I want?
      *I want to finally accept myself fully – all of me – remembering that I have always done the very best I could at the time.*

Do this 10 times as quickly as you can and then do the same exercise for the questions:

What do I **need?**
What do I **fear?**
What do I **hope for?**

Don't be concerned about repeating yourself. It simply means that this answer is particularly strong for you. The insights you will gain from doing this exercise may surprise you. They will reveal the deeper truth as to why you are choosing to undergo this healing journey and reinforce your commitment to it.

# *Chapter 2*

## OPENING TO GRACE
## A PERSONAL STORY

W HEN I was deciding where to put the following life story, knowing that it could fit into other sections of this book where I share parts of my life, I chose to have it close to the beginning. From the start, I want you to know who I am, not only as a psychotherapist, author and writing coach but also as a woman who lives with her own struggles and knows the relief and liberation that comes from a committed and continuous healing process. For me, a significant part of that process has been writing my life stories.

### Living With a Mental Illness

One day my mother sat me down and told me she didn't know what to do to make me feel better, that it felt too big for her to carry. She wanted me to go with her to the hospital where some doctors would talk to me.

"They'll know what to do, honey," she tried to smile. "They will make you feel like Junie again. They'll bring back our Junie, I promise," she cried, wiping back tears.

I sat there horrified but couldn't speak. She put me in the car and drove me to the Branson Hospital on Finch Avenue in Toronto. I was in absolute terror as they admitted me. When my mother left me that day I thought my life was over.

"Mommy, please don't go. Please, mommy! Don't go!" I inwardly screamed.

I was an infant trapped in a twenty-year-old body and the only thing that mattered was my mommy was going away and now I would surely die.

Life on the ward was unbearable. I was expected to sit in 'the lounge' with other crazies like me and watch the world go by. Every now and then they would call us into a larger room where we would sit on chairs in a circle. We were asked to talk about how we were feeling. I had no language. I could not talk. The people in the other chairs terrified me. I wanted my mommy. More, I wanted to die. "God strike me dead," I begged from a hollow cave inside me. I hid in my room. They'd come and get me and take me back to the lounge. I'd slip back to my room. They'd come and get me again. There was nowhere to go. I had nowhere else to hide. Nothing was helping – none of the umpteen medications they had me on nor the individual or group therapies. My mother and father came every day. So did Joseph, a man who loved me no matter what. I was told my siblings came as well but I have no recollection of that. I just remember living for the visits from my mom and wanting to end my life every time she left.

At the end of a very long month the doctor told my parents there was nothing else they could do for me. He said that I probably used a lot of drugs while I was away in Europe and that there's no telling if I'll ever come out of it. He went on to tell them that I may have damaged my brain cells irreparably. He said he was sorry but they could take me home now. I knew he was lying. I never did drugs. I couldn't defend myself. There was a veil between me and them. I could hear but I couldn't speak. But I could go home! That was all that mattered. I was never so happy in my life. I was also never so terrified. I was just condemned to a living death – to be this way forever.

Excerpt from *On Her Way Home – A Woman's Story*
June D. Swadron

# *Let's Write*

Now that you've read the above story, write from where you are right now – from what you feel right now. Don't go into the kitchen and grab a donut. Don't make that phone call you've been meaning to make since last Thursday. Grab your notebook and pen instead. Write down whatever comes to you from reading that passage.

Is there someone in your life who lives with a mental illness? A friend, a parent, a sibling, a child? How do you feel when you are with that person? Is it challenging? Perhaps it's you. How do you manage with your own bouts of illness? Write from your compassion, your anger, your emptiness and your losses. Write from your fear, your frustration, your sadness, your acceptance, your grief or your shame. Where do you feel these emotions in your body? And if you are one of the fortunate people who are not touched by mental illness, what event in your life did this story evoke in you? Be gentle. Begin to write.

# Chapter 3

## FINDING THE GIFT

W HEN I was twenty years old I was diagnosed with manic-depressive illness. The excruciating pain and desperation that this illness causes, the sense that there is no escape from it and the inherent hopelessness, has made me want to give up many times. There were occasions when I did give up, but my life kept being spared. It taught me that I am here on this planet for a bigger purpose. I always seemed to know that, even as a child, but for me, it seemed incongruent. How could I be here trusting that I am to do something important with my life, make a difference, when I am hospital bound again and again with circumstances that often felt out of my control?

Perhaps one of the biggest challenges was coming home after being in a hospital psychiatric ward and needing to re-enter my professional life. I was filled with dread. I had to face my therapy clients and students who awaited my return. Rarely would they know where I had been. But I knew. My self-imposed judgments haunted me, judgments that I would never place on anyone else. I gave myself the following drill dozens of times: "Look at you, you're a trained psychotherapist – you should know better; how can you be helping others when you can't help yourself? You're obviously a fraud." Sometimes that voice was relentless. Yet the healthier part of me knew that in spite of the occasional onset of clinical depressions or mania I was good at what I did and my work really helped people.

My path has kept me on a winding journey, akin to a social scientist – wanting to discover, uncover, know and understand the reasons for my illness, to grasp its inherent teachings and put it in a context with the rest of my life experiences. This has been my most important life's work – my mission, if you will. And it always leaves me asking the question, "How can I impart what I have learned in a way that will serve others?"

After returning from another hospital bout for clinical depression in 1999, I knew I was well enough to return to work but this time I decided not to go back right away. I needed to do something different. I didn't know what that would be but I knew it had to be something that would give some meaning to what was happening to me and to countless others who live with this disease.

So, even though I was really scared, wondering what I could possibly do next and how I would support myself, I still chose not to return to work. Instead, I took time out to heal – to be still and ask inside for guidance. Within a short time, I got the message that I was to write my life story in the form of a play and perform it on stage. I couldn't believe it. Surely this message wasn't meant for me. The idea terrified me. I shared this with some close friends who thought it was a great idea but I was adamant that I wouldn't do it. It was like a nightmare that wouldn't go away so I cried out, "God, surely you don't mean me! How can I expose myself this way! I am a professional. I am a counsellor. What will happen to my practice – how will it affect my clients, my students, my colleagues?" But the message wouldn't go away and somewhere deep inside I knew I had to do it. This was what I had been asking for – the something that would give meaning to my life and hopefully bring light and hope to others who suffer with mental illness and their families. I hoped the play would break down some of the myths and stigmas attributed to this illness. I surrendered to the idea, and in time the process began.

Writing the play, *Madness, Masks and Miracles*, started moving me out of my depression. That writing process gave me some freedom to begin coming out of the closet of shame. You can read the full story in Chapter 3, A Time You Were Stronger Than You Thought.

# *Let's Write*

Write about a time in your life that you knew you had to change the circumstances you were in because it was too painful or too destructive to stay where you were. The idea of making a change scared you but you did it anyway.

Describe the details. What did you do to turn the circumstances around? Do you remember the year and your age at the time? Where were you living? What stands out as the most painful or challenging part of that time for you? Were there people there to support you?

What happened once you made the decision to change your circumstances? Write all the details as you remember them. Honour yourself for the strength and courage it took to get you through it. What tools did you use? What were your strengths? Looking back at it from a distance, what did this time teach you about yourself?

*Book 1,*
Part B

# GUIDELINES
# How To Use This Book

*In the beginning*
*There was a writing area, paper and pen and*
*Intention, Courage and Commitment to*
*"Know Thyself"'*

N ow that you know why you are writing your stories, this section gives you a road map on how to write them. For most writers a blank page can be daunting. When looking at an empty page, panic can set in. "Where do I start? What do I say? How much should I say? How do I say it?" To help you deal with those kinds of questions and put your mind at ease, you need to prepare yourself in ways that can help you relax and look at each story as an honouring of yourself and as an exciting adventure. You begin with the first story. That is the only one you need to think about for now. But before you even do that, there are things that will help you get comfortable. Later in this section I describe how to prepare a sacred writing space. This is a place where, as you enter it, you immediately feel motivated and inspired to write.

Also in this section is a meditation that you may choose to do to centre yourself before every writing session. There is also an invocation to use when you are writing about something painful from your past. Both the Centering Exercise and the Invocation are optional guidelines to bring you into stillness and into the present moment. It is a good idea to record them on a tape recorder. Or you can download them onto your computer or MP3 player by going to www.juneswadron.com and clicking on "downloads".

Treat your pages as your dearest friend, one who is ready and willing to accept you as you are. Remember not to judge yourself or your writing when you put pen to paper (or keyboard). Judging yourself will slow you down or worse, make you quit.

There are many themes in this book to write about. They can be written in whatever order calls to you. However, for the first story, I suggest you begin with "Gratitude". The reason for this is that your story of gratitude will be your touchstone – the story you can come back to when you're writing the stories that are difficult to tell. When you return to gratitude, you are right back in present time and all that you have to be grateful for today. From this perspective, you see that the painful story you have just been writing about is in the past, and it can no longer hurt you. Gratitude keeps us grounded in today.

For each of the story selections, I offer memory-prompting exercises that will assist you in remembering the details. For instance, in writing about a significant move in your life, some questions I might ask you are: Why were you moving? How did you feel about it? What year was it? How old were you? Who were the supports in your life at the time? What were your goodbyes like?

In some cases you will be guided through a healing process to help you not only tell your story but also release any negative feelings that you still carry with you.

## The Healing Power of Intention

Having a conscious intention toward something – whether it's about moving through our day with mindfulness, remembering to be patient when we are caught in traffic or whether it is to be kinder to ourselves and others when we're in the middle of a conflict – the very act of having intention will bring about right mental and emotional alignment in order to achieve it. We are choosing to move through our world with consciousness – knowing that what we focus on grows. Our intention gives the Universe a signal that we are serious about what we want.

When you begin to write your life stories, choose to have the intention to let go of anything that is stopping you from having a happy life, free of resentments, anger, shame and guilt. Have the intention to forgive the people in your life who have hurt you – forgive them and yourself. Hold the intention to see the gifts and lessons in every story and especially hold the intention to love and honour your life. Honour yourself for the amazing human being and spirit you are. Honour yourself for the courage it takes to write your life stories with the conscious intention to heal your life.

# The Healing Power of Courage

It takes a great deal of courage to go back into old pain in order to release it and move forward. Yet it is necessary for our ultimate growth. You will find that the benefits outweigh the fear. Courage is often propelled by an honest commitment to heal our pain. Courage means that we feel the fear and do what it takes to move forward anyway. We take our pens and write into the hollow places that scare us and still continue to write until we are done. We uncover truths that have been buried deep inside us, perhaps for years, and the healing begins. We leap in an act of faith knowing in our hearts that the net will be there. And it is. The universe smiles at us and rewards us for our courage. Synchronicities – or "God-winks" as I like to call them – begin to happen. The telephone rings and someone with whom you have wanted to make amends for a very long time is on the other end of the line, and instead of shouting at you, they say they've called to ask for your forgiveness.

Yes, courage has many unseen promises and rewards, especially the confidence to keep on keeping on.

# The Healing Power of Commitment

The following quote by Scottish explorer William Hutchison Murray is one of the best reminders I know to keep me putting pen to paper, to trust the process and to not give up. It is quoted from his 1951 published works, *The Scottish Himalayan Expedition*.

> "... but when I said that nothing had been done I erred in one important matter. We had definitely committed ourselves and were halfway out of our ruts. We had put down our passage money— booked a sailing to Bombay. This may sound too simple, but is great in consequence. Until one is committed, there is hesitancy, the chance to draw back, always ineffectiveness. Concerning all acts of initiative (and creation), there is one elementary truth the ignorance of which kills countless ideas and splendid plans: that the moment one definitely commits oneself, then providence moves too. A whole stream of events issues from the decision, raising in one's favor all manner of unforeseen incidents, meetings and material assistance, which no man could

*have dreamt would have come his way. I learned a deep respect for one*
*of Goethe's couplets:*

*Whatever you can do or dream you can, begin it.*
*Boldness has genius, power and magic in it!"*

Commit to writing your life stories. Look back at the insights you
gained from the self-awareness exercise you did. What did you say you
want, need, fear and hope for regarding writing your life stories?

Say "YES" to the process and continue.

# GUIDELINES
# FOR WRITING YOUR LIFE STORIES

## Creating a Sacred Space

THERE'S NOTHING like having an inviting, friendly, beautiful writing space to inspire you every day. It doesn't have to be big, just welcoming. Make it personal. Make it yours. Light a candle. Bring out your favourite incense. Bring in colourful flowers, precious stones, shells you collected on the beach, crystals, a favourite prayer or affirmation or anything else that will make your writing space special. You may want to put a photo on your writing desk or next to your computer of a special person or pet and imagine them smiling at you as you write. (Pets do too smile!)

Or conversely, you may want to keep it very simple and not have anything in your space. For some, having special items may be distracting.

Also, tell your family what you are doing and ask them to please respect your new writing area and that the books, photo albums and letters you placed there are not to be touched.

Respect and embrace your sacred space.

## Organization

I have found the best way to stay organized is to keep everything in a three-ring binder or folder so your writing is all under one cover rather than using loose sheets that could get lost. Make sure you number your pages. Use separate tabs for each life story. Also keep separate folders or large envelopes that you label for each story to create order with any memorabilia you are collecting such as photographs or family documents you wish to include.

## Computer or Handwritten

As to whether to write by hand or use the computer, do whatever you're most comfortable with. The benefit of the computer is that later, after your story is written, it makes it much easier to go back and make changes. You can cut and paste and delete or add without any difficulty.

If you are using the computer, be aware of the temptation for distractions like surfing the net and checking emails. Focusing only on your writing as soon as you sit down is critical to your success. To help reduce distractions, you may choose to turn off your connection to the Internet during your designated writing time.

Whatever your method, unplug your phone, make sure you are not hungry and keep a bottle of water at your writing table.

## You Do Not Have To Be a Great Writer

You don't need to be an accomplished writer to write your life stories. You don't need to have taken writing courses, have a certificate or degree in writing or any other such thing. You just need to be able to be honest and write from your heart.

Let go of perfectionism, spelling, punctuation, grammar and having to do it 'right.' Instead drop into your belly and try not to think about the writing at all. When you are thinking, you are judging, planning, figuring out what to say next. This writing process calls for stepping out of your own way and not editing as you write.

It is about being fully in your body, allowing memories to flow from your head to your heart to your hand and onto the page. That being said, some of the stories in this book have been edited for punctuation and grammar. That was done after the fact – not during the author's creative process. Only some of these stories were written by accomplished writers.

Marion Woodman, in an interview in *Common Boundary* said:

"After much thought, I realized the trouble I had writing that bleak Friday afternoon was due to my approach. I was trying to analyze, trying to explain rationally. I was failing miserably because I was approaching the task through my head. I had to drop into my belly."

Nathalie Goldberg in *Writing Down the Bones* states:

"In writing, when you are truly on, there's no writer, no paper, no pen. No thoughts. Only writing does writing – everything else is gone."

# Your Writing Style

You are unique and there is no right or wrong way to write your stories. You will notice that the true life stories that are inserted throughout the book are written in different styles – poetry, prose, letters, metaphor. Free yourself to do the same. Perhaps some of your stories want to come out as fairy tales ... Once upon a time there was a girl who...

Be true to your own method of writing. Even if you have never written poetry before, stay with it if that is how it emerges. Trust and enjoy the process!

# Breathing

Writing is a full-bodied exercise – it is not just the brain and the fingers. It calls for full breath. When you get scared, your breathing becomes shallow and so does your writing.

The more grounded you are in your body, the deeper your writing becomes. When you are breathing from a shallow place, your writing tends to stay on the surface. Breathe from deep in your belly and write from that place. In his book, *Writing from the Body*, John Lee explains:

"To begin writing with the full power of our body's knowledge, we must welcome our life, our breath and our emotions completely. Write whatever bursts forward from the breath. Let the pen follow where the breath leads. We have only to begin breathing fully to show life that we are serious about embracing her."

# Embodying Memories

At times throughout the book, when you are writing about people or events that are disturbing, I offer the suggestion that you do NOT embody these memories. In other words, do not bring the emotion of them into your body. Instead imagine the events on a movie screen where you are at a safe distance from them. Then be an objective observer without emotional attachment to what you see and remember.

# Making Time to Write

It's best if you can get into a routine. Find an uninterrupted space of time to write every day, preferably at the same time. If you can't do it every day, perhaps it's possible to write once, twice or three times a week. Whatever works for you, mark it on your calendar and commit to it. Then turn off your telephone. Share with family members what you are doing so they know to be respectful of your writing time. If you need to, reread "The Healing Power of Intention", "Courage" and "Commitment" to help you get started. Also, carry a note book with you to write down ideas that come to you during the day so you can refer to them when you sit down at your desk to write.

## Ways to Stay Grounded

Although writing about one's life can be exhilarating when recapturing beautiful memories or coming to terms and moving through to the other side of painful ones, it can also catapult you into feeling like your entire emotional foundation is collapsing. It is vital to stay grounded and safe by taking special care to nurture yourself throughout this process. Make sure you eat well, drink plenty of water and get enough exercise, fresh air and adequate sleep. Refuel your sense of humour. Rent a funny movie. Reach out. Call a friend. Roller blade, dance, go for a walk in nature. Keep an attitude of gratitude. Breathe deeply! Read inspirational writings, prayers. Give whatever you are going through over to God/Goddess/Creator. If you are remembering and recording painful events from your past, remember it is part of your past. You survived it and are on the other side of it now. Bring yourself back to this day, this moment, for it is right here, right now that you are safe. Use conscious breath to do this. Breathe deeply and often.

## Right Brain vs. Left Brain Process

This writing process calls for right brain activity which uses pictures, symbols and images and is nonverbal. It is the part of our nature that is intuitive, sensuous, artistic and spontaneous. It works with shapes and patterns. While writing, simply be open to receive. You are a conduit, not a planner. As stated earlier, you write without paying attention to spelling, grammar or punctuation. This is a function of the left brain. It is verbal, linear, logical, rational and cognitive. This is the part of the brain you will engage if you decide to go back and edit. It is not for now.

## Clustering

Clustering is a fast and effective way to remember the details of your story before you start writing. It is a great way to bring back memories and access your right brain through word association.

Instead of writing lists which are linear, for example: then I went here and this happened, then that happened, etcetera; draw a circle in the middle of your notebook. Draw lines coming out of the centre circle to other circles. In those circles write the first words that pop into your head. If those words trigger another thought, draw a line to another circle and write the thought. It is an excellent tool to help access the memories of these events.

See the diagram on the next page.

# Memory Prompts

Every writing topic in this book also has memory prompts attached that will help you recall the details of your story. There are a number of ways you can use the memory prompts.

Before writing your story, record the memory prompts onto a tape recorder. Be sure that while recording you pause for a few seconds between each question to allow time for the memory to surface and become clear. When you are ready to write, simply close your eyes and listen to the prompts. Begin to recall the events with as much detail as possible. You may stop and write as soon as a story comes to mind and then go to the next prompts until another story comes to mind. Or, you may choose to listen to all the prompts before writing anything.

If you do not tape the memory prompts, then read them slowly. With each question begin to recall the events with as much detail as possible.

You can use the memory prompts to build a cluster from which you can then write your story.

Note: To save time and for easy access and enjoyment, I have recorded all the memory prompts. They are available to download on my website, www.juneswadron.com

A major advantage to listening to the prompts rather than reading them is that you can sit back, relax and let your imagination run free. It will open the channel for more thoughts, symbols, feelings, senses and information to come forward. Reading is more of a left-brain activity and may not engage your memory in the same way.

As mentioned previously, the majority of stories in this book have been written by my students. They listened to me reading the prompts while their eyes were closed. This method brought them more fully into their personal experiences and allowed easy access to their memories.

# CLUSTERING

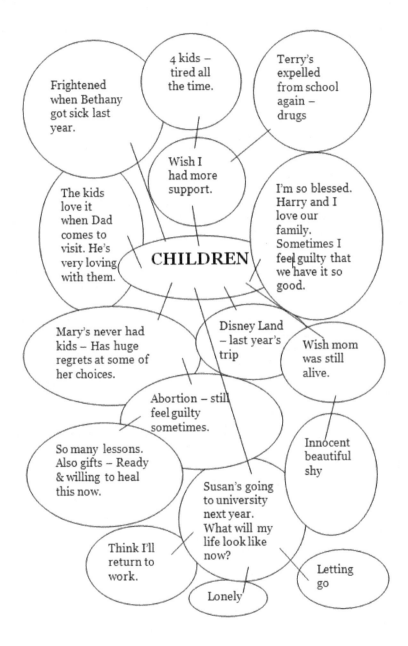

# What to Do on Designated Writing Day

Turn to the themes of the book in the Table of Contents and choose which story you want to write about. When you go to the chapter, the first thing you will see are true life stories written by a selection of authors plus many of my own stories. These are followed by memory prompts that will help you recall your own story.

Sometimes you will be guided to read the Centering Exercise in Book 1, Part C or the Invocation, Book 1, Part D before writing your story. This is optional.

Write your story from wherever your energy is. Breathe into the memory of your personal life story and everything that transpired. Sensing what you were aware of, what the people looked like and what time of year it was will all have an impact on the story you are remembering. Were the streets slushy, was it windy and cold or did your story begin in sweltering heat – the kind where your clothes stick to your skin because of the dense humidity? You are in your story now. The heat depletes your energy. You are practically falling asleep. You need to get somewhere. It is urgent. How do you do it with this scorching heat melting you? You can no longer tell if it is from the outside in or the inside out. You have to leave. The clock is ticking. Will you make it on time? You want to sleep. What will he say? You are melting. You splash water on your face. You take a cool cloth and rub it all over your blistering body. Slowly you feel the energy returning. For the first time today, you think you might make it. Write into it. Write into your details.

The more detail you bring to your story, the more it will help you see clearly. Details will evoke even more memories. Remember, "Show us, don't tell us." is one of the first rules of writing. In other words, bring yourself deeply into your story with detail, dialogue and anything else that will make it real. Breathe deeply. Breathe in joy for what you are about to uncover, discover, transform and transcend.

Are you ready? Is your writing space welcoming? Do you have a full glass of water next to you? Remember, you are not alone.

# Choosing Whether or Not to Publish Your Stories

Many people want to write their life stories but wonder whether or not to publish them. If you are writing the stories to help you heal certain issues, then I recommend you work through the writing exercises in this book as if you are NOT intending to publish them. The exercises offer an opportunity to write the stories the way you remember them and help you let go of the ones that no longer serve you – the times in your life that, when you think of them, you feel sad or angry, fearful, remorseful or stuck. Writing through to the other side of these stories will help you transcend negative feelings and shift your perception. If, during the writing process, you are concerned about publishing and afraid of what people will think of you, you may be tempted to with-hold parts of your stories or write them in such a way as to conceal the truth as you remember it.

The first writing of your stories is a process that requires you to be completely honest. Writing for your benefit only is truly liberating. It allows you to write in an unrestricted manner which will take you to the other side where catharsis awaits you. After you have written these stories just for you, then you can decide whether or not you wish to publish them. Your insights could possibly encourage, comfort or in-spire others.

There are some stories that I have written and made the choice not to include here. The writing gave me the desired healing outcome, es-pecially as I was able to read them out loud to my therapist or friends who love and accept me unconditionally. These were stories of abuse that involved people close to me and I was concerned how making the stories public would affect them.

Also, I believe that everything in my life has happened for a reason. Perceived wrongdoings have been great teachers. They have helped me grow stronger and provided an opportunity to forgive and offer un-derstanding and compassion to myself and others. The writing process has provided a vehicle that offered a safe place for my thoughts and feelings.

To publish or not is a personal choice and there are no right or wrong answers.

If you wish to publish your life stories and are concerned about how people may react, there are ways around it. You can change the names of the people involved. You can also choose to write a novel and use true life circumstances as part of the characters and events in the book, or you can write under a pseudonym.

In my story of forgiveness in Chapter 13, I changed the names. I was also very clear that the events in the story are my perception and not necessarily the perception of the other people involved. Their version of how things happened may be very different from my own.

# Book 1,
# Part C

# CENTERING EXERCISE
# BEFORE WRITING

I F YOU arrive at your writing table in distress after racing home from work and being frustrated by traffic, or simply have lots of things on your mind, this centering exercise will help calm and relax you before you begin to write.

For the best results, consider recording this meditation so you can close your eyes and fully relax into this process. Speak slowly. You can also download a recording of it, along with all memory prompts at www.juneswadron.com.

## Centering Exercise

Get comfortable in your chair and begin to focus on your breath. Take some deep breaths in from your belly and let go. As you are exhaling, let go of tension and worry. Let go of any thoughts that you have. Let go of anything that is preventing you from being here right now and breathe. Gently bring yourself into this moment. With every new breath, breathe in joy and peace. Breathe out tension or worry. With every breath you move into a deeper state of relaxation. Breathe. Now scan your body. Notice where you are carrying tension. Next imagine your breath moving into those places to release and soften, fully letting go. You are becoming more relaxed with every breath you take.

Now in your mind's eye, take yourself somewhere in nature where your spirit feels at home – somewhere you have either been before or somewhere your imagination takes you to for the first time. Go there with all your inner senses fully alive and awake. Breathe in the beauty of this natural setting. Notice what you see in front of you. Observe all the details. Notice what you see in the distance. Slowly turn and look in all directions. Notice what time of day it is. Are you at a beach or in a forest? Somewhere else, perhaps? Listen to the sounds. Is there an ocean, a river, a creek near you – a meadow? What sounds do you hear? What colours do you see? Breathe. Notice how good you feel in this beautiful place. Every time you come here, you will feel better and better. This is your safe place, your very own inner sanctuary. This is the place of letting go of all worldly concerns. Here there is nothing you have to do, nowhere you have to go and no one you have to please. Allow yourself to be fully present to all that is around you. In this exquisite inner sanctuary, this place of beauty and stillness, you can simply be. You feel renewed here. You are happy and at peace.

Enjoy your time here. Know that this is your spiritual sanctuary and yours to come home to whenever you choose. It will always be here waiting for you. A place of stillness, outside of personal and worldly concerns where you can reconnect with your Higher Self. This is a sacred place where you join with Universal love and Intelligence and bathe in a radiant sea of golden light and love. Take another deep breath and let go.

When you are ready, you can come back to your sacred writing space, relaxed, renewed and prepared to begin to write your story.

# *Book 1,*
# Part D

# INVOCATION – OPENING TO THE GIFTS

## St. Francis affirms the following:

*"It is in giving that we receive,*
*In pardoning we are pardoned,*
*And in surrendering we are born to eternal life."*

T HE FOLLOWING invocation is to be used before writing any story that holds pain, grief, fear, shame, sorrow, regret, anger, hostility or resentment. The Invocation will help you let go of all that no longer serves you by allowing you to be held in the hands of God. (You may choose to replace the word God with another name that feels more comfortable for you – i.e. Light, Universal Intelligence, Love, The Creator or Spirit).

Once again, I suggest recording the Invocation so you can close your eyes and fully relax into this process. If you prefer you can download it from my website, www.juneswadron.com.

## Invocation

As I prepare to write the following life story, I let go, step aside and let God in. I am open and willing to receive the highest truth with respect to all that has happened to me. I acknowledge and accept that the people and circumstances in my life were brought to me for my learning, healing and growth.

I am open to the gifts that the people and circumstances in this story offered me. I receive these gifts easily, graciously and with gratitude. I am letting go of any negative thinking that would cause me to deny the blessings that this life story offers. As I write my truth, I open myself to receive complete healing.

I take ownership and responsibility for the choices I have made. I love and forgive myself for any choices that hurt me and/or others. I am also ready and willing to forgive those who I perceive have hurt me in any way. I am willing to see the innocence in myself and in them. I take a deep breath in and let go of any fear or tension I may be carrying.

I open to Universal Grace and Intelligence, helping to restore any imbalances for my highest good. Through the writing and remembering of this story and appreciation for the inherent gifts that were offered, I open to return to a state of deep peace, health and joy. I remember that everything I have experienced is for my soul's growth and evolution. I breathe in light and love. I give thanks as I begin to write and remember… (name of story) e.g. The Story of My Mother.

# *Book 2*
## STORIES

# *Chapter 1*

## GRATITUDE

### Introduction to Writing
### Your Story of Gratitude

THIS IS the story that you will be invited to come back to when you are writing others that may be more difficult. It is the one that will bring you into today and remind you of the goodness that is present here and now. It is the story that may help ground you, help you to remember that your life is no accident – remembering it all – the trials and the triumphs. In this story you begin to see the gifts in all of it. You remember you are safe in this moment and, in many ways, abundantly blessed.

Gratitude is an attitude. It is an attitude that no matter what is going on in your life, you are able to recognize the good – that which is working – the events and moments that warm you, bring you joy and help you see and acknowledge those things that lift your spirits. They are everywhere if you just let yourself be open to them. Have you ever walked down the street on a day you felt particularly sad or lonely and a stranger smiled at you and in an instant your heart opened? Even such a seemingly small gesture can give meaning to your day.

Gratitude is a mindset. It is a way of showing up in the world breathing in the beauty that is around us even in times of pain and sorrow. There are gifts to behold here too. Gratitude is also the first spiritual law of abundance. As we appreciate and are grateful for where we are and what we have right now, we create the conditions for abundance to show up. Living in gratitude raises our vibration and we become an open conduit for God's grace to enter.

Melody Beattie expressed it this way:

"Gratitude unlocks the fullness in life. It turns what we have into enough, and more. It turns denial into acceptance, chaos to order, confusion to clarity. It can turn a meal into a feast, a house into a home, a stranger into a friend. Gratitude makes sense of our past, brings peace for today and creates a vision for tomorrow."

Perhaps you are not in a state of gratitude at the moment. Perhaps you are feeling lonely, or afraid, or angry with your life circumstances and gratitude is the last thing you are feeling. I understand what that's like. Even though I keep a gratitude journal that I like to write in every night before I go to bed, and I generally find at least a few things that have given me pleasure that day for which I can give thanks, and often many things, this is not always the case. Recently I was feeling angry and resentful toward someone and it flooded into all the other areas of my life. That night in my gratitude journal I wrote "I am grateful for this day to be over!" That was the most I could muster. I immediately shut the book, shut off the light and tried to sleep. Sometimes though, when I feel like this, I make the choice to look back at earlier pages of the weeks and months prior and I am reminded of the many wonderful things that do make up my life. This helps to open my heart again and bring me back into a state of thankfulness. Then, when I turn off my light, I move into sleep in a much more relaxed and peaceful way.

# These Hands

by Marya Nijland

*Looking at my old wrinkled hands, my thoughts are floating far away to my beginnings....*

*These hands were playing with my dark brown bear, the only toy I really loved. I used to carry him around the house and tucked him in bed with me such a long time ago. What a feeling of gratitude for the safety and love I received when I was so vulnerable and fragile.*

*These hands stroked my little brother who was born in August of 1945 when I was 7 years old and who came after my first brother had died on March 31st of that year. That baby was so treasured by all of us and especially by me.*

These hands explored….in my teenage years. There were several exciting sexual discoveries. I felt alive and full of adventure…throughout my life my hands were my sexual tools.

These hands learned to write stories and essays in High School. They were helpers to my inner thoughts.

These hands made love to the four people I have sexually loved in my life. My heart fills with joy and gratitude, still at this very moment.

These hands were folded in prayers and meditations over and over in rough times and times of gratitude.

These hands played the harmonium as a child and now in later life they are touching the black and whites of my beloved piano helping me to compose new melodies, a new found love.

These hands have known poverty, rolled up pennies and dimes, wondering how to make ends meet. Now, having no financial worries, I am so grateful that I am able to help others now and then.

These hands still stroke my husband's old beautiful face with his funny little beard. There is no better face in this whole wide world than his! I am so grateful to have such a great companion!

These hands have made fists to demand justice for human rights, equality and freedom. They have expressed anger and frustration. Now these fists have straightened out to hands that make banners and write letters of protest. I am grateful that I can make a difference.

These hands were made for writing, crafting, baking, making music and above all loving and holding hands with people here and all over this world. And they reach out to hug my friends as they enter our front door.

I am thoroughly grateful and if I die tomorrow, I hope these friends will say: "Marya – she was a woman who said YES to life!"

I am sighing a deep sigh of gratitude. My heart is overflowing!

## Rejoicing in the Union of Love

### by June Swadron

For what am I grateful?
For fresh sheets flapping in the summer wind and angels conceived in laughter on fresh fallen snow and the music that I dance to on my living room floor

*and the phone that rings when a friend thinks of me first. And for my mother and her quirkiness and her cigarettes and contagious laughter; her pony tail and hoop earrings, high-heeled-up-to-the-knees boots over her black spandex and her cleavage proudly poised under a sexy low-cut sweater and would you really care that she is 80! And the trees that stand strong and reassure me with their courage just to be. And the majestic mountains outside my window that change with every sun and every moon.*

*And gratitude for my eyes that allow me to see this glory because of God's nudges to get me here – 3,000 miles across the country at age 49 with just my cats. And a 4-block walk down a cherry-blossomed street that ends at Lost Lagoon. It is here where I have claimed 'June's bench' to dream and journal and watch the baby ducklings swim by. And they live there among the others – the herons and swans, the eagles and ravens, the shrubs and flowers of every colour and scent. And if Carson were here he'd name every one – each tree, each leaf, each bird – for he knows them intimately and teaches them to me.*

*And I am so thankful for the work I do that allows me to keep my heart open on days I don't want to – and the miracle of finding myself again when I join with others, who in our tears and pain and joy and ecstasy breathe life in and out of ourselves and each other, and we rejoice in the union of love.*

*And for what else am I grateful – I only need to read back my gratitude journal to be reminded of the gifts of each day. And perhaps, the most notable of all, is that in my times of torment, in my darkest, most frightening hours, God enters into me and carries me and I remember that I am not alone.*

## Blessings along the Way

by Annie Lavack

*I am grateful for who I am and where I'm at right here, right now. I love my beautiful sweet heart. It's been mangled and torn, broken into a thousand little pieces and then put back together again. Healed and mended and better than before. It's a kind and compassionate heart that opens wide and loves deep.*

*I'm grateful how even in the darkest moments when the pain has seemed unbearable I have always been able to see the light and know that all is well. I love how fearless I am. I will step into the biggest ring with the fiercest giant knowing fully that love, truth and God will triumph.*

*I am grateful that I can see how every heartbreak, every trauma, every tear has created a foundation so strong that it can never be touched. And I love how I know that even if something came along and blew it into a million pieces that something even stronger would be built in its place.*

*I am grateful for the road I have travelled and the journey I've made. It's been hard & long, treacherous & terrifying and there were times when I wasn't sure I'd make it...times when I didn't think I had it in me to keep going. But Spirit picked me up, carrying me from the inside and I let myself be lifted. I let myself continue down the path – sometimes kicking and screaming! – but I kept going, moving forward to a better and better life.*

*I am grateful that in those dark and lonely times I listened to the voice that said, "It won't always be like this." because it was right.*

*There is more love, more goodness, more hope and more beauty than I could ever have imagined. And I am grateful that I can see that!*

*Right now there is so much gratitude inside of me that I can't seem to break it down and speak to smaller parts. All I can feel is the fullness of it. How light and happy I am.*

*I am grateful for Tyler's little cat Velcro. For his curiosity, his mischievous ways, his guts and his innocence.*

*I am grateful for this sacred space in which I sit and write. Clear, pure and holy. I can feel the presence of God the minute I open the door. Whatever stress or confusion may haunt me in the moment, I walk in here and I feel peaceful and content – one with myself.*

*With so much gratitude filling the space inside me and so many things, events, situations and people that I could speak about – I start to wonder how I can ever bring this exercise to a close. When do I stop writing? How do I finish without sounding like I just cut myself off mid-thought or mid-sentence?*

*Well I guess that leads me to another gratitude. I am the creator – the beginner, the middler and the ender – of every piece. Much like my life I have creative license to go where I please and stop when I choose. It's simple really – and when I trust the rhythm of the process I realize that all things have a natural end. I don't have to figure it out, seize up or try to control it. Just relax and let it flow. And for that, I am truly grateful!*

# *Let's Write*

Begin to look at your life as it is right now. The following memory prompts will help you recall the things for which you can be grateful. Read them all the way to the end before you start or begin writing after any of the prompts that call to mind something for which you are grateful. If you downloaded the prompts at www.juneswadron.com, stop reading and listen to them now.

Let's begin with your home – where you currently reside – no matter how big or small. Notice how it supports you, keeps you warm, shelters you from the cold.

In your mind's eye, walk in the front door of your house or apartment and lovingly move from room to room blessing each one saying, "Thank you." Take a new look at what fills each room – the furniture, the paintings, the colours and the energy that fills your home and makes it yours. Bless all of it. Notice what you really like or love about it. Notice what you would want to change while being in full appreciation of what is there now.

Now think about the supports in your life – the people who love you just the way you are – and how you can love them just the way they are – your partner, your parents, your children, grandparents, grandchildren, siblings, nieces, nephews, neighbors, colleagues and special friends. Say a silent thank you for the richness you feel because of their presence in your life. Perhaps you have a mentor or teacher, past or present, who has believed in you, has given you the loving support you needed – either in kind words or deeds – encouraging you to take the next steps. Acknowledge these people in your heart now.

Now reflect on the work you do. What skills and talents do you bring to your work? What is your work teaching you? Who are the people who are there with you? Bless each of them and say thank you to your work for helping you to pay the bills and giving you an opportunity to contribute.

Do you do volunteer work? How is this act of giving honouring you? Who are the people involved? Bless them. Bless yourself. Give thanks for this opportunity to give and receive in this loving way.

Do you have a pet or pets? How do your pets enrich your life? Breathe in the joy and delight of this. Say a silent thank you to them for their innocent and loving nature – yes, loving you unconditionally. Love them for their open and tender hearts, for the comfort they bring you again and again.

Now think about nature – the places of beauty that constantly gift us and bring us home to ourselves. It is often here that we resonate with the part of us that is pure beingness. Here we do not strive or hunger for anything. Instead our hearts open wide while walking through a forest, listening to the sounds of songbirds or watching a sunrise or sunset.

Do you have a favourite place in nature – a place where your spirit feels at home? If so, imagine yourself being back there right now with all your senses fully awake and alive. Give yourself ample time to enjoy this experience. This is another one of God's greatest gifts to us – the ability to use our imaginations, and in this case, to go back to a time and place to recreate an experience of love, joy and inner serenity.

Now think about yourself. What God-given talents and gifts do you have and express in the world? Do you have an appreciation for art, music, dance, laughter, creativity? Give thanks for the ability to enjoy these things. Consider the random acts of kindness you've given to others and that you too have received.

Next, how does your spiritual life feed you? Are you noticing the synchronistic events that are at play – the phone ringing when you think of someone you love and there they are, the money coming in just when you wondered how it ever would, the book someone lent you ages ago that just fed you exactly what you needed to hear to inspire and uplift you. This is you in Divine Co-creation with the Creator. There are no accidents. Breathe in the glory of this.

Now consider all the things in your life that you have to be grateful for. Living life with an attitude of gratitude brings joy, love and abundance into our lives. Love begets Love. Joy begets Joy. Gratitude begets Gratitude.

Move to your writing table and begin your story of appreciation and thanks. And remember, when you are writing the stories that are difficult, return to this one. Let it bring you back into today and all that is good and beautiful in your world.

# Chapter 2

## TEACHERS AND MENTORS

### The Key

by Sharon Pocock

*It's about the key. It always comes back to the key. The key is physical. The key is mental and emotional and metaphorical. It's always about the key.*

*I'm standing in the drab, grey corridor, waiting to open the door. Savouring the moment. Building the anticipation. Feeling my heart race and my skin tingle and the hairs on the back of my neck stand up.*

*The key is a gift to treasure. It's not mine for keeps, but I have temporary ownership and I guard it with care and with pride. Perhaps too much pride, because nobody else has the key. It's there for the asking. It sits in full view, but it seems like I'm the only one who can see that it's real.*

*Like the corridor, the door is grey, heavy and scarred, like some battered safe from an old black and white Western. But I don't need to bring dynamite. I don't need safecracker's hands to unlock the door and discover its treasures.*

*I'm thinking about you as I open the door. Thinking about black curly hair, about a smile, about the intense look on your face when you're answering a question. And that's what made the difference. You always took the time to answer the question. That's why you gave me the key – so that I could ask more questions and find more answers and discover whole new worlds.*

*It started so simply like all great journeys do. We talked about Mockingbirds and slow, southern summers and the boogieman who lived in the house next*

49

*door. I can hear your voice, like Scout's narration, leading me onward, enticing me to take the steps and turn the page. I sat in the courtroom and watched from the balcony and in my head I stood with the others as Atticus passed. I slid into a world I hadn't known existed and you were there to guide me. That was the start of the journey.*

*Looking back, the foundations were always there. At home, adventures and excitement lined the shelves, sirens waiting to tempt and ensnare. They didn't have to work too hard. One look at the gaudy spines and exciting titles and I was gone. Like Eve with the apple, I stepped into the garden and I wallowed for a time. Dennis Wheately, Alistair MacLean, Hammond Innes – adventures of daring do, of chiselled jaws and damsels in distress and baddies vanquished in the final chapter. And they were fun, but I wanted more. I wanted to think and discover and challenge and question. I knew the bad guy wasn't always beaten and that good men didn't always save the day. I knew that damsels sometimes didn't need saving – that they kicked butt and flew planes and made choices. And that's what you gave me and that's what I treasure – choices.*

*In my mind's eye I can still see the door and the key and I step forward and turn the handle and step over the threshold. You're right behind me, giving me pointers, showing me maps of safe routes and well-trodden paths and where the dragons lurk. At my feet there was a long beach and a conch shell and a pair of broken glasses. On the second shelf, the shadow of a jungle beckoned a journey in hearts of darkness. Up in the far corner I can see the tips of the Himalayas and hear the sound of cannon fire and the screams of battle, hand-to-hand.*

*The shelves go up and up, but you hand me a ladder and I start to climb – step by step, shelf by shelf, book by book – new worlds, new adventures, new ideas – a new me. And as I climb, you grow distant and small, framed in the doorway of that magical room – so innocuous on the outside, but like a Tardis within. I look down from my eerie at the top of the ladder and you wave and wish me luck. You don't look back and I can't climb down to follow. I doubt if we'd recognise each other now. You are a vague figure in my head, tangible only in my dreams and in the recesses of my memory. A magician revealing wonders to a child. And what wonders you revealed.*

*So here I am, still on my ladder. So many steps below me and so many still to climb. I've fought dragons in Middle Earth and run through the Bibighar Gardens in the flash of the summer rains. I've danced the minuet with Mr. Darcy and listened to Dracula's siren call. I've cracked codes and picked locks and crossed borders and worked out who was Tinker, Tailor, Soldier and Spy.*

*We'll probably never meet again, but for that short year you threw a switch and the light shone brightly. Now standing on my ladder I can see the future and the past and sometimes, if I stand on tiptoe, I feel like I can touch the stars.*

*So I close my eyes and see you in my dreams and we talk about Mockingbirds and slow southern summers and childhood's end. Then I wake up and you're gone, but one thing always remains. You always leave me the key.*

# Mr. Logan, an Angel of Kindness

by June Swadron

*The following story is about loving kindness and a time when a true angel appeared in my life and lifted me from the depths of darkness into the realm of hope and miracles.*

I dedicate this story to my Grade 6 teacher, Mr. Logan. Mr. Logan was the first person in my young life who consistently reflected back to me that which made me feel good about myself. Before him, was a teacher of a different kind, Miss S., the one who crushed any self-confidence I may have found.

I was 11 years old and the youngest child in a family that was grossly dysfunctional. In between the good days which I prayed would last, would come the inevitable barrage of fighting followed by days of mom's angry, silent rages. My parents fought over not having enough money, my sisters dating non-Jewish boys, my brother being a rebel and me and my laziness and depression. I hated life. I hated school. I always wanted to run away. But at eleven, where to?

I was a terrible student and Miss S. made sure I knew it. I had already honed the habit of dissociating, fantasizing, daydreaming, going far, far away – certainly never at my desk paying attention. I wished I had been one of those kids that poured all their pain into their schoolwork, burying themselves in books and acing everything because it was the one place in the world they could excel. But that wasn't me. Reading wasn't encouraged at home and I didn't seek it out. I seemed to be afraid of everything and it showed. And Miss S. used it to humiliate me. When I failed a test, she would announce it to the class. When I didn't have my hand up, she'd choose me to answer the question. This would cause me to tremble and shake because she'd come over to my desk and put her sharp finger nails into my ear and squeeze. Then she'd pull me up out of my desk that way and demand an answer. Finally when she knew she wasn't going to get one because I could hardly breathe, she'd release her nails from my ear and shout for me to stay after school.

*She'd tell Mark to stay after school too. He was berated as much as I was. When everyone had rowdily left the classroom, she'd make us both stand up straight in front of her. Then with a look of pure disgust and sarcastic intonation, she'd admonish us with these words: "You two are pathetic and stupid! You're an embarrassment – a disgrace. I promise you I will fail you both. Now, get out of my sight!" This happened on a regular basis.*

*Mark and I would leave the classroom and walk outside with our heads down to avoid the perceived stares from the kids playing in the school yard. We'd walk quickly past them, shrouded in shame, wishing we were invisible. Once on the street we'd walk together in silence. When we got to the field, we parted ways. Mark continued down Baycrest Avenue. I needed to cross the field and the creek to get to the street where I lived. I walked slowly, hoping to delay whatever was waiting for me at home. Would mom be raging or loving? I never knew.*

*True to her word, at the end of the school year, Miss S. marked, "F A I L E D!" in big red letters across my report card. Mark found the same thing on his. It was one of the worst days of our lives. We both dreaded going home.*

*I don't remember what my parents said or did when they read my report card. In my fantasy mom was reassuring and comforting. I often had those fantasies – it was what I yearned for. And sometimes my wishes came true. Sometimes she was remarkable. She could be so nurturing, so kind, so wise. But inevitably, the sardonic side of her nature would return and would take over. Dad was quieter.*

*Soon it was summer. School was out and I knew the other grade six's in my class were excited about going on to Ledbury Park Junior High School in the Fall where they would have their own lockers and get to change classrooms between periods and have different teachers for every subject. I could only imagine how excited they'd be. Not me. Not Mark. We'd have to trudge back, shame-faced, to the same public school, back into grade six again with kids a whole year younger.*

*And then it came: September – and with it, the first day of school. I hardly slept the night before. I was planning my escape. Had there been street kids in Toronto in those days I'm pretty certain I would have been among them because it was a familiar notion to run away. (Even when I was eight or nine I would run away from home – but never too far. I'd hide in the stairwell of our six-story apartment building. It was as far as I could go because it was late and dark and I'd be too frightened to be out alone in the night.) And here I was, age twelve with the same sickening feeling to run as I thought about going back into Miss S's classroom. This time I wanted to run and never come back. But somehow I walked to school the next morning instead.*

*Once there I was instructed to go to room 6-B. I did and a miracle awaited me. At the front of the class stood the well loved Mr. Logan. I knew from the previous year that kids in his class always seemed to be happy. He had the best reputation. He was also young and handsome and wore a warm, genuine smile, laughed easily and exuded an aura of kindness. It seemed too good to be true that he would be my teacher. I was afraid they made a mistake and I would be sent across the hall to Miss S.'s class. Once everyone was seated, Mr. Logan did a roll call. I held my breath. He was going in alphabetical order. ...Sammy Olstein, Sylvia Peters, David Rosenberg, June Swadron, Deborah Timberley... Oh, my God! Was that really my name he called or did I imagine it because I wanted it so badly? It took a moment to sink in but yes, it was true. He did call my name and then he called Mark's. We looked at each other and both breathed a deep and grateful sigh of relief.*

*And so it was. Mr. Logan became my teacher that year and it was the best thing that had ever happened to me. Not only was he kind, but he was also joyful, gentle, patient and sincere. On top of that he made learning fun. And best of all he liked me. This I knew because of his constant kindness, praise and encouragement. He took extra time with me after school on subjects that I found difficult. I became inspired to read and conscientiously do my homework – something I had never done in the past. I wanted to learn and I did. Soon my school work started to improve. I was beginning to learn that I could learn and that I wasn't stupid after all. And as my marks improved, my confidence grew and I was able to stand a little taller. At the end of the year I held the highest percentage in that grade 6 class – a feat I wouldn't ever have believed possible.*

*I will never ever forget you, Mr. Logan. In a sea of pain, you were my refuge. More than anything else, you made me believe in myself. You gave me hope and the courage to go on.*

*So sir, wherever you are, I thank you from the bottom of my heart. That 12 year old girl who still lives inside me, the one who was given back her life all those years ago, will never forget you. You were my heaven-sent angel. My gift from God. My mentor, my teacher, my friend.*

*Today, I try to do my best to live up to your way of being. My intention is to always motivate, encourage and care for others in my teaching and therapy practice by offering kindness and respect. I know that our souls flourish this way. I also know only too well how we shrivel, back away and die a little more inside every time we are criticized and judged. The young child in me couldn't have known back then that Miss S. must have been a very unhappy woman to have treated children that way – but as an adult I can recognize it as such and know that every act of cruelty and aggression is a call for love.*

*A million thank yous, Mr. Logan, for teaching me the value of every-day human kindness.*

# *Let's Write*

Has there been someone in your life who impacted it in such a way as to make it easier, gentler, better or somewhat kinder? Someone who took the time to be with you and uplifted you so you were able to look upon the world with fresh eyes? If so, imagine that person in front of you now and begin to recall the day that you first met.

How old were you? What is his or her name? What were the conditions in which you met? Did you like each other from the start or was it a relationship that grew over time? How long was this person in your life? Is he or she still in it? What was it that made your relationship particularly meaningful or special? What were some of this person's qualities that meant the most to you? And now consider some of the specific ways he or she influenced your life. What did he or she do or say that made a difference? How did your thinking, behaviour or attitudes change as a result of his or her motivation?

If that person had not entered your life, do you think you would be the same today? If not, why not? In what ways do you think you would be different? What were you like before you met? What path did that person's influence put you on that you may not have chosen otherwise? Have you been able to pass some of what you learned on to others? And since we are all teachers and students at the same time, in what ways do you think you may have influenced or benefited your mentor? What truth or awareness did you bring to him or her?

Is this person still alive today? If so, have you considered thanking him or her for the life-altering gifts you were given? We never know for certain how people feel about themselves. Receiving a letter of appreciation, thanking and acknowledging them by sharing how they made a positive difference in our lives could be the very thing they need to bring about a renewed sense of hope, peace, joy or well-being. Consider finding out where this person is today and offering your heart-felt appreciation, possibly even through this story you're about to write.

And now allow your heart to open to the wonder and splendor of the Universe – how Providence sends us remarkable people to guide us and show us the way just in the nick of time! Sometimes they come for just a day or a month or a year but their impact lasts a lifetime. It is grace that brings these people to us. If you have been fortunate enough to have had a "Mr. Logan" in your life, then wrap yourself in gratitude and feel the love enfold you. Consider writing your mentor a letter. Even if he or she has since passed, it is both healing and gratifying to do this. Love moves beyond the veil. Your grateful energy is being sent.

# Chapter 3

## A Time In My Life When I Was Stronger Than I Thought

### The Creation of Madness, Masks and Miracles

by June Swadron

*On August 1st, 1998, I moved into my brand new apartment in the West End of Vancouver having just made a 3,000 mile hike across the country to move to my new city and begin my new life. Leaving Toronto, the home of my birth, was very difficult in some ways and exhilarating in others. The hard part was saying goodbye to family and friends. The exhilarating part was making my life-long dream come true. The first time I went to Vancouver was in 1971 as a young hippie and I spent a summer which I had never forgotten. Over the thirty years I would return there time and again because I fell in love with the mountains and the ocean and the way they made me feel inside. The summer before moving there I was visiting Vancouver again and one day on Ambleside beach I made a pact with myself that the next time I came to the West Coast I wasn't going to leave after two weeks. I was coming back to stay.*

*From the time I made my decision to move it felt like I was in a state of grace. And this feeling of being in the flow continued for me for many months after I arrived in Vancouver. It was with heart, joy and trust that I watched the mystery of my new life unfold as it would. Within two months I had full workshops up and running. I was walking the sea wall every day and emailing* my family and friends back home, joyfully telling them how good my life was. And it was. Until that old familiar foreboding set in about 9 months later and I could hardly believe what was happening to me.

At that time I was beginning to build a healthy private psychotherapy practice, facilitating corporate seminars for the Canadian Mental Health Association and running three weekly groups. Then it all started to fall apart. I tried the usual methods I have learned to use over the years to help me move through panic attacks and the onset of clinical depression – things like yoga, healthy food, proper sleep, psychotherapy, walks, journaling and reaching out. But this insidious monster continued to creep up on me until I could barely function.

I have come to learn that once it hits that level of chemical imbalance in me, no matter what healing tool I practice, it does not make much difference. Still, I managed to "keep it together" for my work and outwardly to the people with whom I was developing new friendships. I was wearing the masks which I learned to put on fairly early in life in order to feel accepted in my home and in society. However, the amount of energy it took to wear the disguise, which was beginning to wear thin, soon became overwhelming. When the groups I was facilitating all came to a natural conclusion I began to isolate more and more and held myself hostage in my own home. I could barely get to the grocery store across the street and it terrified me to even do that. The panic, the obsessive suicidal ideation and hopelessness took over.

One day I finally summoned up the courage to go to a mental health walk-in clinic and tried to explain my situation to an intake worker. She seemed genuinely kind as well as sorry as she told me she couldn't help me because I didn't fit their mandate. Because I presented well and did not have the stereotypical look of a street person, I was not considered ill enough to be seen by one of the psychiatrists or psychologists on site. She suggested I go to the emergency of the nearest hospital. That was beyond what I knew I was capable of. Instead I went home and wrote my suicide note and put in front of me the many vials of antidepressants and sleep medication that I had brought from Toronto that were no longer working. I didn't want to die, but I didn't know how to live one more minute with the panic, depression and despair and a mind that could only be described as a torture chamber.

I have a very strong faith and believe I have been walking what I consider a spiritual path for most of my life but if I needed proof that I was being watched over, it was certainly given to me that night. At the very moment I was about to end my life, what I can only describe as a force, seemingly outside of me, lifted me from the computer where I had just written what I truly believed to be the last thing I would ever write. An energy I had not known in many months, drove me from the computer to the bathroom where I found myself violently tearing open every vial of pills and flushing them – one by one – down the toilet. It was several moments later that I had the realization that my only means of escape was now gone and the despair hit even harder. I don't know how I found my way from the bathroom to the bedroom or even much else but I do know that two days later I admitted myself to St. Paul's hospital where relief awaited me. And it was here that I completely surrendered to the situation and let myself be taken care of. The nurses and doctors were compassionate and kind. Within a short time the medication they gave me began to help. The side effects of dry mouth and trembling hands were hardly a concern from that perspective. I was alive and I was grateful.

Soon I needed to go back to my life on the outside. But something on the inside of me had shifted. And this is where I can honestly say, I was so much stronger than I thought.

In the past, I have jumped back on the bandwagon as fast as possible as though I'd never skipped a beat. I'd be back in my world seeing clients and delivering seminars. If I did it fast enough I could pretend no one knew where I had just been and I sure as heck wasn't going to tell them. I wasn't prepared to risk being ostracised, criticised, seen as a failure, incompetent or bad. I was giving enough of those messages to myself. Even more, considering the work I do, I gave myself the additional pressure of "I should know better". After all I've done the work and gone through years of personal therapy. I am educated, have a clinical designation with The Ontario Society of Psychotherapists and am a certified life skills coach. How could this happen to me? Why do I have this illness and why can't I heal it? I equated it to a character flaw, a weakness and something I was personally doing to make it happen. My sense of shame and guilt was enormous. The internalized stigma has been much worse than any external judgments I have ever felt. Still, I have come to know only too well the stigma that does go along with mental illness and that, unfortunately, is what keeps the masks on tight.

But this time I decided I wasn't going to hide any more.

When I left St. Paul's Hospital, instead of running back to work, although it was terrifying not to, I knew that I had to do things differently. I didn't move 3,000 miles across the country to begin again at this stage of my life and go into old, unhealthy patterns. In an attempt to put some of those stigmas to rest, I did what I believe I was divinely guided to do even though I rejected it for a long time. When I asked the question, "Where do I go from here, God?" the reply I got over and over again was to tell my story. I was mortified. "Not me; you can't mean me", I'd cry. But eventually I listened to my inner promptings and they became a play; one I co-wrote, co-produced, played the lead part in and for which I even wrote the lyrics to every song.

Julia Cameron's book, The Artist's Way, was the catalyst that helped me take the leap. It was the brilliant processes outlined in her book, to which

*I devoted myself faithfully, that eventually gave me the courage to make it happen.*

*I called the play Madness, Masks and Miracles. It was about the madness or the dark night of the soul that we all go through as we take our human walk on earth, the masks we wear to hide the madness, lest we be ostracized, criticized or marginalized and finally the miracles that let us take off the masks and be our true selves.*

*The play got enormous support. Even though I'm somewhat embarrassed to toot my own horn, I have dug up my favourite accolade to quote right here on these pages. I remember how I took a terrifying experience and channeled it into a creative theatre piece that premiered at the World Assembly for Mental Health in Vancouver, hosted by the Canadian Psychiatric Association (CPA).*

*Dr. Michael Myers, the then President of the CPA had this to say:*

> "This play is a winner. June Swadron and her writing team and actors engage the audience immediately and throughout with what it's like to have a mental illness in contemporary society. We feel the anguish and confusion, we witness the denial in co-workers and family, we experience the shame of the sufferer and the multiple losses and we learn painfully about the limitations of our treatments. Yet this production is not cynical or depressing. It is moving, inspiring and intensely evocative. A gift. A call-to-arms. A must-see for every Canadian citizen."

*After the play was over, when the last curtain call came down, I did not recognize the enormity of what I had just done. Even though there were dozens and dozens of letters of praise, I still did not love myself enough at the time to acknowledge the magnitude of it. Now, five years later when called to write a story about being stronger than I thought, this story jumped out at me. Today I am taking a healthy stand that says: "Yes, I did that!" When my depressions come as they tend to do, I will try to remember how resilient I can be. I will choose life and thank God for all the blessings that I receive over and over again. I will be comforted by the knowledge that I know I can make it. I always have and I always will. I do it with my spiritual beliefs, with poetry, with music, with friendships, with nature, with my work and with love.*

*I am reminded here of Marianne Williamson's famous passage that she wrote for Nelson Mandela's Inaugural speech:*

*"Our deepest fear is not that we are inadequate. Our deepest fear is that we are powerful beyond measure. It is our light, not our darkness, that frightens us. We ask ourselves, Who am I to be brilliant, gorgeous, talented and fabulous? Actually, who are you not to be? You are a child of God. Your playing small doesn't serve the world. There's nothing enlightened about shrinking so*

*that other people won't feel insecure around you. We are all meant to shine as children do. We were born to manifest the glory of God that is within us. It's not just in some of us; it's in everyone. And as we let our own light shine, we unconsciously give other people permission to do the same. As we are liberated from our own fear, our presence automatically liberates others."*

When I was finally able to commit to writing and performing the play, even though my shame-filled ego was still terrified at the thought of coming out in public with my personal story of mental illness, it provided a safe place for others to also share their stories. People with a mental illness as well as their caregivers, friends, children, parents and co-workers stood up and disclosed what was in their hearts and what was relevant to them.

Perhaps this book with my personal stories of bi-polar illness will help some people come out of their own closets of shame. Perhaps they will proudly affirm their inner courage, strength and resilience instead. This isn't just my story. It's so many of our stories. When the statistics tell us that 1 in 5 people in North America will suffer from a clinical depression at some time in their lives, we can't continue having a "we versus them" society. It is my hope that each of us be kinder and more tolerant with one another because underneath each of our masks we are all innocent and loving beings. It is only when we feel safe enough to shed these masks and speak authentically from our hearts that the madness ends and the miracles begin.

## Recuerdos De La Alhambra

by Janet Lawson

*The week has been difficult, though I always thought I would investigate this idea of My Strength. First, I'm thinking that I never allow myself to really stretch to my limits and that is why I feel I have never tested my strength – I live below the level of its expression. But in the tub this afternoon with George – another 'wisdom bath' – tears came readily as I told him of two possible times. Both are so painful that it's no wonder I avoid them and try to find a simpler sample.*

*Like being in Granada at last! – Recuerdos de La Alhambra, the composition by Tárrega that inspired me to learn classical guitar so that one day I could play toward its beauty. Carved in stone above one of the entrances was:*

*"Dale limosna, mujer, que no hay en la vida nada como la pena de ser ciego en Granada." (Roughly, Give him alms, woman, for there is no greater tragedy in life than to be blind in Granada.) Finally I got myself to that Moorish master-piece, taught myself enough tremolo to approximate the melody, sought out the gypsy musicians by night, bought the dream guitar and decided to venture to the monastery in the hills above this most beautiful city. I took the bus as far as it would go, followed general directions and cut across the fields and climbed. All was magical. Living out the dream begun at fifteen when in music I en-countered beauty bigger than my pain.*

*From nowhere appeared one of the gypsy musicians – can he accompany me, he asks. Oh, my life is charmed! I get to try my few words of Spanish with a real gypsy guitarist while we trek towards the magical monastery, older than the hills we climb. We are so high, so remote, the conversation is as pleasant as my tourist Spanish allows. Then out comes the knife along with the demand that I drop to my knees and service him with my mouth. How can this be?! This is not in my fantasy! He's got his lines all wrong! He says that's obvi-ously why I am here. I suddenly see myself through his eyes – a blonde twenty-six-year-old foreign beauty who doesn't know dick. Well, one thing I know for Absolute Sure is I am not going to suck on his! And here on this mountainside is where I first discovered – one of many episodes, several of which I landed in due to my naiveté, or as they used to say in a court of law, "she was asking for it" – that I WAY prefer righteous rage to fear. How dare he sully my dream?! I am writing this script and I can improvise my way around this nasty little twist you little shit!*

*I became more fluent than I could, telling him in rising voice and stature that he did not have the right to such a demand. I became one large loud woman who claimed to this strong young wiry proud gypsy and to his own hills that he and his ways had better do some quick learning. As my torrent of words escalated I saw and felt the power of my will. The tables had turned. He knew it and I knew it, knife be damned. In the middle of nowhere, on steep pastures high above the city whose image of beauty had once been saviour to teenage mire, a tall slender young Canadian woman chased a tight tough younger-still Spanish gypsy downhill fast, screaming "Policia!!" when we both knew there was none to hear. He just wanted to be away from this crazy creature – not what he had bargained for and certainly not worth the trouble.*

*The monastery remained whatever it was. Not visited by me. When I fi-nally reached a road I followed it down. Downward would take me to Granada, to my room, to my handmade guitar, to my dinner and safety and sanity. I came upon a village where a very small and ancient toothless man led his burro down the road. Would I like to ride his burro? Alright, a choice: do I stay scared or do I welcome the sort of reality where kind people offer special moments? I slowed the heartbeat, swallowed the suspicion and climbed aboard thinking, ok, these Spanish males can redeem themselves. Clip clop clip clop in the hot Spanish sun, a few words of broken conversation, feeling calmer and open to charm once again. Yes, this is very nice. Until a gnarled hand cupped the ass riding the ass. No danger, just derisive self-laugher – I have been alone in Spain for how many months now?! Will I never learn?!*

*Decades later now, and yes, I think I can see better how to be and not to be when in Rome. And yet... I retain and exercise my still fierce belief in my right to be a woman exploring her own planet on her own terms.*

# One Step at a Time

by Debbi Jones

*One month shy of my twenty-first birthday, I married Eric Johnson. Deep, deep in my subconscious, I knew I didn't love him but it would be twelve years before I would admit that to myself. Why did I tell myself I loved him? Here are my best guesses: I had this unconscious need to fix someone and he needed fixing, I wanted my life to be settled, I wanted to be needed and I wanted to be loved. Once I had agreed to marry him, I didn't have the guts to call off my wedding. Thus it was that I vaulted the door shut on my real feelings and forged on.*

*Eric was hired on the Provincial Police Force just after we got married. He was posted in the city where we were living at the time. I was slated to begin teacher's college in the fall of 1976.*

*Sometime during the first year of our marriage, we began to romanticize about life in a small town. We put in for a transfer to Blue Stream, a tiny town in the most northerly part of the province. Eric left for Blue Stream in January of 1977 and I stayed behind to finish my teaching degree. I applied for, and got permission to, complete my final practice teaching session at the Blue Stream District High School. I joined Eric in late April.*

*It's rather complicated, but the fate of my first year of teaching was forever altered because of the principal of the Blue Stream District High School. His name was Paul Sampson and he was a tyrant. He was short with a stocky body and mean eyes that liked to bore into you for the fun of watching you squirm. He was the incarnation of every negative stereotype attributed to very short men. He was a bully, arrogant and a power-obsessed control freak. The year I* moved to Blue Stream, I had the unpleasant task of trying to earn his favour in order to be hired for a fall position. I worked extremely hard throughout my practicum and then again when I took over a Life Skills class during the final few weeks of June when a teacher suddenly quit. Mr. Sampson tended to have that effect on teachers.

A former Vice Principal of the high school, Walter O'Brien, became the principal of the local public school. Like most everyone, Walter hated Paul Sampson, his former boss, and the feelings were graciously returned in kind. Knowing that Paul was enjoying playing cat and mouse with me, Walter called me up out of the blue and asked me if I wanted to be interviewed for a full-time elementary teaching position. I was terrified by the very thought that in the fall I could be living in this small town but not have a job.

I am a city girl, born and bred. Life in a tiny mining community with less than 3,000 people spread out over fifteen miles was a shock to say the least. This hint of civilization was surrounded by hundreds of miles of spindly spruce trees that housed wolves, moose and bears. At that time, there were about ten stores in town, as well as a Polish Hall, a Legion, a movie theatre that soon closed down, a few small schools, five churches and, of course, the two gold mines. It took over an hour of driving down a very windy, single lane road to reach the Trans Canada Highway and five more hours to reach Winnipeg. I was 1,200 miles away from my friends, my family and everything that was familiar to me. Mosquitoes and ravens were the size of cats and dogs. The first summer I was there, my eyes puffed up and closed over because I had no immunity to the ravenous black flies that swarmed the air night and day.

Without hesitation, I accepted the interview for the elementary teaching position and became the proud owner-to-be of a split grade three/four class in a tiny five-room school. The principal would drop by occasionally – something that became more frequent once he started having an affair with the grade seven/eight teacher, another first year rookie who was half his age. I had not stepped one foot inside a grade three or four class since I was nine or ten years old and in those grades myself. I knew absolutely nothing about elementary teaching. Despite this fact, by the time September rolled around, my classroom was a virtual elementary paradise. Using my own money, I found a rug and cushy pillows and built a puppet theatre equipped with puppets. I furnished a reading library full of the latest cool books from the Children's bookstore in Toronto. The desks were arranged in an imaginative way. I had the students' names creatively designed on cardboard tags. I had posters on the walls, sayings artistically written on the bulletin boards and coloured chalk waiting anxiously on my chalk ledges. I also had no clue how I was going to get through a day. What the heck was I going to do with the curriculum guides I had been given? No exaggeration, they might as well have been written in Mandarin.

*After Labour Day, the school year began and my stress level went to heights I had never before experienced – twenty-four hours of relentless cortisol, adrenaline and fear raged through my body. At the end of the day, when I was alone in my classroom with the door shut, I would sit at my teacher's desk and cry. Every night I would stay late after school and then carry most of my binders and books home. All evening I would hope that somehow a miracle would happen and I would know what I was going to do the next day. I was completely out of my league and so far beyond my comfort zone that I was paralyzed most of the time.*

*It was in the midst of all this, in early October when I was barely sleeping a couple of hours a night, that Eric came home one morning after doing a night shift and sat on the edge of our bed. He looked at me with an odd expression and said calmly, "I don't think I want to be married anymore." We had only been married 18 months.*

*I was barely able to respond. I recall stumbling into the bathroom, bending over the toilet and either retching or feeling as if I would. I distinctly remember going to school and walking around as if I had been hit by a train. I felt completely alone. I was over a thousand miles from home without one close friend or confidante. How I got through that day and that week, I still don't know.*

*During the next few days Eric and I must have talked but I think I mostly became silent. I struggled to figure out how to respond to something as foreign as this experience. I was the one who had always made everything work out for myself. How could I fail at something so quickly if I was giving it my best, my all?*

*To my surprise, after a few days I became quite calm, almost matter of fact. A sense of peace emerged. Acceptance. I asked myself what needed to be done. I found a room to rent in an old Nurses' Residence. I worked out exactly what I would need to do to establish myself on my own. And through all this, I got up every day, went to school and continued to walk the labyrinth of my first year of teaching things I knew absolutely nothing about.*

*Less than two weeks later, one afternoon when Eric was home, I sat down with him and told him my plans. I recall that he was very quiet, likely processing this calm, confident woman before him. I wasn't begging him to stay with me. I wasn't falling apart at the thought of being on my own. Suddenly he fell apart. He said he was sorry, that he had made a mistake and that we should try to work things out.*

*It was a crossroad.*

*When I married I totally believed I would make my marriage work the way my parents had – through the good times and the tough times. When he asked me to try again I could not imagine being the one to give up. I had been hurt beyond belief, but I felt I could not abandon a vow I had made. So I stayed. Nonetheless I had given myself a glimpse of the strong and powerful woman I really was deep inside. It would be twelve more years until that woman would emerge again but it was the beginning of learning how to believe in myself.*

*In that tumultuous year, I also proved to myself that I could handle any kind of teaching challenge. My grade three and four students survived the ignorance of their rookie teacher, leaving me with a swarm of loving notes, hand-drawn pictures and little gifts from Avon. I would go on to become a teacher who, over the course of her career, taught every grade from Junior Kindergarten Phys Ed. to Grade 13 Advanced Literature Studies. I would become a Department Head of English in a large city high school and a master teacher who would make it her mission to help many young teachers begin their teaching journey. I would one day, to my surprise, be given a prestigious award of teaching excellence. But all of that was only because I found the strength to take one step at a time throughout that year when I was lost and alone in a strange and frightening place.*

# Time to Tell

by Nan Campbell

*December 1st, 1982*

*Mrs. Francis (Bert) Wood gets on a bus and leaves Ft. Frances behind. Arriving at the Winnipeg bus depot, she calls her eldest daughter Nancy. Nancy dutifully responds, arrives, loads her suitcases in the back of the van and heads home. One thing is certain – Bert has not returned to Winnipeg to help her daughter convalesce from her recent surgery. Bert declares that she needs help, no one in Ft. Frances will help her. Woody (Bert's new husband) is out of town and she can't stand being alone any longer. Nancy is in the middle of a teaching practicum, winter exams and is trying to make up for the week she lost after her surgery. She is 4 months pregnant with her first child. However, this is familiar territory for her and she immediately goes into crisis intervention mode.*

*In between teaching and exams, Nancy drives her mother all over town, makes countless phone calls and convenes a family meeting with her three teen-age siblings. The desperation mounts as they search for ways to find their mother a doctor, clinic, intake unit, anything, anyone who might be able to help – she is morbidly depressed and in very rough shape.*

*One evening after several days of failed efforts, Bert looks to her daughter and in a trembling voice announces that she is going to go back to Ft. Frances. The next morning, Nancy is greeted by Bert's two suitcases at the door and her mother sitting at the dining room table, shaking, sweating, with a lit cigarette burning away to a grey finger of ash. Bert licks her lips and attempts to sound upbeat, "If it's not too much trouble dear, could I get a lift to the bus depot?"*

*Heart sinking, Nancy resigns herself to what seems to be the hard truth: this is her mother's life and she is responsible for her choices. For a fleeting moment Nancy thinks that things might work out. "Okay Mom, let me just warm up the van and we'll get you off to the bus."*

*Nancy slams the door of the van and heaves the suitcases on to a cart. "That's fine honey, I'll take it from here. I'll be fine. Say good bye to the kids for me." Bert forces a wan smile from her puffy, vacant face. She pauses to fish out a cigarette from her purse, lights up and without another word or glance, heads into the bus depot.*

*December 15, 1982*

*"Nancy is that you? Bert's daughter Nancy? Well how are you doing dear? I hear you're going to have a baby. Oh this is Millie Wood, you know Woody's mother."*

*Alerted by the high-pitched tone in the voice at the other end of the line, Nancy knew something was wrong. "Mrs. Wood, is everything okay with Mom?"*

*"Oh dear, I don't know how to tell you this Nancy, but your mom passed away tonight, well we think it was actually last night, or maybe some time yesterday."*

*"Passed away? You mean she's dead? How?"... Nancy felt herself tumbling into a surreal pool of liquid sounds. Millie Wood was jabbering away, describing the gruesome details of the neighbor seeing something strange through his kitchen window, calling the RCMP, trying to get into the house, trying to find Woody, finally contacting Millie about entering the house, breaking through the door and being greeted by a horrible sight.*

*"Dear, she hung herself. You know that big exhaust fan in the kitchen ceiling? Well imagine her hanging from that fan, just hanging there in her nightgown like a limp rag doll. She used the dog's chain and I imagine she had to work pretty hard to get the whole contraption rigged. The chair that she stepped on was kicked over underneath her. No one is sure how long she'd been hanging there. I guess her shadow is what caught Billy's attention next door. He pounded and pounded at her door trying to get in and then he called the police. The police cut her down and now she's at the funeral parlor. Nancy? Are you still there?"*

*"Millie, is Woody there?"*

"Well yes he's back in town dear, but he's a real mess as you can imagine. This is a terrible situation for my poor son. I've had to go ahead and make all of the arrangements myself. We're going to have a service on Friday morning and there will be a luncheon back here at your mom and Woody's place. Will you kids be able to make it to the funeral?"

"Make it to our own mother's funeral Millie? Of course we'll make it. Uhhh Millie thanks for calling and for taking care of things."

Nancy hung up the phone, took a deep breath, sighed, rolled her shoulders back and picked up the phone to call her dad. "Jesus Nance, I'm sorry. Who's going to tell the kids? Are you going to go to the funeral? I'll loan you a car if you need one.... "

"Dad I'm going to tell the kids. I'll send Greg over to pick them up right now. I'll talk to you later when I know more."

With Cindy, Joanne and Ross all lined up on the couch together, Nancy didn't know where to start. "This is about Mom isn't it?" Cindy got right to the point. "She's dead isn't she?"

"For fuck's sake Cindy!" punched Ross, "Why would you say that?"

"Well you guys, Mom is dead. She died yesterday. It was suicide." Nancy could not bring herself to tell her brother and sisters how their mother had finally killed herself. It seemed too violent to tell these vulnerable young teenage kids about her hanging from that dog chain – she was having a hard enough time dealing with the image herself.

"Overdose?" Joanne offered up meekly.

"How else would she do it?" barked Ross trying to be the tough brother in the face of this insanity.

"So the funeral is on Friday, Dad has offered us a car. We'll book into a motel for the night and be in and out as fast as we can. How does that sound?"

"Awesome!" spat the combative Cindy, "Another Campbell family road trip." The four siblings looked at each other, Joanne's lip quivered, Ross wiped away a tear, Cindy looked to Nancy and they all dove into a collective wail of sorrow. "She finally got it right you guys, she was desperate, there was nothing we could have done and do you realize that this was her 21st attempt? Really it has to be for the better, she's finally at peace..." Nancy grasped at ways to make sense of the whole thing, to try and somehow mend the torn souls of her fragile sisters and brother.

The Campbell Four loaded up the station wagon and with Greg, Nancy's husband at the steering wheel, they departed on the merciless trip to Ft. Frances. They arrived close to midnight and checked into the motel. They tried to get some sleep before the surreal circus act tomorrow in which they would perform in the centre ring.

There was a collective inhale when the four Campbell's entered the chapel. They were greeted and asked if they would like to spend some time with their *mother before the service. There was a viewing in the sanctuary. Nancy had not accounted for an open casket and responded with a swift no thank you. Cindy managed to sneak away saying she had to go to the bathroom. When she returned to the family she was ashen. "She definitely didn't overdose you guys. Nancy you knew didn't you, why didn't you tell us?"*

*So, right before the service, Nancy was compelled to explain to her brother and sisters how their mother killed herself. "I guess she really meant business this time," was all she could muster as consolation. John White (former neighbor and family friend) had once been Bert's psychiatrist and he was the one to give her eulogy. His words were kind and compassionate. After the service, he spoke to the Campbell children. He told the children that there was not a thing they could have done to prevent this. His certainty was comforting and those words would serve to support each child as they worked through the events of their mother's death.*

*Each one of Bert's children moved through their grief in a unique way. Nancy shut the door on tears from the moment she heard the news of her mother's death. It would take her 13 years and her own suicide attempt before she was reduced to the very pool of sorrows she had been stepping around for the entire prolonged aftermath of that fateful December day in 1982.*

*February 12, 2009*

*Yes, I overcame this rather insurmountable obstacle – against all odds. It is not so much her death that I have overcome – it is her life. As I have been writing through her death thinking that the bizarre tale of her demise is the object of my overcoming, I realize that is not it at all. I have overcome being my mother's daughter. I sit here in wonder that I have overcome this legacy of tragedy and hopelessness.*

*In writing, I move from overcoming to becoming.*

# Let's Write

Begin to journey back to a time in your life when you were stronger than you thought – when you overcame obstacles beyond all doubt. There may be several such times. Still yourself, breathe and allow one of these times to unfold before you. You needn't strive for it… just let it gently reveal itself.

Notice the circumstances of that time appear on the screen of your mind. Do not embody this experience. Simply observe what was happening from a safe distance. This is an opportunity to be a loving and compassionate witness to a younger you – an earlier time when a situation arose that called for strength, courage and conviction to see you through.

Before writing your story, consider reading "Invocation – Opening to the Gifts". See Book 1, Part D.

When did this situation occur? Do you remember the year? How old were you? Where were you living at the time? What was happening just prior to the events of this story?

Were there red flags warning you of what was about to happen? Did you see it coming? If so, how did you prepare for it? Or maybe it was something that was going on for a long time and you knew you had to make serious changes regardless of what you perceived the consequences might be. Perhaps there were no red flags, no events over time, but something that you were called to respond to immediately.

Bring the details of this time up on the screen. Notice what was happening. Was there one situation that was difficult to manage or was there one darn thing after another other akin to Murphy's Law?

Were there others involved besides you? If so, what part did they play? What kind of interactions were you having together? Were you in any danger? Did you have to protect yourself and/or someone else? Who were the supports in your life at that time? Were you, in fact, feeling supported or were you bearing the weight of it on your own? Is it your style to get through things mostly by yourself or do you reach out to others in a crisis? What did you do this time?

As time continued, did the situation get worse, more complicated? And then, how in fact, did you eventually handle it? What actions did you take to make it better, to make it easier? What skills did you use? What strengths did you utilize? At which point did you know that you were going to make it? And once you did, once you got safely over to the other side, how did you feel? Exhausted, spent, grateful, relieved? Some people crash after a crisis is over. Did you?

If you haven't done so before, take this opportunity now to fully acknowledge yourself for succeeding against all odds. Congratulate yourself for your resilience, for staying with it all the way to the end, for all the resources you drew upon and for your courage and strength. If there were others who helped you through this time, say a silent thank you to them.

Has this experience taught you that you can handle most other challenges that have come your way? Do you have more confidence knowing that you can surpass difficult situations using the skills, wisdom, resilience, humour, strength, courage and faith that you drew upon in this situation? Perhaps your success also came from instilling stronger boundaries or reaching out to others. Embrace these attributes for they are yours and you can still rely on them today if need be. They have served you well and will continue to do so.

And finally, what has this experience taught you? What are some of the gifts and lessons you received and how can you pass them on to others?

Begin now to cluster your memories of this time or move directly into writing your story. And remember, you are on the other side of it now, so enjoy the process while looking back and realizing how strong you truly are.

# Chapter 4

# A Significant Relationship

## Jesse

by Ange Frymire

*I have waited all these years. Bang! On August 21, 2005, I walked into a BBQ party and there you were. Two years later, here you are. I blush, I feel nervous, I feel as though it's our first date. You are so refreshing. You are an oasis for me. You are a stop sign, a flashing pedestrian crosswalk, a blazing fireplace and a plush rich Arabian carpet that invites me to swim in oceans, soar through cumulous clouds and sink into a cushion of bubbling, illuminated love. Love that still can't find the words to express how we are. Of how you have lit up my days and evenings and travelling. How I can hear you in the silence. Of how I inhale you in the dark and touch you when you're sleeping in your home that is nestled in the pines.*

*You, Jesse. You who I could not meet, would not meet, did not meet until one and a half years after I was told about you. When I was ready, when my heart knew that the power of my love for me could be shared with a love for you.*

*You...who talked to me for four hours the first time we met.*

*You... who invited me into your simple and complicated life.*

*You... who share your mind and welcome mine.*

*You... who listen to me, hear me. You who show love, acceptance and commitment.*

73

*You...of whom I've written so many words and have barely written any depth.*

*You...who are a gift to me from my god and goddesses. I am so grateful for all that you are, do, think, feel, see, walk, laugh, love and be. Thank-you, oh so dearly...*

# Bring Me All of Your Dreams

by Nathalie Vachon

*Bring me all of your dreams, dear husband*
*Bring them*
*Set them on our bed*
*And let's lay beside them*
*Picking one up at a time*
*Measuring its proximity to your heart*
*We will write them like love letters on our walls*
*Read them out loud*
*And pause*
*To appreciate the most cherished ones*

*Bring me all of your dreams, dear husband*
*Pick them from trees*
*From childhood*
*Let them be the wind, let them be the sun*
*And I will cradle them in my arms*
*Sing them a swallow's song*
*Raise them like doves*
*White, glorious*
*Reaching up and forward*
*Flying delicately over the past*

*Bring me all of your dreams, dear husband*
*And I will carve time with you*
*Put do-not-disturb signs on our doors*
*As we let the storm stay outside, however loudly it yells*

*I will build a fort with you out of blankets and couch cushions*
*For the dreams you have, dear husband,*
*Come from the child inside of you*
*And oh,*
*How I love that little boy*

# Cherished

by Julia Jirik

*Dear Auntie Phyl, I miss you so. You've passed over but I still feel you strongly. If it weren't for you, dear Auntie Phyl, I might never have known what it's like to be loved, cherished and adored.*

*When you took care of me while Mom was in the hospital, a loving, lasting bond was formed between us that even death cannot break.*

*I was the only child in your and Uncle Frank's life and you cuddled me, praised me and played with me with wild abandon. No one had ever smiled at me so much. Thank you for your love and attention for so many years. You made it clear that I was never a burden – only a source of delight.*

*I recall coming to spend time with you and uncle Frank in your immaculate old Tudor house with a yard resembling Butchart Gardens. Your wonderful sense of order and cleanliness were such a tonic for me.*

*A delightful memory of the two of us shelling freshly picked peas on your porch and sharing "grown up" conversations stays snugly with me. How I loved being the apple of your eye!*

*As a toddler, I enjoyed the wonderful pink knitted outfit you made. When I was older, the beautiful summer dresses you created transformed me into a princess in my imagination. The scent of new fabric was euphoric. Thank you.*

*When I stayed with you, I had my very own room complete with freshly picked sweet peas from your garden because you knew I loved the scent.*

*I loved watching you with your smile, bright red lipstick and dyed blonde hair. You seemed like a slim, English-finishing-school Marilyn Monroe. I wish you had known how beautiful you looked through my eyes. You probably did. Children have such a way of innocently expressing through their facial expressions – such clear mirrors.*

*You knew how to play. Smile. Have fun. We loved dancing and romping around the house. It gave me such a wonderful sense of aliveness and freedom. Thank you.*

*When we would go for rides in your big ol' 1938 Dodge, driving down the road at a breakneck speed of about 5 miles per hour, a tingly sense of adventure surged through me. We were friends. Sisters. Women. Age difference did not exist. A sense of fairness and equality were wonderfully mysterious gifts you gave me which I delightfully unwrapped and still cherish. Through your eyes, I saw my goodness, lovableness and potential.*

# *Let's Write*

This story is about a significant relationship in your present day life or a significant relationship you had with someone in the past that you would like to write about now. You can write about a partner, a relative, a friend or someone else. Someone whose love and caring has made a meaningful difference in your life. Your life has been fuller, richer, kinder, because of him or her. If there are several people who are significant, who have impacted your life in this way, for now, just choose one. Imagine that person being here with you right now. Bring him/her up onto the screen of your mind now. And remember.

When did you first meet and what were the circumstances of your meeting? Was it through a mutual friend, a family member, perhaps at work? A chance meeting at the library or park? What were the circumstances? Do you remember what year it was? The season? How old were you? What were your first impressions? Consider the details of your first encounter. What attracted you to her or him? Or were you attracted? Or did that grow over time as you grew to know one another?

What stands out about the feelings you had or the conversation you had the first time you met? Did you have a sense he or she would be in your life for a long time? As you got to know one another, what kinds of things did you find you had in common? Your values, things you liked to do together?

Once again, listening deeply within, what is the essence of this relationship? What makes it significant for you? What makes it rich and exciting or gentle and caring? What are some of her or his most endearing qualities? What are the things that you love – that make your heart sing? What stands out as one of the loveliest times you spent together?

Almost all relationships, even the best ones, also have times that are challenging, when buttons get pushed, when things are said that are hurtful or when insecurities arise. How do you get through these times? Is your relationship built on a strong enough foundation of love and respect that allows you to trust that whatever comes up can also be resolved? Do you move through difficulties with honest discussion or by just not sweating the small stuff or have you agreed to disagree or realized you'd rather be happy than be right? How do you transcend the more challenging times with this special person in your life….if that is a factor?

Is this person still in your life? If not, how and why did the relationship end? Was it a move? A break up? A death? What was the ending like for you? How did you deal with it?

Consider all the things you like or love about this person. Embody the feelings. Bathe in them. What have you learned about yourself as a result of this special and significant relationship? In what ways has he or she impacted your life?

Bless the time you are sharing or have shared. What do you wish most for this person?

Begin to write about your significant relationship. You can also write a letter to this person. If she or he is not in your life today, you still can write a letter letting them know how much you have appreciated them.

# Chapter 5

## A Significant Move

## No Going Back

by Christie Eng

*Portland Crescent remains for me the resting place for my ideas about child-hood; the ideal neighbourhood, perfect summer days. It still feels like the place where we all came from. I was born in Regina and lived there on Portland Cr. until I was eight. Jan was a baby when they moved in and Bill and Carolyn were born there too.*

*I have different images of Portland Cr. At first, the houses were new, the trees small. It seemed a flat dry place with rough gravel driveways. In other memories it was lush and green. The trees we planted as tiny sticks as chil-dren, grew to provide shade, a different micro climate. Behind the row of houses across the street was a field of Saskatchewan gumbo. At one end was a pond. A source of mosquitoes, it was a science world of pond weed and minnows.*

*I have a picture in my head of the street being narrow. The neighbours seemed so close. We all barbequed together. We could ask anyone's Mom or Dad for help. The boundaries of family seemed blurred, as we all seemed to be one family, called "Portland Cr".*

*I remember playing on the clothes line stand across the street. It was metal and there were metal rods welded together to provide a holder for the laundry basket. Were laundry baskets so standardized in the 1950s that this concept seemed to make perfect sense? We used to pretend that that square of welded* metal tubing was a toilet and that if you flushed yourself through you would come out in another world, a world where all the rules were different. We made up the rules as we went along. Actually I think we spent most of our time making up the rules, as that defined the imaginary world we were sharing.

I had to become real when we moved to Calgary. I remember that our parents recognized that it would likely be a big adjustment for us when we moved. They probably felt as shaken by it as we did. The move was necessary because you went where "the company" sent you.

Leaving Regina was momentous! I felt like a big mistake had been made. I spent hours in my bed, in Calgary, tucked into my corner with two windows, my head on the glass, rain streaming on the other side, matching my tears, watching the traffic on Crowchild Trail. I don't know if there were many nights that I cried myself to sleep this way, or if they are just prominent in my memory because of the magnitude of feeling. I planned what I would pack. Deliberated over leaving a note, counted the headlights. There were so many, at least one of them must be going in the direction of Regina. I thought about what to wear to keep the rain off and to be seen as I stood by the side of the road. I contemplated as far as arriving on Portland Cr. The reception I would receive.

I guess that that was when I realized that there is no going back in life. Where would I stay? Who would be living in our house? Even though all of those other families felt like family in a neighborly sense, I knew that staying at their houses would be awkward. My family wouldn't be there. The people I was closest to were here, with me.

It didn't make it any easier that we had moved into a neighborhood of rental houses. The street seemed wide and barren. The lawn was dry and weedy. The house had had a daycare in it before we moved in and there were scratches in the doors and floors. Everything needed a coat of paint.

There was a girl that I played with across the alley who was my age. We played together a little and I felt comfortable enough to cut through her yard on the way to school. But she was selfish with her toys and had the rules of her games all made up before I got there.

In school my teacher was serious and angry. The work was half a year behind my accelerated program from Regina. I was bored and she accused me of daydreaming and sloppiness. This was indeed a different world from the ideal I had left behind. But there was no going back.

Having had the realization already that even the families on Portland Cr. were different from my family, visiting friends in this neighbourhood was truly an adventure. The girl across the alley was an only child. She had lots of toys but her mother seemed dry and bitter. One family had newspapers. Having been invited to come over after school, my new friend and I walked into a small front entrance way. I wondered if they were doing a renovation and had begun to stack stuff there on its way out of the house. Then we walked into the living room. But there was no room, it was all full. There was enough space to move between the stacks and stacks of magazines and newspapers. There were stacks from the floor to the ceiling. There were stacks on the furniture. I have a vague memory of bewilderment. Did she say or did I invent a story that her Dad needed all of this for his work? Was it political in some way? We walked through a short hallway, narrowed by stacks of paper, to the cluttered and tiny kitchen. I remember feeling lucky. All the time my friend had a big smile and I could tell that she was loved. Then her eyes lit up. "My Dad made my room for me, do you want to see it?" Where I hadn't seen them before there was a little set of attic stairs. Truly this girl was the most treasured member of this family. At the top of these stairs was the sweetest little fairy room. The house was small and this room was tiny, but it was sweet and pretty and she had it completely tidy and organized. The piles of paper stopped outside her door.

The move to Calgary, (although the year in that house and neighborhood never became comfortable), taught me that my home was with my family. I learned that every family has its own culture. I began to spread my wings and explore new streets where I didn't know every corner, every minnow pond. I learned that some people are not good friends and that families very different from my own can still experience the depth of love we had in our home.

# The Metal Beast

by Doris Trinh Lewis

*Some memories never fade. I remember the first time I set foot on Texas soil. It was a cold morning in May, 1975. We arrived early after a long flight. I stepped out of the airplane and saw in front of me a clear, clear blue sky. It was so blue and open and I took it as a good sign of new hope, new possibility for the new life we were about to enter.*

*I couldn't say for certain how long it had been since we left Vietnam because my family had a temporary stop over in Guam – three to four weeks or so. Everything was like a blur – as if participating in a play; somehow unreal, yet still playing a role and moving through the day. Looking back I marvel at the innocence and naiveté of children. I was finishing 11th grade in Vietnam. The war was at its full height yet my life was very sheltered and protected.*

*Night after night going to sleep with the sounds of distant bombs seemed a natural part of life; as natural as the sounds of crickets in a summer night.*

*One day during morning class we heard a shrieking sound tearing through the sky and then a loud explosion. I could see fear in the faces of the teachers. The delight was (for me at the time) that we got to go home early – very early – because school was immediately closed for the year instead of it ending at the normal time which was at the end of June. The loud explosion came from a North Vietnamese jet dropping a bomb on the Presidential palace. I did not feel fear or panic even though the adults were whispering more and exchanging worried glances when we walked into the room. We saw a story on the TV news about wealthy Chinese business men getting caught trying to leave Vietnam in their big boats. The rest of the time in Vietnam was like a dream.*

*One day my mother called us together and announced that there was a change of plans. Instead of waiting for me to graduate from high school and then go to college in the United States, the whole family was going together to the United States. And in two days! We had only two days to pack and only two small bags each in which we had to pack all our belongings. We were instructed not to tell our friends we were leaving.*

*How do you pack everything in two bags? What's most valuable – certainly not money. I took a taxi drive and gave the driver $500 Vietnamese currency for a $20 ride. This was all the money I had after emptying my savings account and buying a pair of shoes. Why shoes? Maybe I was afraid I wouldn't be able to find anything that would fit me in the U.S. I also took a few pieces of clothing and pictures of my grandparents. One picture was of my grandma holding me as a child.*

*I managed to say goodbye to one friend. I bought seven bracelets and gave them to her to give one each to the others. She gave me a quizzical look, full of questions, but did not ask any. I don't remember her face but I remember the street in front of her house. It was like seeing a picture in a movie. I am there yet it is unreal at the same time.*

*Next I remember walking up a metal ramp of a cargo plane – and then right into the bowel of the metal beast. Looking back, this was like Jonah being swallowed by the whale and taken to his destiny.*

*My new life began that morning in May – a clear blue sky. A promise of hope. A new beginning.*

# Seoul, Korea

by June Swadron

*Thursday, November 07, 2002*

*It was only six or seven months ago, I think, when I first seriously considered coming here. Before then, I thought he would come home. Or even if he didn't, I couldn't see any reason to go there. None, really. I mean, what would I do? How would I live? And besides that, how committed was he to this relationship? I wasn't convinced he was committed enough to protect me if I needed help, if I got sick, if I felt lonely. After all, he left. How committed was he while we were together? In the end, not much. Mind you, if there's an end, no one's committed that much.*

*We were lucky, I suppose – or I used to suppose. We were lucky, because we turned it all around the week before he left. We dug deep into our hearts, found our centres and remembered the reasons we fell in love in the first place. I sent him off with blessings of every kind and a true belief we would walk together again. He wrote me beautiful words in my journal the night before he left – saying we are on a different fork of the same road that will eventually meet up again....far more poignant than that – far more poetic. But it meant that his heart was open and he was holding me in it. We were holding hands across the world.*

*I had big plans for my play – the one he just finished producing. The one about mental illness. The one that's striking me again these days. Not the play – the illness. The foreboding, the panic, the body sensation that stops me in my tracks, all but paralyzes me. So here I am – forced myself just now to get onto this computer and start writing. Start anywhere – tell my story. This one. Tell it like it is. No more lies. No more denials and burials of deeper truths. Not pretty? Well, neither are the books and stories I've been reading these days – they seemed to get into print. Maybe people don't want happy stories. I do. I want one. I want to live one! I want a happily ever after one! My God I want to live my own happy story. I thought I would be by coming here, to this foreign land to be with my beloved. I worked so hard to make it happen. But I'm getting ahead of myself.*

*Before the Big Decision, I was going to take my play, Madness, Masks and Miracles on the road, across Canada – the States even. We had performed* the play in Vancouver at the World Assembly for Mental Health to 400 delegates from around the world with brilliant feedback from the President of the Canadian Psychiatric Association and he wasn't alone. Such ironies – he thought my play was outstanding but couldn't find me a shrink to see when it was all over. Couldn't find me someone who was just willing to talk to me without drugging me up. Go figure.

I needed help badly. The play and all the hats I was wearing – the stress it took to produce it, act in it, sing in it, co-ordinate the actors, stage managers, memorize and rehearse lines, get the venues – all of it, how the hell did I manage it all? But I did, and not alone. Lucas helped and we went broke. The World Assembly for Mental Health had promised to pay all our expenses but reneged in the end. It was brutal. So we spent every penny we had – and all our credit cards too – to pay for rehearsal space, actors, musicians, videographers, printers, the master of ceremony, the stage manager – the works. And then it was done. The curtain came down to a thundering applause – but not for long – the curtain came down once again on me. The panic attacks returned. And my illness struck even harder. So, Lucas left. He said he was sick of mental illness. He was going somewhere where people didn't have those words in their vocabulary, where people were just – were just what? "Normal," I think were his words. It came out in anger after my shrew-like attack the morning after the play – "How the hell are we going to pay the rent!" I shrieked. He screamed back, "Can't you give me one fucking day to enjoy our success! One fucking day!" Four weeks later he was on a plane to the other side of the world. Who could blame him?

Somehow I got motivated on my own. I fought the panic attacks and was going to take my show on the road. I engaged a willing group of supporters to help me produce it somewhere else. And seemingly just when were getting going, I lost steam. I just couldn't do it. I was faking it again – pretending to be fine when I was fumbling and treading water. I lived with the fear and shame of them finding out. I began to identify with Lucas. I didn't want to know about mental illness any more either. I wanted to put it back in the closet. I didn't know how to face the outside world. The calls were still coming in congratulating me for such a tremendous feat but I could hardly make it out of bed in the morning.

So I ached because I had no motivation now and my best friend and lover was gone. The music stopped. But our emails continued.

And one day, he said, "Junie, I'm not coming home. My contract's up in a few months but I'm not coming back. I love it here. Come to Seoul. Join me. Be with me. Please."

"What'll I do there, Lucas?"

"You can write. You can teach. I don't know. Just come."

So I fast tracked an ESL course, put the play to bed and boarded a plane.

*And here I am.*

*I have just re-read what I wrote shortly after I arrived here. In spite of the culture shock, I still carried hope.*

"As if awakened rudely from a comfort dream the street venders oblivious to my susceptible senses, calling out their wares as if all were blind, while uncountable numbers swarm about...I feel alone, yet not afraid.

Nothing is familiar. Gone now. Gone are the oh-so-sweet pussycat kisses and fur-to-face hugs. Gone the charitable smiles and voices of friends spanning 3000 miles upon a North American continent, gone along with the ringing of the telephone bringing news, being part of, included. Gone the community of those I love, who loved me, other than what rushes through my blood and pulse and words punched upon a computer screen ineptly describing that which words cannot. Ever.

I am alone. Yet not. Stranger in a strange land. How often this phrase has been used by others before me. Lonely Planet. Lonely traveler. Woman-child, very old lady in this culture where the baby boom only happened in the late 70's and 80's and these 20 somethings are oblivious to a pumping heart inside anything older....except to notice the different colour of skin, hair, eyes – and then stare unashamedly.

35 calendar days later. I am used to it now. And only now and again do I show any sign of notice. Last night I did. Last night I was not interested in the well-dressed drunk man's smile or blatant "How old are you?" He was fascinated by my looks. Lucas was standing beside me on the speeding subway train and heard me return just as blatantly with "It's none of your damn business!" The whites of his teeth and upturned lips quickly disappeared at this unheard of female verbal outbreak.

"He just wants to know so he can know how to talk to you," Lucas tried to explain.

I didn't want him to talk to me was the truth. Not after his opening question. It came only one day after a new Korean 'friend' wanted to know if my siblings, who she knew were all older than me, were still alive. I guess I hadn't recovered.

I have stopped feeling attractive, pretty. Sometimes I still felt that way back home – even beautiful some days. But then my mother's wisdom came back. "Junie – people are never old when they are happy." She's right. My mind flashes to Annie Needleman. We were in the Clarke Institute together in the early '70's. She must have been in her 80's when I was in my 20's. That woman sat every day devouring three newspapers – Toronto Star, Toronto Telegram and Jerusalem Post as though starved for information and then passionately described and discussed everything she'd read with all of us fortunate enough to be there. Annie Needleman was definitely not old!

Yesterday I taught at a university. Two classes. 50 young woman who are studying to be English kindergarten and elementary teachers. I came to the interview a week ago for something else and was given this job instead. The sum total of information about the course I was about to teach was the theme and title – "Creative Dramatics for Children's English" leaving me to invent an outline and pray it would go over. I was informed just before stepping into the classroom that they speak very little English.

So much for full days of laborious outline-making. As always, (just like the way I pack my suitcase) I have a surplus, more than I will every need – only now I have at least double – perhaps three times as much as I could ever use since the time will be spent simply explaining my words.

Still, once again, and for the first time in several calendar months and undetermined psychic time, I was in my element. I was communicating with eager recipients – wide-eyed and thirsty for English and information – it was easy to spark it with humour and fun and laughter and – my God – I did not feel old then. I did not feel old at all. I felt as young as they were. I felt alive and happy. Yes, mom is right. You are not old when you are happy."

*And today is a markedly significant one as it is Sunday and I needn't be on a subway racing to and fro. Such luxury – still in my flannel pajamas at 10:18 a. m. Lucas is making coffee.*

# The Pain and the Relief

by Anne Sture Tucker

*"We are getting a divorce." The words are coming out of my father's mouth. I hear the words alright, but they don't mean anything. I don't understand them. I don't want to understand them. I want him never to have said them.*

*I look at my mother; she is crying. "I don't understand!" I shout and run out of the door. I slam the door behind me.*

*I run to my secret place on the farm where we live. My dog runs after me as though he senses that I need him and he is right. I need him more than ever, my little black lab with the big black dark eyes.*

*I sit down, his head rests on my lap and I cuddle him while I cry. How can they do this to me? It must be a mistake. I am 12 years old; my brother is 10. We have lived on our farm since we were little and we love that place. I have many friends. I like school. I feel safe and secure in the place and now we have to leave.*

*My parents have been married for 18 years. My father is a doctor and every day he travels into the city to work. He leaves early in the morning and comes back late at night.*

*I know why they want a divorce. I know that my mother has serious problems, but it is never anything we talk about. It is as though by not talking about it, it isn't there. Now that the words "We are getting a divorce" are out, it is as though the family secret is not a secret anymore.*

*I look around and realize that I am not alone and I am brought back – my father is watching me. He comes over to me and holds me. He tries to explain, but I don't want him to explain. I have this feeling that it will never be good again – I simply cannot understand that the two people I love the most in this world don't love each other anymore.*

*My father explains to me that I am to move with him into the city. My brother is going to boarding school and my mother is going to an apartment by herself.*

*I worry because I always looked after her. Who will do that now?*

*I am scared that she will not manage without me.*

*My dad kisses my cheek and holds my hand. "It will be ok," he says, but I don't believe him.*

*They have known for a while and soon my life is in boxes on its way into the city in a big truck.*

*The last night I am there I stay with my friend. My mom and dad have left already and in the afternoon I take my bike and ride back to the farm one last time. I travel back the so very familiar way on the tiny winding road that leads to the only place in the world I know as home. I find the key and let myself in – I just want to see the place one last time. It is a need; I have to say goodbye to this place alone.*

*I walk around in the empty farmhouse, go into every room and as I walk all the memories come back to me.*

*My brother and I growing up here – all the good memories of this place, all the wonderful family time, but also the bad memories come back as well. It is like a movie that passes by me.*

*My mother is an alcoholic. We never use that word. In fact, we never talk to anyone about it, not even in our own family. But I know that is what she is. I believe that nobody knows it. Somehow I have made myself believe that nobody can see how things are.*

*More pictures come to me. I see myself and my little brother wearing pajamas sitting on the kitchen table. It is after dinner. We are 5 and 7 years old. Our mom is in bed drunk. We have just found something to eat, what we could find in the fridge. We are sitting on the kitchen table looking out into the darkness. We will take turns and run into the back room all the way down the long corridor, to the end room where we can see if there are any cars coming towards the farm. We are waiting for our dad to come home.*

*Suddenly he is there. We see the lights and I feel the relief growing bigger as he comes closer. I throw myself into his arms and I whisper, "Mom is strange today." I see his disappointment, but he pretends nothing is wrong.*

*All the memories come back to me. I don't know how long I am there, but I suddenly realize that it is dark outside and I must go.*

*I remember locking the door and feeling like I am starting something new.*

*I ride back to my friend and on the way I think that it is not all bad. I get this sensation that when I move my life will be normal. I don't have to lie anymore. I don't have to be scared to have friends home with me, because my mom won't be there drunk. I don't have to look after her anymore. It is a relief.*

*The next morning I hug my friend goodbye and we promise each other that we will always be friends. I hear my dad honk his horn and I run out and get into the car that will take me to my new life.*

# *Let's Write*

Begin to journey backwards to a time in your life when you moved from one location to another. Choose the one move that holds the most energy for you at this time. Allow that one to enter your consciousness and be with it now. Allow yourself to remember the details as clearly as you can.

When was this move? Do you remember the year? The season?

How old were you? What was happening in your life at this time? Bring in the details. Why were you moving? Where were you moving from and where were you going to? Were you moving countries, cities or simply from one home to another within the same city? How were you feeling at this time? Was it a happy time for you, filled with anticipation and excitement? Or was it a scary, challenging time? Perhaps it was both. Were there others making this move with you? What was your relationship to them? How were you feeling about the other person or people involved?

Were you feeling supported? Were you a support for them? Perhaps you were alone. If you were, who bore witness to your move – the supports in your life at the time? How were you travelling? Car, boat, bus, plane? Something else?

How long did it take? How did you feel about leaving where you were? Were you ready to go? Who were the people you were leaving behind? What was your relationship to them? Were you going to be seeing them again? Were they sad you were leaving? Were you? What were your goodbyes like? Were they genuine? Wholesome? Full? Were they guarded, shallow, perhaps empty?

And what about the new home you arrived at? Were you happy to be starting again somewhere new? What was beginning again somewhere else like for you? How did you feel when you arrived? Was it a different culture as well as a different community? Was it a different language than you were used to speaking? What were the obvious differences that you noticed even if it was the same culture and language? What was new and different? What was seemingly the same?

What did your new home look like? Walk through the rooms of your new home. What was it like then? Can you see it? Feel it? Was it relatively easy to settle into your new environment or did it feel strange? What were the neighbours like? Did you feel welcomed into a community of new friends or was it a place where you felt alone and isolated?

How long did it take you to settle – to feel at home? Did it ever feel like home? What about the people that were in your life at the time of your move – the ones you left, the ones who came with you, if any – are they still in your life today? Did distance make it easier or more difficult to be in relationship with them?

As you look back now on that move, what made it significant for you?

Bring the memories of this time onto a page of clustering or simply start writing your story. Write from the person you were when you made that significant move. Then come back into today and write what you learned from it and in what ways it impacted your life.

# Chapter 6

# OCCUPATION/CAREER

## Hitting the Brick Wall

by Esther Hart

*In the late 1980s I gave a talk called Success Without Guilt. The response was overwhelming. For years afterward people would refer to the talk and say that they would never forget what I said. Lyn even recommended me to the Royal Bank to speak at a dinner recognizing graduates from one of their programs. I thought I had found my calling and the speaking engagements would come pouring in.*

*IT DIDN'T HAPPEN!!!*

*So I convinced myself that it had been an ego trip and that I was not meant to be on stage. A few years later I had the opportunity to re-evaluate my life. My marriage had ended, I was without a job and I was free to do whatever I chose with the rest of my life. I have never been so terrified. When you have lived your whole life living up to other people's expectations it is frightening to start making all your decisions for yourself. Not only do you have to accept responsibility for your failures, you also have to accept responsibility for your successes.*

*I kept hearing "Live your passion and the rest will fall into place". I wanted to live my passion but I couldn't figure out what it was. Finally through a long process described in my book,* Journey to Personal Freedom, *I came to real-*

*ize that speaking was my dream and that out of disappointment I had buried it very deeply. I realized also that I had not been ready before.*

*This time I put my full commitment behind becoming a world-famous inspirational speaker. In July I contracted with Uncommonknowledge to represent me and we planned an event in Vancouver to kick off a national tour. I spoke to my angels and told them that I would prepare the work and they had to sell the tickets. I was finally on my way to fulfilling my mission.*

*IT DIDN'T HAPPEN!!!*

*Not enough tickets were sold and the event was cancelled.*

*It could have felt like hitting a brick wall. I could have been devastated, disappointed, discouraged, angry, furious, confused. Instead I sat on my couch and prayed, "There isn't anyone on the planet more willing to do what they came here to do. Just show me what it is and I'll do it."*

*Part of the answer was to write this story as a newsletter article to let people know that there is no shame in changing plans. When we are willing to do what is in our highest good and put our full commitment behind it, everything we do is perfect. Sometimes a closed door is to save us from a possible disaster. Sometimes a closed door is to redirect us to a much more rewarding situation.*

*I have stopped banging on closed doors. Instead I take the angels by the hand and let them guide me through open doors. I live every moment in joy knowing that everything that comes to me is a gift.*

*I know that my gift is to speak to people and I know that when the time is right the appropriate opportunities to speak to large audiences will present themselves. In the meantime I live every day sharing the joy of my freedom with everyone I meet. If I ever have a day when I feel that I would like to accomplish more, I do a meditation that radiates love to every part of the universe. In the end I know that sending out love is far more powerful than any speech I could give and I know that I am living my purpose.*

# "Accounting for Business" to "Accounting for Life"

by Azim Jamal

*I used to be an accountant and a senior partner in an accounting firm where I had spent twenty years of my professional life. I made a comfortable living, providing for my family and myself.*

*During those twenty years, I did some volunteer work, primarily in the area of motivational and inspirational speaking. Every time I spoke in this capacity, I discovered boundless energy and lost track of time even though I was not paid to speak. These engagements changed me. I learned so much about myself, about life, about purpose and about others. I would have paid to get a chance to speak!*

*In the early 1990s, a recurring thought would not leave me alone. What if I did inspirational speaking for a living? This would mean doing something I really loved doing, something for which I had talent and that would make a difference. Why not? What is stopping me from doing this?*

*I had to make a choice. Either I live a life that I really want to live, or I live a life that others want me to live, a life wherein I will not perform to my fullest joy and potential. I persisted in thinking that my circumstances were not right, that I had to support two kids and that I had to provide for my spouse and my retired parents. Surely I could not abandon my responsibilities and go into a venture that many people described as risky, even irresponsible. Nevertheless, my inner voice responded, "Yes, writing and speaking professionally may be risky, but some speakers and writers do very well. In the time of Shakespeare or Rumi, one probably did well and made it big after one died. Today, excellent writers can do well during their earthly passage." I pondered the shining examples of Deepak Chopra, Pavlo Coelho and Stephen Covey. Another voice cried, "Yes, but these are the very few among the hundreds of thousands in the writing and speaking field." My inner voice responded, "Why can't I be one of the few who make it? What is going to stop me from going all the way?"*

*I began to feel empowered. I understood that it was up to me, not anyone else, to succeed. It was not that I had two young children, nor was it the fickle writing market that would determine my fate. It was entirely up to me to make the choice. If I believed I could do it, then I would do it.*

*But how was I going to convince my spouse whose support I would most definitely need? How was I to convince my parents whose blessings I would need? How would I make my parents understand that, after all those years of investment in their child and all the education they had provided me, I would now end up in a fickle and risky business that would drain me of money and time? How do I get my children on my side, cheering for me and being proud of their dad? These thoughts were daunting.*

*The fuel to make a jump into my new career came in 1997.*

*As part of my volunteer assignment I visited a family of fourteen Afghan refugees who lived in one hut, to interview them about their financial needs. While I was doing that I heard heartbreaking stories. I heard how they had survived from war to war; not gone to school for many years; seen their father killed in front of their eyes; walked without shoes in the mountains for nineteen days in cold weather with just the shirts on their backs; given birth to children on the mountain; come to Karachi and had no rights to stay there. Fourteen people stayed in a hut smaller than my child's bedroom in Vancouver; several worked for fourteen hours a day selling corn on a trolley in the hot blazing sun, making $1 per day and not even having enough to pay the rent of the small hut; kids held their Nan (bread) as if their life was at stake. I saw mosquitoes everywhere, the kitchen and washroom all lumped in one small hut.*

*All of this despair and I was still offered dry nuts in the hut even though they had nothing for themselves. They give dry nuts to any guest. They know the beauty and joy of giving, that richness is not defined by what you have, but by what you give.*

*After 20 minutes, I was emotionally wrecked and felt physically sick; there was a sense of utmost despair in my body. My energy was drained and I felt totally helpless! I could not bear what I was seeing.*

*I was there for less than 30 minutes, but it seemed like an eternity. I absorbed the experience but could not take it any longer so I walked to my cab, which was waiting for me.*

*In the back seat of the cab, I was sobbing like a baby (like a two-year-old crying on the floor having lost his mother). I cried and cried and cried. I felt very little, humbled and helpless. I was shivering and sweating at the same time . . . I felt like I had been shaken to death.*

*If I can point to a defining moment in my life, it would have to be the twenty-five-minute cab ride back from the hut to the Marriott Hotel. I reflected on how I could help these people. I began to understand that it could not be through my accounting practice, because I was not passionate about accounting.*

*I began to realize that my gift was not in accounting but in speaking and writing.*

*After the cab driver dropped me off at the hotel in Karachi, one of the very first people I met at the hotel was my colleague, Aziz Shariff.*

*Without me uttering a word, he asked, "Azim, what is wrong?"*

*Wanting only to retreat to my room, I told him, "If I had to die for one cause, I would die for this cause."*

*As I went back to my room to cry and remain sleepless, I was reflecting on my statement, "I would die for this cause." Never in my 43 years had I had a feeling of willingness to die for any cause. In hindsight, I can see how one's life really begins when one is willing to give his or her life for a cause that is larger than self.*

*After a few months and many lengthy and difficult discussions with my wife, I felt we were able to create a shared vision of my new career. This was the single most important turning point in my journey to achieve the dream I had conceived after visiting the refugees. Spending time with my wife and business partner to get their support and buy-in was worth every second. They helped me face the enormous challenges ahead.*

*I soon realized what a mammoth task I had ahead of me. Nothing was working. It seemed like it took me forever to finish writing my first book, only to find out that writing my book was the easy part.*

*The marketing and selling of the book was a hundred times harder. The more I worked, the bigger the hurdles became. I was ready for the challenges, not being swayed by them but rather going through them like a bulldozer. I kept my eye on the goal and nothing fazed me. On February 17, 2000, I went to the Chapters bookstore in Richmond near my house. I wanted to check if my book 7 Steps to Lasting Happiness had made it to the bookstore. I typed in "7". There were seventy hits for books of 7 something, but my book was not listed there. So I entered "happiness". Seventy books on happiness and related topics appeared, but again my book was not on the list. I entered "Azim Jamal, The computer blurted out "Author," I thought, wow, finally something*

*"..........................................Author Unknown!!!"*

*That was depressing. I reckon I had clocked about ten thousand hours towards my mission. At my accounting rate of $200 an hour, I was out by $2 million in opportunity costs. I could not even get a book into the bookstores, let alone sell it. How was I going to help Afghan refugees if I could not even help myself?*

*My experience at the Chapters bookstore was the lowest moment of my career — all of my money was gone, thousands of hours spent and yet no sign of my book in the bookstore. My passion was at its lowest ever. I began to walk away from the computer, completely dejected, when I noticed a small book amongst the thousands of books staring at me. I thought, no way, not a chance. I have been reading an average of two books a week and look where I am. I'm not in the mood to read another book! A thousand and one thoughts entered*

*my mind at that juncture – the many humiliations, feelings of being an abso-
lute loser, wasting of my prime years, how could I be so stupid – I never felt so
hopeless in my life.*

*As I found my way to the bathroom, it seemed as though the book was fol-
lowing me like a light, a beacon in my personal darkness. A book is not supposed to follow you, right? I had a choice to go to the bathroom or go to the
book. I decided to obey the "magic" or "unknown pull" and went back to the
book. It was the story of Og Mandino author of* The Greatest Salesman in
the World *which sold ten million copies. I was again inspired.*

*Today I am a full-time international inspirational professional speaker,
management consultant and executive coach. I have spoken to more than 1
million people in 26 countries. My work has been recognized by some of the
leading thinkers including Dr. Deepak Chopra, Dr. Wayne Dyer, Jack Canfield,
Ken Blanchard and Brian Tracy. My book* The Power of Giving *(co-authored
with Harvey McKinnon) hit #1 twice on Amazon and on one occasion toppled
Harry Potter! The big question to ask is, have I realized my dream?*

*From one perspective, the answer is absolutely not! I'll never quite arrive.
Every time I reach 'there' from 'here', then 'there' becomes 'here' and I have
another 'there' to aim for. So, throughout my life I aspire to new goals that keep
me going. From that perspective, I'll only really arrive when I die.*

*From another perspective, the answer is a resounding yes! I am doing what
I love doing; I am really passionate about my work, losing track of time when I
am engrossed in my work. I am traveling around the world speaking frequently.
I have the full support of my spouse, the blessings of my parents and the cheering from my children. Moreover, I am making a difference every day to myself
and to others. I am doing what I had the promise to do when I was born. If I
were to die today, I would have no regrets. In this sense, I have arrived.*

# *Let's Write*

Are you living your passion? Does your work make your heart sing? Do you get up every morning looking forward to the day ahead? Or do you get up resenting what you do – wishing you could be earning a living doing something else – but this is what pays the bills?

What do you like about your occupation/career and what don't you like? Do you work alone – are you self-employed or in a one-person office? Or do you work with a team of people?

In what ways does your job bring out the best in you? What skills and talents do you bring to it?

Perhaps you are feeling stuck with what you're doing. Do you have dreams of doing something different? Are you taking courses or studying something that will lead you in the direction of your deepest desires?

My father worked as a projectionist in the movie theatres for 30 years and they gave him a gold watch when he retired. I don't know when the novelty of watching movies wore off, but I know he wasn't happy doing what he was doing. He wasn't inspired but it was a secure job and fed his family. That was the way then. A person (usually the man) worked at one job all his working life and then collected a gold watch. For my father, it was his *raison d'etre*. Also jobs lasted in those years. Today it's expected that people will change jobs as well as careers. Many people go back to school and learn to do something else – especially in economies where people are being laid off by the thousands. It makes people re-invent themselves. Many people ask, "What is it I really want to do?" and then find creative ways to make it happen.

Sometimes they look at what excites them such as their hobbies and see how they can turn that into a money-making venture. After her accident, my friend, Teya could no longer do the massage work for which she was trained. She loved jewelry and started designing earrings and necklaces. She also put her creativity into desktop publishing. She now makes her living doing both and loves it. Life sometimes begs of us to change what we are doing and start again at something else.

In 1980 there was a recession and I was working as a freelance writer and having a hard time making ends meet. Alan, a lawyer friend of mine suggested I become a court reporter because it was interesting work and it paid well. So I enrolled in the local community college to learn the art of verbatim reporting, as well as court practices and procedures.

A year later I began working at City Hall on Queen Street in the heart of downtown Toronto. Within the first month or so, I knew it wasn't for me. I did not want to be in a daily adversarial environment – especially when I had no opportunity to evoke change, only repeating verbatim what other people said.

It was the dissatisfaction and frustration of not having a voice that led me back to school again. This time it was Atkinson College, the night school at York University. I studied there as well as enrolling in other schools that specialized in particular areas of psychology and psychotherapy. After five years I was qualified to put out my shingle as a psychotherapist, certified as a Clinical Member of the Ontario Society of Psychotherapists. During those years in school, I continued as a court reporter in order to pay for my tuition and books.

Because writing was always of paramount importance to me, along with my therapy practice, I began facilitating writing workshops as part of a creative and cathartic healing process. I feel so blessed and grateful to do what I do.

How about you? Do you feel that way about your job or career? If not, can you allow yourself to find the gift in where you are right now? And if there is to be a change, can you trust it to come at the perfect time?

Write about your jobs or careers and where you are right now. If you are looking for work, this is an excellent time to write down the things that excite you – what you are passionate about – and through this process begin to put your ideas into action. If you're at the stage where can't find your passion, be kind and gentle with yourself and trust that the journey of your life is unfolding perfectly. Write into your feelings about this.

If you have changed careers, what was the crossroad that lead you there – the circumstances that took you from one job or career and set you on another path?

If you are retired, you may wish to write about the career you chose and how it impacted your life. What did you learn from it? Are there insights you would like to pass on to others?

Or you may wish to write about your retirement. How do you occupy your time now? Do you miss your working life or are you happy that you now have more time to do the things you enjoy? What is the best thing about retirement for you? Are there things that present challenges? Write about this phase of your life and how it is impacting you.

Gather your writing utensils and begin to write the story of your life's work – or the different jobs you have held over time.

# Chapter 7

## SPIRITUALITY/RELIGION

## A Little Rock and an Unfinished Poem

by Joy Emmanuel

*When I meet with my osteopath (bone doctor) he always asks me what's been going on. We explore many levels – body, mind, and spirit. I tell him my "story," acknowledging both the shadow and the light.*

*One day, after listening to me talk, he shared an image that had come to him as I spoke. He saw a student with head bowed, and with great reverence, offering the master a cup of tea. Then the master, also with great reverence, offered the student a cup of tea. I laughed, saying, "Yes, I can see that image and I have a little something to add. I see the cup of tea that the master offers the student is sitting on a plate and beside the cup is a little rock – that's the part I am having trouble embracing. Right now, my cup of tea comes with a little rock – and a koan." We both laugh.*

*In Buddhist traditions a koan is like a spiritual riddle that a master gives the student to ponder. It can contain dynamite insights meant to crack open your little ego-mind and take you into the depths of your soul. The one I received went something like this:*

*Rockness,*
*Light crystals, entombed,*
*Waiting with Grace.*

*The osteopath's parting guidance was to be curious about the little rock, not to try and figure it out, but just hold it in a place of curiosity.*

*Three months before this, I had lost my job. A job I had loved. Simply put, a new director came on board, decided to go in a new direction, and puff - my position was eliminated. Ouch! It was a big shift. It meant letting go of an exciting project I had initiated; now the new director would carry on without me. There was also the loss of connection both with new developments in the field and with co-workers – funny how people stop seeing you. I was no longer on the "inside", now I was an "outsider". Although I could see that being "kicked out of the nest" was bringing new opportunities, before I could fully embrace them there was the matter of this little rock on my plate and some deep feelings that were hard to reconcile.*

"Little Rock,
*May I find the way to embrace you,*
*So that the hard shell of my heart may be broken open."*

*The last week of work, I said to my colleague, "I feel like I am becoming a ghost." I was erasing my footprints, clearing my desk and saying goodbye. I was, in a way, dying into change; letting go of an identity, a way of showing up, letting go and moving into the unknown – a place that held strange feelings of emptiness and, at the same time, was a place of possibility.*

"Little Rock,
*May I hold you close until I have looked deeply*
*into the pores of your being.*
*May I remember that what is hard today*
*can be the foundation for tomorrow."*

*"Are you happy?" a friend asks. How do I respond? Am I whole? That is the question I preferred to answer. How do I meld happiness and wholeness in a response that speaks to both questions? I offer a reply and let it go where it will. I appreciate the expression of caring and recognize, I have tender places.*

"Little Rock, sometimes I let you grow into a great boulder
*and you are the whole story,*
*But you are the past,*
*You are a part of my story but maybe soon,*
*I will be ready to let you go."*

*Sometimes good books come into our lives at just the right time. I went looking for a birthday gift for my sister and came home with a book for each of us.* Tracks *is a true story of a woman who travelled across the Australian desert by herself, with four camels, when she was in her twenties. Oh! What guts! I am amazed by her courage and strength! I am consumed by her incredible journey across the desert and deep into the core of her being. I am inspired by her ability to be present to her fears and give herself permission to come undone – shedding layers of the socialized self, releasing expectations, old feelings and patterns.* Tracks *kept nudging me toward the depth of my own solitude and allowing the unravelling to unfold.*

> *"Little Rock, you are just a step along the way.*
> *You are the bones of the earth beneath my feet.*
> *I may hold a small part of you,*
> *but you have carried me across galaxies."*

*Another book came unexpectedly through a friend. It was called* Broken Open *and was filled with stories of other travellers navigating their way through difficult times of change. It reminded me of the blessings in the darkness and, like the North Star, the stories kept pointing me toward – rather than away from – the dark night of the soul; encouraging me to be present to these parts of my story.*

> *"Little Rock, you are the flower*
> *Buried in the cave of darkness,*
> *Like Persephone going into the underworld,*
> *discovered the rebirth of her soul."*

*Today, I was sitting in a rose garden on a lovely spring day in May when the sound of bagpipes drifted into my consciousness. The last time I heard bagpipes was at my mother's funeral. The piper led our family into the church service. We had asked him to play Amazing Grace and that is the very song I was listening to right now. With that memory, came the tiniest little shower of tears, like the tenderness of spring rain.*

> *"Little Rock,*
> *You are the memory of time beyond life and death,*
> *You hold day and night – dark and light –*
> *without judgement."*

*Each day brings another step into the unknown moment of now. Bit by bit, the tides of change wash away everything – both what I hold dear and what is hard to accept. The little rock part of me knows that even this story is but one line of a wild, and precious, unfinished poem.*

## "Glimpses" on a Spiritual Journey

by Eric Hellman

*For the last six days, Vancouver – the city I live in as I write this – has been almost entirely engulfed in fog. It's a fog so thick I can barely see the ground from my 25th story apartment, let alone the 1000 acre park across the street, or the panorama of mountains I normally look upon several miles away.*

*A few minutes earlier, I looked out from my desk and all I could see was a 'solid' wall of grey-whiteness. Then a moment ago, the view shifted. Now, below eye level is a carpet of thick, grey-white clouds as far as the eye can see. Above it, everything is clear. There's the deep blue-black of a clear sky at dusk. A dim orange and pink hue on the horizon. The mountains stand dark in their silhouetted shapes against the cloudless sky. And lights are now visible on their slopes – a twinkling city that seems to start half way up, with dots of a ski resort at the very top.*

*Half my view is totally clear. The other half, totally blocked. It's like sitting atop a cloud, with a view of Shangri-la. To me, that's a bit like spirituality.*

*In the 'normal' daily world, our view and experience of life is rather dim. Sure we see what's around us. The stuff and the things and the people of life. But there's also a kind of fog. A questioning about why we're here and what it's all about. Feelings of separateness from others, nature, even ourselves. A kind of going through the motions – "doing" without much meaning – that leaves us rather lifeless. Or a yearning to "veg out" and leave the world behind.*

*Then there are those stark moments – clear skies of vision, twinklings of insight, peak or mountain-top experiences and hues of "aha, wow and ahhhh" – that show us there is so much more. We become refreshed, invigorated and alive, reminded of the fullness, the joy and the beauty of life.*

*These can happen anywhere, in the commonest of activities: singing, dancing, making love, walking through a forest, putting one's hand in a cold running stream. Having an insight into a challenging problem or looking into the eyes of a new-born baby. In those moments, we see and touch something beyond the form and experience the spirit or essence of life. For a time, everything seems clear. We know who and what we are. There's no question why* we are here. Then the fog rolls in again and we forget – and wonder if it ever really happened.

For me, spirituality is about finding and exploring what lies beyond the fog; the starry lights of our hopes and ideals, the powerful emotions and subtle energies that move and shape us and the cues on life's horizon that point us in new directions. Knowing inside that we are more than we appear to be, we search the possibilities of our being and yearn for a deeper intimacy and connection with others and all life. This is some of what excites me on the spiritual journey.

Yet the journey is also about going through the fog. That can mean opening ourselves to the darkness and the confusion of life. Breathing into the sadness and the pain. Being present to the fear and craziness that stare us in the face every day. It's discovering that both the fog and the clarity aren't just in our outer world; they are within us. And it's about finding ways to cope, heal and remember our 'truer self' in the midst of it all.

*My First Glimpse*

My first real glimpse beyond the fog came on the shores of a lake one day, when I was still in my late teens. I had always loved nature, but on this afternoon, standing on a warm sandy beach by myself, basking in the sun and gazing out on the brilliant blue waters, I experienced a connection with nature beyond anything I'd ever experienced. It felt like I was dancing with the light and the water, without distance or time in-between. And with it came a clear knowing that I needed to go into environmental work – which was strange for me, as I was just two days from entering a Math and Science program at university.

Returning home, I changed my program of study – then eventually universities – and for the next nine years pursued my environmental calling. And I loved it. It gave me the opportunity to talk about something that deeply mattered to me, initiate innovative projects and engage with the community. I would go anywhere, any time, to talk with people about my favourite subject and what we can do to make a difference.

"Spirit" had called me that day – though I wouldn't have used this word at the time – and I gladly responded. But it was not too long before my path would change again, in another, even more unexpected, direction.

*A Gift... and a Curse*

As much as I loved my work, I also found myself in deep conflict – partly within my field (environmentalists were often at odds with business, government and one another) and particularly in a young marriage. The daily disagreements, upsets and arguments had me drowning and lost inside; the emotional pain was becoming unbearable. Trying everything I could think of to resolve the problems – marital counselling, personal therapy, trial separation, group therapy – the only thing that helped was something called "A Course in Miracles." A self-study program using Christian language, it introduced me to a spiritual way of looking at life and to the practice of forgiveness. By applying it to my work and marriage, I was finally able to find the peace and healing that I sought.

Thus the Course was a great gift to me, another experience of seeing beyond the fog. But it also came with a curse; something that would become the most difficult challenge I'd ever faced.

Having been raised by a father who put religion down – and also being a "good boy" who obeyed his elders – for me studying a book with words like God, Jesus and Spirit felt like I was reading pornography. I would hold it close to my chest when reading it in public and hide it in my drawer at work, pulling it out only when I thought I wouldn't be discovered. I told almost no one about it, as the thought of being seen as "religious or Christian" petrified me to the core.

And there lay the paradox, the challenge. Despite my terror of being exposed and judged, something in me kept studying the Course AND feeling calmer, clearer and more at peace. It also helped me to see the world differently, with more compassion, acceptance and forgiveness. And soon I ached to find a way of bringing it into my work, to share these new insights on how we could create change and heal from a deeper level. After about a year, I started to do so... and that's when my 'greatest fear came upon me.'

A Lock on my Heart

This time, instead of my colleagues and friends responding with open ears and a willingness to explore – as had happened in environmental work – they reacted as if I'd lost my mind. "What's wrong with Eric?" was the most common response, if not simply dead silence. People just didn't want to go there. Even my father took me aside and said, "There are some things you just don't talk about." Rather than take it in stride, I then reacted with fear, hurt and rejection. My self-respect collapsed. Feeling like a stranger in a strange land, I made a decision: I would continue my spiritual work and new ways of thinking as fully as possible. But I would not share it with anyone. It was not safe. And I would not risk such rejection again.

For someone used to communicating his heart, soul and passion with others on a daily basis, it was like putting a lock on my heart. And that's how I lived for 25 years. Intently pursuing a spiritual practice and way of life – and suppressing my voice and beliefs in almost every way I could.

In retrospect, my decision should have come with one of those warning we see on TV: "For professionals only: Don't try this at home!" For while it led me on to great things – new relationships, work and projects, and deeper insights into life's problems than I'd found anywhere else – it was also a recipe for disaster. Because over time, my internal split grew too large. My desire to express my spirit conflicted with my choice to suppress it. My business ebbed, my new marriage collapsed and my expression in the world declined to a trickle. I even feared looking people in the eyes, lest my dirty little secret become known.

*In the midst of the fog of life, it doesn't seem like a grey-white cloud. It can appear to be both terrifying and impenetrable; at least it did for me.*

*Writing my way out…*

*It's only over the past five years that I've begun finding my way out of this dilemma. And that began one summer's night while I was watching television.*

*Feeling antsy inside, the thought that I needed to say or do something kept pushing it's way up in my brain. I squirmed, changed channels and resisted as much as I could, then eventually succumbed. Walking over to the computer, I sat down and started to type whatever words came into my mind. Then a deeper feeling rose up, demanding to be expressed – and I started to pour my story onto the keyboard. Out came the words and the pain, the experiences and the insights, all the things I wished I'd been able to say for 25 years and never felt I could tell anyone.*

*It was the beginning a new stage in my journey. I began coming out of my "spiritual closet".*

# The Architects Dream

by Michael MacGowan

*You are the great artist*
*And I your willing canvas*
*Each line has been carefully drawn*
*Blue skies*
*Emerald forests*
*Chiseled mountains*
*They adorn my heart's*
*Mysterious crown*

*You know your work well*
*For you create beauty*
*Where nothing exists*
*I am the timeless thought*
*Sculpted from loving hands*
*Born of eternal spirit*

*I watch and see you everywhere*
*I sense you in everything*
*In sunlit skies you blaze*
*In sleepy green oceans you flow*
*The beasts of night*
*Sing songs to your holy moon*

*You carry love on lofty wings*
*Like a wind swept song*
*Blowing through a rain drenched meadow*
*No matter where I go – I see you*
*No matter what I think – you see me*
*In the darkness of night*
*I feel your gentle touch*

*My mortal flesh*
*Testifies to your craft*
*Life's sacred strand*
*Sets my solitary path*
*Beyond my brittle bones*
*Within my naked heart*

*Your blueprint holds court*
*For I am the architect's dream*
*Every nail and dowel is set*
*They fit this perfect mystery*
*And secure the truss*
*Of my flesh bound spirit*

*And those whose faith falls short*
*They shall live out their days*
*Alone and abandoned*
*For your truth*
*Sits silent and patient*
*In cracks between the lies*

# *Let's Write*

This story is about a spiritual experience – a time or times in your life where you have entered a place of expansiveness, of deep inner knowing – a feeling of tranquility, joyfulness and bountiful love. Here there is no trying, no striving. You are simply being. Here is home. You have entered the realm of your own divine nature.

Worries, struggles and challenges fall away in this place. You are in harmony with yourself and with All That Is. You are in a heightened state of beingness or awareness or state of enlightenment or bliss.

Sometimes it comes without warning – a spontaneous knowing that you have entered into a higher state of consciousness because you are experiencing a peace beyond all understanding.

Awakening and transcendence are often born out of darkness. Without warning a light appears through a tiny opening of possibilities. A new sense of hope arises. Sometimes it reveals itself in the stillness of breath through meditation and prayer. A yearning speaks from deep within our soul – sometimes pleading, "Dear Spirit, I feel lost and afraid. Tell me, please, where do I go from here?" Messages from unexpected sources begin to greet us. Sometimes it requires time and patience. Sometimes answers come in an instant. As new hope emerges, despair lessens. We experience a shift of consciousness and we find ourselves energized in a whole new way. Our inner joy begins to re-awaken. From the yearning has come a profound inner knowing. Gratitude and humility are often what we experience next as we are gently guided just where to go from here.

Sometimes for me it happens when I look into the eyes of an infant or a child and I experience a sudden outpouring of love. Sometimes it's walking in the stillness of the forest, or holding the hand of a loved one and feeling a holy bond between us. Sometimes exquisite music brings me to this state or gazing out and into the billions of stars in the nighttime sky. Often indescribable joy surges through me in a moment of sacred communion with an animal. Our souls are touching and in those moments nothing else exists.

I have come to believe that heaven is not a place we go to after we die. It exists here and now. Our true divine nature is joy, peace, expansiveness, beauty, freedom and love. And when we are in alignment with these states of consciousness, everyday miracles occur.

We have heard it said that we are not human beings having a spiritual experience, rather we are spiritual beings having a human experience. We are in the world but not of it. When we have what we call a spiritual experience or a moment of awakening, we are often left in awe and deep gratitude because we are reminded where our true Home is.

Sometimes our hearts ache at this homecoming because we have yearned for it all our lives. It takes us beyond our day to day human experience where there is so much pain and suffering. When we touch upon the Grace of Infinite Source, when we are living truly in the moment, in the pulse of exquisite nowness, we move out and away from the madness and the mundane.

We, as human beings, strive to know our true spirit. We ask the existential questions, "Who am I? Why am I here? Where am I going? What is my purpose?" We seek that which shall bring us Home again. And when we find it, right here on earth – when we open to the profound beauty that awaits us in every moment, we align with who we really are. We naturally want to share this awareness. We want to bring our joy and our light – our love and our compassion – our forgiveness and our kindness – our hope and our gratitude – to every living creature on our path.

Has there been a time in your life when you experienced a sense of peace or joy beyond all understanding? A time that left you with a profound knowing that you are far more than your five physical senses? So much more than your mind, your body, your thoughts and your emotions? Where were you? How did this experience come to you?

Perhaps there have been several such times.

For me, our spiritual essence is the only thing that is real and when I remember that, when I bring my day to day experiences into that knowing, I open myself to the universal mystery of life – into the field of all possibilities. It is during these times that life flows, when synchronistic events are the norm and I am awake to the beauty that lies within me and all around me. Yes, when I am living the truth of my divine nature, all striving stops. I am home – no matter what my outer world looks like.

The simplicity of the following poem – whose origin I do not know – resonates true and makes me smile.

*Who Or What Is God?*

"What is God?" a voice asked, "Who or what is God?"
The pine trees sighed softly, "I Am."

Deep in the jungle of grass and weeds, a tiny ant paused and declared. "I Am"

From a million light-years away, the burning answer of a star came, "I Am."

A turtle poked his head out of his shell and said, "I didn't understand the question."

"Who or what is God?" the voice repeated.

"Oh," said the turtle, tucking his head back into his shell, "I Am."

The voice asked, "Who is God?" The ocean roared, "I Am."

The trees swayed, "I Am." A little newborn child cried, "I Am."

Then a voice said, "Will the real God please stand up?"

And the entire universe

Quietly stood up.

Gather your pen and paper and begin to write how you experience spirituality in your life.

# Chapter 8

## YOUR BIRTH STORY

## Birth Days

by Nan Campbell

*May 23, 1959, Saskatoon, Saskatchewan*
*"Jim!" Bert called out to her husband after lighting her cigarette, "I just got off the phone with Dr. Burt's office and they said I'm supposed to check into the hospital this afternoon. They don't want me going past two weeks with the baby so today's the day. We're going to be new parents after all honey! If this baby is born tomorrow it will be a Victor or a beautiful Victoria! What do you think honey?"*

*Bert walked down the hallway from her bedroom into the baby's room. The crib was all set with crisp new sheets, the mobile was hung and the change table and dresser were freshly painted with little stencils of lambs frolicking across the drawers. The yellow and white gingham curtains swayed gently in the May breeze. This was a good day to have a baby, Bert thought as she drew in long and hard on her Pall Mall. She opened up the drawers to confirm one more time that all the diapers were indeed in order, the sleepers were lined up and the tiny little booties were ready for their new baby. All the girls from nursing school had got together to surprise her with a baby shower. The Campbell family was set for the arrival of their first-born.*

*Jim and Alberta Campbell were an up-and-coming Saskatoon couple. Jim was a Saskatoon born-and-raised young man recently returned from college in*

*Flint, Michigan where he had trained to be an authorized General Motors deal-
ership consultant. Bert was from Swift Current and she had been attending
nursing school at the University of Saskatchewan. They had met at a Lion's
Club social and the romance pretty much kicked off that evening two summers
previously. Jim had spent that first courting year finishing off his training with
GM while Bert finished her nursing classes. In the spring of 1958 she had her
first episode. She was supposed to finish writing her nursing exams; instead
she tore off back to Swift Current and only returned to Saskatoon in June for
their wedding.*

*Jim wasn't entirely sure what had overcome his bride to be. She said it was
just a case of nerves and that she would go back and finish up her exams as
soon as they were settled in their new house after the wedding. Well, "as soon
as" never arrived and now instead of her being an R.N. at the Queen Elizabeth
hospital, she was going to be having their first baby there. This had been a
strange year for Jim, not at all what he had anticipated newlywed life to be.
Bert was pregnant pretty much within a month of their honeymoon and it had
been a whirlwind of doctor's appointments, moving into the little two bedroom
bungalow on Fifth Avenue, cocktail parties around town with their friends and
more doctor's appointments. It seemed that Bert struggled with her nerves a lot
more than she had led Jim to believe. He never knew who he would be coming
home to at the end of a day – his vivacious bombshell of a wife, a sad, sleepy
girl curled up on the sofa or a whirlwind home decorator with a bottle of vodka
in one hand and a roll of wallpaper in another. For the most part she was a ton
of fun and he had grown to accept her down days as just part and parcel of
living with Bert.*

*So today was baby day! Jim called his Grandmother to let her know that
they would be heading off to the hospital soon. His folks had moved to Florida
earlier that year and he had been keeping pretty close to Grandma what with
Dee Dee having passed away last year and all. He loved the old doll and he
knew that she pretty much worshipped the ground he walked on. "Grandma?
That you? I just wanted to let you know that Bert and I will be heading off to
the hospital pretty soon. Dr. Burt said that he thinks today is a good day to
have a baby. I'll call you as soon as we know if we have a boy or a girl. Do you
need anything? I could drop by for a while for a visit later."*

*"Well Mrs. Campbell, we'll just get you settled in here and Dr. Burt will
be along shortly. He said that we were going to help this little one along by
giving you a bit of a nudge. I suspect he'll break your waters for you and that
should speed things up nicely. You run along now Mr. Campbell, you'll be a
new Daddy by the morning." Jim was indeed a new Daddy by the morning.
According to the nurse, after Dr. Burt's visit the contractions started rolling
in pretty regular. Early in the morning, they took Bert into the delivery room,*

knocked her out, did a little snip to help the baby through and, with a little help from the forceps, his brand new baby girl entered the world.

"Would you like to come to the nursery to see your new daughter Mr. Campbell?" Jim and his grandmother followed Mrs. West the head nurse along the hospital corridor to the nursery. "Oh my, she's a big girl sir – 8 pounds 9 ounces. You don't often see such big babies coming out of such tiny mothers. That's why Dr. Burt had to use the forceps you know. A classic Dr. Burt special, nice clean cut, in and out with his number 3 forceps, then stitch her up tight as a drum. Mrs. Campbell will need to rest here for a few days. She's sleeping in the recovery room right now. It often takes a while for the anesthesia to wear off. I'll let you know when she's ready to go to her room – for now you and Betty can visit with your new daughter. Betty, is this your third or fourth great grandchild now?"

"Jimmy, she's absolutely perfect!" Betty Campbell gently rocked her newest great grandchild while her grandson looked on in amazement. "What are you going to call her?"

"Well Grandma, since she was born on Queen Victoria's birthday, the 24th of May – how about Queenie? Queenie Campbell has a ring to it don't you think? I once had a beautiful German Shepherd named Queenie."

"Jim Campbell, you will not be naming your daughter after a dog!"

"Well, Bert had mentioned that if the baby was a girl and she was born today, we could name her Victoria but I think that sounds just plain stuck up. What do you think?"

"Here dear, you hold your daughter for a while and soon I bet the right name will come to you. That's it, gentle now." Betty handed the squirming little bundle over to the tentative arms of the new dad. He snuggled her into the crook of his arm like an old pro. "Why look at you Jim Campbell, you are a real natural with her. Can you see the way she is looking at you?" Betty didn't need to say another word; Jim was already thoroughly enchanted by the charms of this three-hour-old perfect little blossom – his daughter.

Jim took his two girls home to the Fifth Avenue bungalow four days later. It was going to take Bert more than a few days to be up and around so Jim had taken a week off of work. His in-laws were due to come to Saskatoon in a week or so. Until then, Jim was pretty much on his own with Bert and Nancy Lynne. Yes, Nancy Lynne – the perfect name for his perfect little girl. When Bert had woken up from the delivery, he had suggested the name that had come to him while first rocking their new daughter. Granted she might have still been a bit groggy, but Bert smiled and nodded her head which led him to believe that she agreed with the name. He didn't mention that Nancy was his first fiancée's name – it didn't seem to matter – it suited his baby perfectly. She was registered as Nancy Lynne Campbell – born on May 24th at 9:06 in the morning!

*Jim soon had the new mom and baby settled into a manageable routine. Rise and shine, bath and a bottle for Nancy, toast and coffee for Bert. A quick load of laundry tossed in the washer then Jim loaded the baby into the carriage for her morning stroll around the neighborhood. Grandma Campbell would drop by for a bite of lunch and a visit with the baby and new mom. While Grandma was holding down the fort, Jim would run and do a few errands returning for naptime. Afternoons would come and go, dinner was whatever Bert felt up to and then it was time for the evening bath and the nighttime bottle.*

*Jim was particularly proud of his special nighttime routine with Nancy. He had it timed perfectly so that he could give her a bottle while enjoying the late news. This was not just any nighttime bottle. Jim had devised a sure fire method that guaranteed Nancy would sleep through the night. He mixed up a batch of formula, added a few tablespoons of pablum so it was pretty thick, then the secret ingredient was a shot of scotch – baby size mind you but just enough to send her off to la la land for a good eight hours. The real trick was getting this sleeping potion through the nipple into his baby girl. Simple! He heated up a nail and just made the hole in the nipple large enough for the thick evening feeding to pass through without a hitch. He really loved being a new dad, especially in the peace and quiet of the evening – just Nancy and him and the late night news. Who knew that fatherhood would be such bliss?*

## It's Never Too Late to Be Born

by Annie Lavack

*"Fine...go to the hospital but they're just going to send you back home again". I heard the disdain in his voice, the judgement, the impatience. I tried to wait...I was about to entrust this doctor with the birth of my first child and I sure didn't want to piss him off. So I waited, sitting on the toilet hunched over in pain and crying until I couldn't hold on anymore. Fuck it! Let them send me back home if they want, I couldn't wait another minute. I was scared, uncertain and in desperate need of some reassurance.*

*The contractions were a minute apart when we arrived at the hospital, everything I had learned in prenatal class was gone and I had no idea what breathing I was supposed to be doing. The nurses kept shushing me and telling me not to push – until they saw I was fully dilated! Suddenly I was no longer* an emotional and annoying woman who wouldn't listen, but a mother about to give birth...and guess what? My doctor was nowhere in sight. In fact he didn't even show up until an hour after Tyler was born!

I remember looking down at my son and feeling nothing. Even as I write I can feel that deep dark void of nothingness. There's no sound, no light, no air... just a never-ending black hole going deeper and deeper and deeper. I longed to feel something, to bond with him. I knew all about the mother/child bond and how important it was. The health of his entire emotional life was dependent on a strong healthy bond between us and the more I felt the emptiness the more it began to fill with fear. I became acutely aware of how separate we were and how alone I felt. It should have been the happiest day of my life but I was miserable. I didn't love his father, I wanted to but I didn't. I had a ring on my finger, a man by my side and a baby in my arms and the truth is I had no idea how I was going to survive.

Tyler was born five weeks early and his sucking reflex wasn't developed enough to allow him to eat properly so the doctors had to insert feeding tubes through his nose. There was constant concern about how little he was eating and the nurses kept bombarding me with questions to try and figure out what was wrong with him. They talked to each other but no one really spoke to me directly and I was so scared that I could hardly breathe. I pretended to be happy, sure that everything was fine, but inside I bounced back and forth between worry and numbness...worry and numbness...and in the end I chose numbness.

Did I always feel that way? No. Did I feel that way longer than I would have liked to? Yes. Sometimes I wonder how I managed. But the truth is I know how I did it. I looked at my son one day...saw that sweet, spunky little boy and decided that we both deserved so much more. I dove into that dark abyss and went searching for myself.

Now, instead of guilt I feel compassion. I applaud the commitment I made to give us a better life and the courage it took to actually do it. When I see the love and honesty in our relationship and I hear him talk about his childhood and who he has become because of it, I honour the truth of who he is and I applaud that woman who changed her life.

# Welcome Little One

by Rebecca Kennel

*So you finally made it, little bald baby. May 12, 1951. Saturday night. 11:00. You tried once before, changed your mind, then three days later decided to brave it. You should have come through the first try and you could have been twins with your double cousin Pam. Then she wouldn't have been able to hold her superiority over you all those years. Oh well, now you can claim to be younger, which is just as sweet.*

*The 26-mile trip over the bumpy rural Montana roads must have helped ease your way. And your Dad made that trip every evening for five days to come and see you and your Mom, while Wendell stayed at the farm with Grandma Mullet.*

*Grandma and Grandpa Kauffman would come up after church on Sunday to see you – the 23ʳᵈ grandchild. They would also visit Pam and her mother, your Aunt Gladys. There was probably a whole stream of relatives coming to visit both of you. Uncle Morris and Uncle Cliff would make jokes about your bald head. Aunt Jesse would have come in from the ranch and Aunt Jerry would come up. And Aunt Cele. And Aunt Lucille.*

*Thursday you made the trip back out to the farm. How did it feel to drive onto the yard and smell the scorched brooder coop that burned the night you were born, the kerosene heater tipping over and starting it all ablaze? Is that a way to announce your arrival into the world?*

*Wendell would have come running out on the porch as the car drove up, a two-year old eager to see what a little sister looked like. You would be carried in up the steps to the porch, then in through the screen door to the separator room, then into the kitchen. The bassinet was set up in the bedroom with stacks of carefully folded cloth diapers, the receiving blankets, the knitted booties and caps.*

*Then Sunday you would go to church as you would for every Sunday for the next 17 years, this time to Red Top. Your Mom would try in vain to tie a ribbon to the few strands of hair on your head. And after church, you would be invited to someone's house for dinner – probably Uncle Cliff and Aunt Ann's, your first introduction to a few of your many cousins; Rolly, Donna, Judy and Gloria.*

*Life was good in the Red Top valley. Your Mom would take you to watch your Dad play softball at the field shared by the church, the school and the community. You would go along on the hunting trips – deer and antelope. You would go to the church picnics in Evan's Grove. And every Sunday you would go to church and be bathed in the sound of voices lifting their acapella praise to the Lord – delivering their prayers and their gratitude directly to heaven's door.*

# *Let's Write*

This birth story is one where you can go back and celebrate your own birth. No matter what your early life was like – whether you were adopted, had parents that absolutely rejoiced the day you were born, or you were born into poverty or a one parent family, here is your opportunity as an adult to go back and give love to the precious baby that was you.

What do you know about your birth? Where were you born; what city and country? What was the day of your birth? What was happening historically and what was happening in your personal family at that time? Were you a wanted child? Was there a celebration or were you "another hungry mouth to feed"? Did you have sisters and brothers? Where did you stand in the family? What name were you given? Were you named after a relative? Write about the details as they've been told to you. Were your parents together? Were you adopted? If your beginnings were difficult, I suggest you do the following first:

Go back to Book 1, Part D, "Invocation – Opening to the Gifts" before beginning to write. Read it, then open your journal and read the following prompts:

Travel back in time to the day you were born – the moment you took your very first breath. In your mind's eye, from the adult you are today, imagine yourself taking that precious baby into your arms and holding her or him and giving her or him all the love in your heart. Welcome her or him into the world and tell your infant self how happy you are she or he is here. Rock that sweet baby that was you in your arms, comforting her or him, perhaps singing a lullaby. Tell her you are so glad she was born a girl. Tell him you are so glad he was born a boy. Tell her or him how loved and appreciated he or she is.

Hopefully, this was, in fact, how you were received into the world. Welcomed and loved. However, if that wasn't how it was for you, describe how it was in actuality. What was going on in your home with your mother and your father? What were the circumstances? Were you an unwanted child? Were you given up for adoption at birth? If so, were you adopted at some point? How old were you? What were your adoptive parents like? Perhaps you lived in foster homes. Did you ever reunite with your birth parents? What were the circumstances of your birth? How did those circumstances impact your life and how do you feel about it today?

Now what if you were to imagine for a moment the possibility that your mother and father, in fact, truly did love you with all their hearts but they were too ill or afraid or broken to give you what you needed and deserved? Are you able to open your heart and consider that underneath the many layers of their pain, they loved you unconditionally? I wonder what they were going through to not have had what it takes to love and cherish their very own precious child. So right now, you have an opportunity, no matter what the circumstances were, to imagine yourself being completely loved and cherished by them. This exercise can help you heal the pain that you may have been carrying your whole life. Imagine a movie screen in front of you and there upon it are your mom, dad and yourself. First see your mother holding you and gently rocking you. See the loving smile on her face as she looks adorningly into your eyes. How does that feel inside your body? Be with this feeling for a few moments and breathe. Now watch her lovingly place you in the arms of your dad and see the joy, wonder and awe in his face as he holds you. Now, feel yourself fully bathing in the love of your parents feeling safe, protected and cherished. Breathe this into your body. Know as you do this you are breathing life and celebration back into this precious child – who is You!

Now, when you are ready, begin to write the story of your birth into this world.

# Chapter 9

## ABOUT MY FATHER

### It's Okay to Love Your Father

Excerpt from *Journey to Personal Freedom*
by Esther Hart

*As a child I was taught to believe that the Bible was to be followed literally as interpreted by people like John Wesley and my father. There was only one way to "salvation" and very few people were on this narrow path because the restrictions were so rigorous. Not being on the path meant being doomed to destruction and the fires of hell. I learned to believe that I could either be a good Christian and expect to be persecuted by the "unbelievers" or I could condemn myself to hell. Even if I chose to be a Christian, however, if I had an impure thought at the instant of death, I could still go to hell. I grew up in a state of fear that was fostered by my father's fear. It's no wonder since my father's minister told me that on his deathbed my father was still fearful that after a lifetime of trying to be the best Christian he knew, he could still go to hell if he died with the "wrong" thoughts in his mind.*

*When I was 13 my father bought a dry cleaning business. I don't know if it was coincidental but, between then and the time I left home at 19, something changed. The details aren't clear but I remember being very upset because one day at dinner he would tell us that he had been upset about something and had formulated a plan for how he would kill all of us and then himself. The next evening he would be telling jokes. One of my strongest memories of that time* is lying in bed at night, not wanting to go to sleep until he had passed my room because I thought that, if I didn't, he might kill me in my sleep. I felt that once he had gone to bed I was safe. I don't recall him ever physically harming any of us so I don't know why I took his threats so seriously. Recently a therapist explained that sometimes it is easier for a child to handle actual physical abuse because they know what is coming whereas threats leave everything to a child's very vivid imagination. I realize now that my father must have been in a lot of pain to have made those threats because I believe that he was really a kind man.

I went home for the summer after my first year away and again my father talked about killing. Then when I was preparing to go back to school he came to talk to me. He apologized for not being a good father, told me about growing up with an alcoholic father who beat his mother and asked me to forgive him. I told him that I wasn't as concerned about how he treated me as I was about the way he treated my mother. He berated her because he said she didn't teach the children to respect him. I always used to tell her where I was going and with whom. But if she told him it would upset him and she would get in trouble for not controlling me. She told me that eventually when he asked her where I was she would say, "I didn't ask." She knew where I was but didn't want to tell him, or lie to him, so this was her solution. If it weren't for wanting to spare my mother from his anger, I probably would have been a far more rebellious child. He also blamed her for everything that went wrong in his life. One day I was there when he blamed her for something. After he left I said, "He's right, you know." We liked and respected each other and were used to getting support from each other so I think this statement came as quite a surprise. She said, "How can you say that?" I replied, "You should have kicked him in the butt the first time he misbehaved and he would respect you and himself more." She responded, "I wasn't raised that way. I was raised that the man is the head of the house." Somehow at 19, I had the insight to add, "There are very few people strong enough to have everyone around them ask, 'How high?' when told to jump." I am not one of them and neither was he. That summer I was dating a young man who was Catholic and my father expressed concern that I was putting my soul in danger. He wanted me to promise that I was giving my life to Christ so that he could feel at peace.

I watched the agony of my father's continuous state of guilt and fear and knew when I left home to teach in Thompson at 19, that I couldn't live my life that way. I had to find a belief system that gave me at least some hope of living up to my own expectations. When I got back to Thompson I wrote my father a letter. I told him that this letter was between me and him and I never wanted to hear that he upset my mother because of it. I told him that I would never deliberately hurt him but that I knew what I wanted from my life and if in pursuing my dreams I should inadvertently hurt him I expected him to forgive me the *way he had asked me to forgive him. I advised him that it was much tougher for my younger brother and sister growing up than it had been for me and if he expected to have any hope of them believing what he preached, he better start showing them by his example that it was possible. My mother confirmed that he never mentioned the letter to her but that he carried it in his shirt pocket until the folds were so tattered that it was falling apart.*

At their 40th *wedding anniversary, in front of a houseful of family and friends, my father stood up with tears running down his face and told how the letter had started a change in his life. At first he had been so angry that he wanted to come all the way up to Thompson to kill me. Then something happened and he started to pray and go back to church. After that I really began to believe in miracles.*

*Years later I went to an astrologer and told him I was there to talk about a name change. He said, "No. You're here to talk about relationships." Then he asked that "stupid" question. "Does the man you're seeing remind you of your father?" It was on the tip of my tongue to make a seriously vehement denial when my mind stopped dead in its tracks. I said, "Yes. There are things that remind me of my father." As I allowed this possibility to percolate I realized that more than his reminding me of my father, I was responding to him the way I responded to my father and I had done the same thing with Neil when we were married. I was reminded of the time a therapist had told me that we equate love with the characteristics of the first people from whom we expect to receive love — usually our parents. Is it any wonder then that I expected criticism from Neil and took many things he said as negative judgments, that I felt I couldn't measure up to his expectations and that above all, I didn't feel safe in the relationship.*

*That night as I lay in bed "the voice" said very clearly, "It's okay to love a man who reminds you of your father." My body started to quiver and tingle. Before the tingling had stopped "the voice" said, "It's okay to love your father." Now my body started to shake. Immediately "the voice" continued, "It's okay to love you." I burst into tears and even as I write this the tears are flowing. We're always taught to love others but what is really powerful is when we finally give ourselves permission to love ourselves.*

# Counting Down the Years

by Sharon Pocock

*I kneel in front of grey granite and separate the flowers with care; focus on every delicate petal and thorn. Red roses for love, respect and courage. Aloe for grief. Iris for faith, hope, bravery and promises. Carnations for remembrance. Ivy is myself – anxious and eager to please, binding the elements together.*

*Every stem brings sentiment and memory and the sun darts through the trees and reflects against the polished stone. I float back.*

*Age 4*
*The school gates loom. I hold tight to strong hands. Too small and shy and self-conscious in my home-made uniform, I don't understand why you would leave me. I feel abandoned until the joyous ringing of the bell and you are standing at the gate. Perhaps tomorrow may be easier.*

*Age 7*
*I look round carefully and start to "borrow" money from your wallet. I rationalize that it is to buy you a better birthday present. Nestled in the back there's a picture of a skinny, dark haired girl with too pale skin and innocent eyes. It is the only picture there. I put the money back and go outside for air.*

*Age 15*
*You turn your back and go away. She cries quietly in the corner and refuses to let out her pain. How can you hurt someone whom you spent so long loving? How can you turn your back on me? I grow up a little and become counsellor and housekeeper. You say you are proud of me, but you don't come back.*

*Age 16*
*The year struggles on and I bend under the weight of unsought responsibil-ity. You visit and must see the fractures visible in every conversation. My love has not faltered, but I am no longer a child and emotion has become tempered with wariness and thoughts of feet of clay. You come home.*

*Age 18*
*The siren call of college beckons. The first in my family to fly and the pride and pain of parting shines in your eyes. My world changes and my rebellion*

*blooms gently. It becomes more visible with every visit. But you remain to listen to me.*

Age 23

*Thoughts of my first flat make me flutter with excitement and anxiety. Proof of my separation and independence, bound up in bricks and mortar and terrifying financial obligation. All of a sudden I am truly an adult and must learn to act as such. I still phone for advice on how to fix the plumbing and you tease me quietly.*

Age 25

*I sit nervously in the kitchen while my love asks formal permission to marry. The ice melts in my drink and my hands are damp with nervousness and condensation. This is the right thing to do, an acknowledgement of responsibility and love. I hear you laughing and the torch changes hands.*

Age 27

*You offer me water to moisten dry lips and a throat tied tight with emotion. As I put the glass down on the table my hand shakes slightly and you ease the web of lace gently over my head. You kiss my hand.*

Age 32

*I hold you tightly and you say goodbye. She suffered so much 'til I just wanted it to be over. I could never say that to you and my guilty thoughts haunt me for the longest time. But final peace needs acceptance and acknowledgement and you know that you must find a new reason for your life.*

Age 37

*Five years on and five years of grieving. Her perfume remains on the night stand and I cannot persuade you to clear through drawers and closets. It is not my place to dictate and suddenly I am a child again.*

Age 41

*Ten years on and ten years of grieving come to a sudden end with the beat of a failing heart. How can a person be there in one instant and suddenly be gone? I wander through the rooms looking for a presence where there is only empty air. Your grief is finally ended and we are left behind. The wheel begins to turn.*

*I trace the name already present on the smooth stone surface, the lettering beginning to fade towards grey and my hand lingers on the still blank space below. We have yet to find a wording fit to prove that you were here and that you were loved.*

*For now, I cling to the thought that you are finally happy again and that is enough to make me smile. I know this tunnel has its light. I refused to believe it once before, but now I know this truth.*

*But for now, every day is my Father's Day and it is my time to grieve.*

# *Let's Write*

As with previous stories, before you begin to write, you may want to read the Centering Exercise found in Book 1, Part C and if there's an opportunity for forgiveness, I recommend that you read the Invocation found in Book 1, Part D.

As you enter into this story about your father, begin by focusing on your breath. Let the natural rhythm of your breath bring you into a state of relaxation. Now, begin to bring up a picture of your father onto the screen of your mind. If you have real photographs of him, you may want to look at them before reading the following memory prompts.

You may not have known your father very well. Perhaps not at all. Maybe you never found out who he was and have not had an opportunity to meet him. Perhaps he left when you were very young. Do you have any memories at all? If so, this is an opportunity to capture them on paper as well as express your feelings. What has it been like for you to not have known him – to not have had him in your life? To not have looked into his eyes? Get in touch with those feelings now and write from your sadness, your anger, apathy, emptiness or acceptance. Whatever those feelings are, allow them to surface now and write from where you are.

If your father has passed away, see the memory prompts at the end of this section. However, I suggest that you continue to read through the following prompts as well, as it will help you to remember specific details about him and your relationship. You can read it in past tense instead.

How would you describe your dad? How old is he? What is his name? In what year was he born and where? How well do you think you know your father? Was he away from home a lot while you were growing up or was he effectively engaged in your upbringing? How is your father's current health? Is he strong and vibrant or does he have some health challenges? How does his good health or lack of it impact your life today? How does he earn his living? Does he enjoy what he does? Has your father stayed with the same job or career or has he changed jobs/careers during his lifetime? Did changing jobs require the family to pick up and move from time to time? If so, what was that like for you?

What kind of relationship does your dad have with your mom if they are still together? Is he physically affectionate? Does he help around the house? Does he ever bring home flowers? What do you like the most about your mom and dad's relationship? What do you like least about their relationship? What kind of communicator is your dad? Does he express his opinions outright? Are there or were there interesting discussions in your home with your father open to listening to your thoughts and feelings or was he more controlling – telling you what to do and think?

What are some of your fondest memories? What qualities in your dad do you especially admire? What qualities about your father do you dislike? What does he like to do in his spare time? Does your father have many friends? Is he a social person or more of a loner?

What special things do you do together – just you and your dad? What is your relationship like? Are you close? If so, in what ways? What makes your relationship meaningful? What are some of the most helpful things you have learned from your father? In what ways have you not been close? How would you like it to be different? Do you communicate regularly? What do you talk about? Have you been able to go to him and tell him your troubles? Is he there for you in that way? Does he come to you when he feels burdened by circumstances? Does your father offer you praise? What do you think he enjoys about you the most? Are there concerns or worries you have about him? What are they?

In what ways do you think you are like your father? In what ways are you different?

How would you describe your dad now compared to when you were growing up? What are some of the significant changes you've noticed and how have they impacted you?

How would you describe his relationship with your siblings? Did he have a favourite? Was it you? How did you feel about it if it was you or if it was one of your siblings?

What wishes do you have for your dad? Are there any negative feelings that come up for you when thinking about your father – things from the past you haven't forgiven him for? What are they? Anger, distrust, resentment, scorn, shame, disgust, hatred, indifference? Something else?

Are you ready to transform these feelings into compassion, forgiveness, healing? Are you willing to forgive your father unconditionally right now remembering that he was doing the best that he knew how to do at the time?

If so, say. "I forgive you dad for all the pain I've felt in my life that I perceived was caused by you. I forgive you and willingly let go of all my hurt, anger and resentment." If that's not true for you, if you are not in an emotional place to offer forgiveness, write your truth about that. I had a wonderful teacher, Leonard Shaw, who used to tell us to say: "I am unwilling to forgive you (Dad, in this case) for your ignorant behaviour towards me in spite of the cost." He always reminded us of the cost to ourselves when we are unwilling to forgive. Besides taking us out of the present moment by holding onto old resentments and anger, it can make us physically ill, angry, bitter and ultimately unhappy. Still – forgiveness IS a process and must be done in one's own time. However, I find it's best to at least have a willingness to forgive, even if you're not quite ready to do it.

What else would you like to say to your father? If there is more, acknowledge that now. What would you like to have him say to you?

If your father has died, you can use the following prompts: When did he die? What was the year? How old were you? What were the circumstances surrounding his death? Was he ill? Was there an accident or something else? What impact did your father's death have on your life and that of your family? Are there still things you would like to say to him? What would you like to tell him? Take the time to say it now.

Here are some options you may want to use for writing your story.

You can write a story about your father and your relationship with him or you can write a letter to him even if he is deceased. You can then write a letter from him to you as you believe his highest loving self would write it.

Remember to write without censoring, judging or editing. Relax into the process and breathe. Write from this place of full breath.

# Chapter 10

## ABOUT MY MOTHER

### Now I Lay You Down to Sleep

by Tom Little

*Her breathing was shallow, barely present. Her eyelids rested heavily, unable to open. He leaned over the bed, kissing her gently on the cheek, found her skin remarkably soft and smooth, her face placid, peaceful. He marveled at how her wiry salt-and-pepper hair fought back against time, belying her years – a sign of his mother's renowned youthful energy. Now he desperately hoped this energy would ride to her rescue, in spite of the damage beneath her skull. The damage that kept her hanging between recovery and....*

*He glanced at his watch: 3:15 a.m.*

*He picked up her limp hand and nestled it snugly in his. He watched her eyelids flutter, prayed that she would come back, even for just a moment. He'd driven for hours over snowy mountain roads to reach their small town, but the nurse on duty had spoken frankly to him, "If there's anything you want to tell her, son, now's the time."*

*"I'm here mom."*

*He had started gently, fearing the cerebral avalanche would prevent him from reaching her. He held her wrinkled hand and stroked her arm, wondering if she could understand.*

*"Mom, if you can hear me, squeeze my hand"... Nothing.*

"*Can you lift a finger, mom?*" *From the corner of his eye he saw the blanket ripple on the far side. He freed her other arm and rested her hand over her heart.* "*Mom,* " *he whispered urgently,* "*lift your finger.* "

*Twitch. Her index finger bobbed.*

"*Great, mom! Can you raise it one time for yes?*" *The digit bobbed again.* "*Good, good... twice for no?... Great!*"

*With damp eyes, aware that time was the enemy, he began what he feared would be their last talk. He spoke from the heart, said that the doctors would do everything possible to save her, to bring her back, but if it wasn't possible, if it couldn't happen... this would be their special time together.*

*She raised a finger.*

*His mother was famous for her blunt honesty, appreciated by those who loved her in spite of its sting. Perhaps it was surviving the Dirty Thirties, helping her family work a prairie farm after her father's death. Or her years as a war nurse, then raising three kids on a pittance in a small B.C. town, her starry-eyed husband's dreams crumbling, trapped in a job he hated. Honouring her honesty, he acknowledged some of her broken dreams, how life had laughed at the notion of the white picket fence, the perfect home and family.*

*He said he knew her marriage had been hard, admired her strength to continue... said that her endless love taught him what was really important... how to love his wife and kids unconditionally... how it didn't stop the hurtful moments, the foolish pride, but was the balm that healed the wounds... the best medicine... the magic. Pressing his forehead to her chest, voice quivering, he said* "*Thank you mom.* " *Her finger moved side to side, as if to say* "*There, there, son. It's OK.* "

*And so it went, recounting shared moments of their lives as her finger eagerly responded. Not wanting to tire her, but wary of the time, he asked her to forgive his thoughtlessness, times that he had hurt her feelings. He recalled several minor incidents, yet something still gnawed, something dark and painful, just beyond his reach. He struggled, but all he felt was a deep and foggy sadness. Laying his aching head on the pillow, he rested a moment, but knew he owed it to her to be truthful. It was then he recalled that day at the Greyhound depot. He was barely 18, packsack loaded, heading for the coast after a disastrous year at the local college. She'd had such high hopes, blind to his quest to hit every party, sample the smorgasbord of liquor and drugs and lose his virginity. After a tearful hug goodbye, she had crossed the street to the post office to check for mail. Just as he was boarding, she came running back waving an envelope.* "*Your marks, your marks!*" *she called, ripping the envelope open. Knowing the letter's contents, he had cowardly planned to leave town, leaving the dirty work to the postal service.*

*Now he recalled the stricken look on her face, the down-turned mouth and trembling lip, the weak wave as the bus door hissed shut. He wondered if she'd forgotten, since things had worked out – college in the east, good job, the move back west, then marriage and kids. Should he even mention it? Her finger was still caressing the top of his hand, sending a flood of warmth up his arm into his chest. Yet something still wasn't right. The gnawing returned. Suddenly a chill shot through him. His heart pounded and his mouth went dry as a wave of grief rocked him. There it was in all its ugliness – the one thing that they had never spoken of, never settled.*

*The wedding.*

*What was it that had caused the whole affair to crash to earth in flames; that weighed like a stone buried deep in their hearts in spite of the obvious success of his marriage and her love for his wife and kids? The truth was, he had deeply hurt her and never bound the wound. Her stoic character had long ago covered the scar but he knew it still pained her. Shuddering, he took a deep breath and began.*

*"Mom, please forgive me for what happened on my wedding day. I know it wasn't the outdoor wedding – after all, it was a meadow in the Rockies – nor all our wild and wooly friends. But we were so young. We hated ceremony. We just wanted everyone to come together and celebrate our love. Remember how everyone circled us in all that sunshine? And after, how we gave everyone a red rose...?"*

*He paused, struck by the memory of one photo from the wedding album – long faces on the bride, groom, his brother, sister and father as they walked from the meadow to the lodge, eyes cast to the ground. His mother, holding a rose, wept bitterly. More like a funeral.*

*"My timing was crummy," he stammered. "We should have saved the 'good news' til after. I thought you'd be excited by the pregnancy. We'd just breeze through college with our baby. No wonder you looked so sad in that wedding photo." She raised her finger, but he knew it wasn't really that. Deep down he knew it was the wedding dance. He broke into a sweat as he recalled how his mother and father had left early, wearing even longer faces than before.*

*Time had run away on him that day. The thunderstorm after dinner, the power failure, someone lit some candles, someone else began strumming a 12-string guitar. The bride sang a few numbers, bravely, beautifully. Someone opened the bar. The wedding dance turned into a candle-lit party and he and his bride went round, buoying spirits. He thought it was going well, that his parents and relatives were mingling, coping. He remembered bringing them some drinks.*

*Then the power came back on and the music started. He and his bride pulled the nearest guests up to dance, he with the bridesmaid, she with her dad. Then his sister grabbed him for a turn round the floor and when his mother-in-law came into view he switched to her. By now most everyone was dancing and it seemed that the storm hadn't wrecked things after all.*

*"It was definitely not a traditional wedding mom. I mean, we didn't even HAVE a master of ceremonies! Sure, there were some toasts to the bride and groom, mostly funny ones. Nothing about family or the parents. Hah! Going with the flow! When the power came back I figured everyone would just dance with one another, kind of like one big circle of joy. I kept thinking I'd dance with you next, but then someone would grab me to dance. Then I noticed you and Dad with your coats on, heading for the door. You said you were tired, but I knew from your face that that wasn't it. I was so hung up on ignoring convention I thought everyone else felt the same way. Talk about a generation gap, huh?"*

The finger rose, fell.

*"Well, mom, I didn't honour you and Dad that night. I'm so sorry. I wish I could turn back the clock and take you in my arms and dance you around that dance floor. I know that's all you really wanted. Forgive me."*

A tear rolled down his cheek. Her finger tapped once, then slowly caressed his hand... *"Never mind son, it's OK. "* He sighed and hugged her tightly for a long time. At last he felt peace and he sensed the same in her – a state of grace. Now, he found himself swimming back in time, wanting to take her with him to a special place he knew they both cherished.

He spoke softly, reviving those bright days when, too young for school and decked in fresh T-shirt and shorts, he'd skipped hand-in-hand beside her to the heart of town. Shopping day.

He reminded her how they always ended up at the coffee shop. He loved sitting at the counter, happily munching a donut while spinning round on the shiny stool. She always chatted gaily with everyone; people seemed to light up around her. And still, the best was yet to come – the owner always let them descend into paradise – downstairs to the 'chocklit factory'.

They remembered the heavenly scent as they clumped down the stairs, that first blast of sweet warm air... remembered two balding brothers, their bushy moustaches above beaming smiles as they mixed the creamy brown nectar, spreading it on the marble slab... how his little boy's eyes widened as they poured coats of warm, rich chocolate over rows of nuts and bright red maraschinos... and always a wink or a pinch on his cheek and a free sample or two.

He realized he had been stroking her inner arm as if mixing chocolate on the slab. A sigh escaped her lips. A sigh of bliss, or was she slipping away? He leaned close and placed a hand on her forehead, felt how cool it was. He smoothed the coarse hair from her brow. Her breath was faint.

At that moment, emotions brimming over, his earliest, most cherished memory came to him.

*"Remember when I was little, mom – running around half naked all the time? At bedtime, you always tucked me in, remember?"* He snuggled her blanket around her chest and moved his lips to her ear. Then, in sing-song

*fashion, he whispered the prayer she'd spoken softly while smoothing his silky hair, trying to calm him to sleep.*

*"Now I lay me down to sleep, I pray the Lord my soul to keep, And if I die before I wake, I pray the Lord my soul to take."*

*She sighed again, quieter now. "Remember, mom? First you'd say a line, then I'd say it." Her finger tapped softly. He kissed her cheek. "Mom, I love you so much." Another sigh – this one his – caught in his throat. His voice cracked, "Can we say it again, mom, like we used to?"*

*Another tap. Hot tears flooded his eyes, rolled down and splashed her cheek. "OK mom, I'll lead, you follow."*

*"Now I lay me down to sleep." **Tap**, tap-**tap**, tap-**tap**, tap-**tap**.*

*"I pray the Lord my soul to keep." Tap-**tap**, tap-**tap**, tap-**tap**, tap-**tap**.*

*"If I should die before I wake." Tap-**tap**, tap-**tap**, tap-**tap**, tap- **tap**.*

*"I pray the Lord my soul to take." Tap-**tap**, tap-**tap**, tap-**tap**, tap-**tap**...............*

*All was still.*

*He brushed his lips across her cheek, was stabbed by the absence of breath from her nostrils. Blinking back tears, he kissed her forehead and began stroking her hair. As he did so, a calmness came upon him and, drawn by something deep within, he shut his eyes and began again, silently:*

*Now I lay me down to sleep... He could hear her soft young voice leading him, all those years ago, his small boy's voice following.*

*I pray the Lord my soul to keep... He clung to her motionless body, following her in prayer for a long time...*

*If I should die before I wake... the gentle lowing of a young mother's voice, a smooth hand caressing an infant's downy head.*

*I pray the Lord my soul to take.*

*When at last his tears stopped and he opened his eyes, the sun had risen. A warm, pink glow filled the room.*

*He regarded his mother's eyes. Closed since his arrival, they were now half open, as if she was merely dozing, taking a moment from her busy day. A hint of a smile graced her lips. It was then that he noticed a newly formed tear.*

*He watched it slip slowly from the corner of her eye, starting its lonely journey down a youthful, rosy cheek.*

# The Legacy

by Judy McIlmoyl

*When I heard of our topic for this writing, I knew I had to write of you. I don't even know your name. My eyes have never been blessed by the sight of your face. I long to know you – a longing deeper perhaps than I have an understanding of. You are my link to the past. To the love that brought me into being. You have a legacy that I will never know. What made you dance with joy? What were you most passionate about? What did you fear most, in the depths of your despair? When you awakened in the morning what were your first thoughts? When you caught your reflection in a shop window, did you ever catch your breath and think of me?*

*Many years went by when I did not let my thoughts come to rest on you. That wasn't allowed. Everything was as it should be. I was with parents who loved me. Enough said. But was it enough? While never given permission to mourn the loss of the living you, you were lost to me. Where were you when I was so alone and so afraid? Is my fear your legacy to me? Is it my gifts, my deep love for nature and all things delicate and tender and easily broken?*

*As time leaves its etchings on me, I look in my eyes and wonder who you are. I do long to know you…as one soul knows another; not by name or even a shared past, but by an honouring of each other's presence here on earth. You gave me life. I was once a part of you and I still am; as you are still a part of me, even though I don't even know your name.*

# Masks

by Sharon Pocock

*I step out of the shower and do the things that women do. Towel dry, moisturize, put products in my hair that promise the Hollywood look and god knows it could do with a little help. Wash my face, then comes toner and more moisturizer. Do I really believe I need a separate cream or gel for under my eyes? I've no idea but the package was cute and the jar looks elegant on the wash stand, promising its own patented fountain of youth. I dry my hair and then the real work begins.*

*Concealer, just a touch under the eyes and hey, if I need it there, it kind of suggests the eye cream is the snake oil I always suspected. A little foundation, not all over, just on the bits that need it. Hmm, maybe it should be all over. A little eyeliner, maybe olive, or grey, or burgundy, or black if I'm in a Dusty Springfield mood. A little blush, just a touch, a suggestion of heat and then the final touch – lipstick. When I was younger it was bold colours, making a statement in a too pale face, but now in my more somber, if not more sober years, I'm safe in natural, and taupe, and suede and all the other names the marketing men created to mean the same shade of dull. It's taken me years to hone these skills. To know which colour to hide behind, what creates the desired mask of the moment. But it wasn't always the case.*

*I think back to a small, shy girl, tongue tied in the face of boys. More at home on horseback than at a teenage party. I didn't know the code words. Couldn't crack the body language and the secret handshakes that make the closed world of a popular teenager go round. I remember standing, self- conscious in a pair of sage green dungarees that I'd coveted for the longest time. I thought I was the bees knees. I thought I was the kick. I walked into the party and thought that I would die.*

*The room was wall to wall with tight jeans and tighter tops. With hair styled within an inch of its life and lipstick in every rainbow colour. I stood there in my token flash of blue eye shadow, clutching at my coke and wondering if I could pluck up the nerve to speak to the boy I liked. Finally I took my courage in both hands and made the move and he smiled and talked about our homework and then he walked away, leaving me stranded in the middle of the floor. I know that people watched and people whispered and probably laughed, but I didn't hear them as I stood frozen, locked in my own humiliation. But I didn't blame him. He was a teenage boy and that's how they were. I blamed you.*

*I blamed you for not teaching me the language, not teaching me the code I would need to open this new door. I blamed you for not talking about lipstick and blush, powder and eyeliner. I blamed you for letting me think that my prized dungarees were suitable armour for a teenage party. I blamed you for all these things – for not giving me the weapons I needed to survive in shark infested waters. I was your daughter and you were my mum and I loved you so much, but I blamed you for not helping me become a woman. For not helping me understand.*

*I made so many mistakes in those black years; fell over my feet in so many ways. I look back and shiver and think of the deep pools I almost drowned in – putting myself in positions where the worst might have happened because I didn't understand the subtext.*

*That was then and I grieve for the skinny girl, so unsure in her own skin, desperate to understand and be understood. Desperate for entrée into this adult world of sophistication and sexual knowledge. But this is now and I finally see the girl for who she was. And I see you in the same blinding light.*

*I was fifteen when he went away and you were drowning, clutching at straws to keep you afloat and I was your anchor in that long turbulent year. Your love had turned his back and found new pastures and my brother didn't want to know. What nineteen-year-old boy wants to admit that the father he worshipped had feet of clay? So he withdrew into the strange dark world that teenage boys inhabit and left us two to cope.*

*We floated in our home-made life raft, keeping each other warm. I cooked and cleaned and I shopped and played housekeeper and counsellor and nurse-maid. And by default you became the child in that time and I became the adult. I put away childish things and entered the adult world. The year passed and after more false starts than I can count, he came back, cap in hand and you finally smiled again. But I continued to cook and shop and be your sounding board because I was now an equal in your eyes.*

*Looking back, that was the root of the problem. In that long year I grew up, concentrating on the mundane struggle of getting through the day. At the end I had crossed the Rubicon and couldn't cross back. My childhood, my teenage years of growth and learning and experimentation had gone – disappeared without ever really being explored, every unanswered question buried in a shallow grave with a sprig of rue on top.*

*I couldn't go back, so I walked forward into life, ill-equipped to deal with the nuances of this strange, new world. But it wasn't your fault. You didn't realize that I hadn't asked the questions. You'd been lost and I bridged the gap and when you looked again you saw a woman, an adult and I allowed you the deception.*

*So I stand here and look in the mirror. Picking up cleanser and tissues I start to wipe away the mask. Stroke by stroke, bit by bit, the walls come down and then the tissue is dirty with beige and red and black. I stand and stare into the mirror, my face clean and bare and finally, I see myself with all my flaws and faults and I'm happy with the reflection. And as I look, I see you too. I finally see the person – not the mother or the wife, but I see the woman, with all your fears and insecurities and joys. I see you and know you did the best you could and I don't blame you anymore.*

## I Honour My Mother

by Pearl Graham

*Dorothy May Spooner was born in 1916. In the 1920's she was thought to be slow. She was unable to learn academically and ended up being sixteen in grade 3. She sucked her thumb until then. At this time she left school and started working for neighbouring farms. My sister Iris became a special education teacher and was able to tell her that she was dyslexic. This boosted her confidence. She learned to read when I was 15; she was 55. She taught me to sew, draft patterns, can food, knit, wash clothes and all things practical. Her home was always full of baking and food. My mother was a very capable woman. It is interesting that my daughter who was seven when mom passed described her to me years later as "Gramma seemed like a very capable person."*

*All my growing up years she baked 18 or 19 loaves of bread every month. She was renowned throughout the family for her baking. Family knew if she showed up on your doorstep for a visit you were guaranteed some baking. She literally glowed when compliments on her wonderful cinnamon buns, cakes or tarts were offered.*

*Her thoughtfulness of giving and serving always astounded me. At her life's end the community recognized her for her many good works and kindnesses. Many of my friends still dropped in on my mother after I left for the city, taking her out to neighboring towns for a day's drive or to have lunch with her. One friend told me four years ago how she had been jealous of my home and family, that it was always welcoming and safe, my parents caring and available.*

*As a child and teen I played with my mom's hands. I would run my finger over the veins in the back of her hands and over her nails. I thought they were beautiful. I have had times where I've looked down at own my hands and in my mind's eye have seen her hands reminding me of her love. There is no one in whose arms I have been more loved. She asked nothing of me but to be her daughter and I was always safe in her presence.*

# *Let's Write*

Begin to reflect on your mother. What is her name? Is your mother still alive? If so, how old is she? What is her date of birth? Where was she born?

Has your mother passed away? If so, when did she die? What was the year? How old were you? What were the circumstances around her death? Was she ill; was there an accident or something else?

How well did you know her? Are there still things you would like to say to her? What would you like to tell her? Take the time to acknowledge what you would like to say. There is a writing exercise you can follow at the end of the memory prompts if your mom has passed away.

Perhaps your mom gave you up for adoption when you were born. Did you ever meet her later in life? If so, what was that like? Do you have a relationship with her today? If you have never met her, how does that feel? Be sure to write into the emptiness of that or your anger, apathy, frustration, regret. Whatever is true for you, write it all. You may want to write her a letter and express how it has felt for you, never knowing her at all.

Now we will continue to go through the memory prompts as though your mother is alive. Read through this section even if she has passed away as it will help you to remember specific things about her and your relationship. You can read it in past tense instead.

How would you describe your mother? Is she kind, thoughtful, affectionate? Is she cheerful, outgoing, a businesswoman or a stay at home mom? Is she forgiving or judgmental? Do you think she's more optimistic or more pessimistic – glass half full or half empty attitude? Does she enjoy the company of others? Is she active in the community? Is she quiet and shy, one who tends to spend time alone? Does she invite people home very often? Did she while you were growing up? Does your mom have many friends? What do they like to do together? Does she have siblings? Is she close to them? What are her interests, hobbies? Does she do volunteer work? What is her education? Did she complete high school or university? Do you consider yourself close to your mom? If you are not close, why do you think that is? How do you feel about it? Do you live in the same city? How much quality time do you spend with your mother or how often do you speak? What do you do together? How would you describe your mother now as compared to when you were growing up? What are some of the significant changes you've noticed and how have they impacted you? How is her health? Are there complications? How does that affect her life? Does it affect your life? Are you her caregiver?

What was/is her relationship like with your father or stepfather if that was the case? How would you describe her relationship with your other siblings?

Fully describe your mom. What do you like or love about her? What do you dislike about her? What are some of your most treasured memories? What are some of your most painful ones? How did she treat you when you were growing up? What were some of the things she did that pushed your buttons? Do they still? If not, how did that change? Did you go to her when you needed comfort? How did she respond? Do you go to her now? Does she reach out to you when she needs comfort? What stands out for you when you think of your mom today? Are there concerns or worries you have about her? What are they? In what ways do you think you are like your mom? In what ways are you different? What wishes do you have for her?

Do you still have some residual anger toward your mom – some things from the past for which you have not forgiven her? Are you ready to forgive her now by considering that she was doing the best that she knew how at the time? If so, you can say the following statements: "I forgive you mom for all the hurts I've felt in my life that I perceived were caused by you. I forgive you and willingly let go of all my hurt, anger and resentments. I love you. And I release you." Take a deep breath.

Is there anything you still would like to say to your mother? If so, acknowledge that now. What would you like to say to her? What would you like to have her say to you? Consider writing a letter to your mother stating anything that has been left unsaid. Then write a letter of forgiveness if necessary. When you have integrated this, you can write a love letter to your mom – remembering each of these are stages – give them the respectful time they need. These writings are for you and your healing and not necessarily meant to be given to her.

If you feel it would be beneficial to go through a more complete forgiveness process, go to the Invocation found in Book 1, Part D.

If you are not ready to forgive your mother for any hurts you perceive she has caused you, you will help yourself if you can say honestly, out loud, "In spite of the cost I am unwilling to forgive you, mom, for your ignorant behaviour toward me."

Recognize that holding onto old hurts and resentments causes you more pain. When you acknowledge this and voice the above statement out loud, it allows the pain to shift. By acknowledging the truth of where you are now, you may find yourself moving forward a little more every day toward love, compassion and forgiveness. Have willingness for this to happen. Willingness is a first step in the healing process. You can also read and follow the prompts in Chapter 13 on Forgiveness.

If your mom has passed away, you can write a dialogue between you and her. First write everything you wish to express, then write a letter from her to you as you believe her highest loving self would say it. You may want to read it afterward to your therapist or a cherished friend or partner.

Now think of your mom as a woman, apart from her role as your mother. What do you think are her hopes and dreams? Do you think she has fulfilled some of them? What are some of the things she wanted to do or have or be but so far it has not happened. Do you think she ever lived vicariously through you or your other siblings? How have you felt about that? What are some of her dreams that were fulfilled? What do you think are some of the most significant things she has taught you?

And now, if you are willing, open yourself to the love in your heart for your mom, the woman who gave you life and begin to write the story of your relationship.

# Chapter 11

## ABOUT MY SISTERS AND BROTHERS

## Dear Sister

by Carol Jean

*Oh that I could dance with you sister, rather than fight and compete and crave what I cannot have from you. I simply want to be seen.*

*But that does not seem safe, for when I show you the real naked me, I am at your mercy. My vulnerability is seen as the soft underbelly with which I have given permission for attack. And so I turn over and become the porcupine. No longer do I throw my quills, but you are now aware of them and do not dare to move closer, as you have felt the deep stinging wounds I have thrown to you. Dare I once again turn over? No. Do I need to keep throwing quills? No. Do I need to change my porcupine form? Yes.*

*So what animal shall I become so we can dance together sister? A wolf with its soul-sounding howl? Will you hear my sound sister? Shall I become the owl and hoot with you with the mind sounds that so delight you? Shall I become a totem pole to meet your needs? No. I must become me. I must become just me.*

*I would like to see your angel wings and I would like to show you my angel wings. I would like to dance with the wings dipping and diving ever so gently as a bird glides on the wing. I would like, sister, to show you my wings and dance with you the dance of life.*

*I would like to sing my song with you. I would like you to sing your song with me. I would like once again – I long to once again – blend our voices in reverence to the Divine in each of us – attuned, blending, making the sounds of light and harmony.*

*Oh sister, hear my prayer and pray for my soul and I shall pray for yours. Bless me sister as I bless you. My love for you swells up and then my heart is filled with the honey of such nectar, as I have never tasted. I long to feel this love over and over and have it become imbedded in my soul for you sister.*

*Dear sister, I want to love you.*

## Two Love Letters

by June Swadron

*Dearest Lorraine-dear:*
*I always call you that. And you still laugh. I even address your birthday cards that I post in the mail to: Mrs. Lorraine-dear R. Why? Because you are so truly dear to me. My oldest sister and my oldest friend. You have always been there for me. Even though our lives haven't overlapped the way they did when we were young and even though I always thought they would because I practically lived in your house as your kids were growing up, nothing has changed the love we hold for one another.*

*The nine and a half years between us made a huge difference to our life-styles and also our views of the world which have also contributed to our separate lives. You married young and have been with the same husband for over 50 years. I didn't marry, have travelled extensively, lived in different cities and countries around the world and lead what some would call a non-traditional lifestyle. You grew up with Elvis Presley, Connie Francis and Paul Anka. I grew up with The Stones, The Beatles and Bruce Springsteen. I was just a toddler when you were dating. And I was only 9 years old when you got married to Allan and then left to live in Europe. A day I cried and cried.*

*But it was before that time that set the tone for the love I've always held for you in my heart, Lorraine. I don't think there was a payday that you didn't come home without a skipping rope, colouring book or doll for me. When Allan used to visit you when on leave from the Air Force and took you for drives in the country, you always invited me along. Mom didn't say, "Take your little* sister with you." You just did it. I was your baby sister and I was precious to you. Well, guess what, you are precious to me as well.

I remember when I was only four and we lived on Basilton Crescent in Scarborough. You had a budgie bird. I don't remember his name. What I do remember was when you were at school, I decided to make a nest for him in my undies drawer. So I puffed up my little undershirts, panties and jammies to make it really soft and then I went to the cage to take him to his new house. I somehow got him in my hands, out of the cage, into our bedroom and into the dresser drawer. He was trying to fly away so I quickly closed the drawer so he wouldn't get out. I wanted him to get used to his brand new house. I wanted him to know how special it was and that I made it out of love. It all happened so fast. I closed the drawer and his neck got caught and I quickly pulled the drawer open again but he fell over dead onto the bed of soft flannel. I was horrified. I screamed. I cried. I was afraid. I hid behind the big television consol in the living room. I knew how upset you would be. I don't remember if mom came in and scolded me or not. I don't know what we did with the bird. I just remember hiding behind the television set so you wouldn't find me when you got home. But you found out what happened and you did find me. And you know what you did? You took me in your arms and cradled me and wiped my tears and told me it was okay, that it wasn't my fault. I learned at a tender age that it was possible to make an innocent mistake and still be loveable.

And your unconditional love for me has never waned. Even though we live three thousand miles apart and our phone conversations are infrequent, the love that we share fills my heart. I love you, Lorraine-dear. God bless you, my sweet, beautiful sister.

Love,
Junie xoxo

Dearest Howard:
What can I say about a brother that I hardly know and who hardly knows me? It used to cause me great sadness that we never got along. Even though we are only three and a half years apart, we could have been twenty years apart for all the contact we had. Maybe you wanted a baby brother and not a sister. You already had two sisters and didn't want another one. Or maybe it was just the fact that I came after you and required lots of attention which took the attention away from you. Maybe it's because we came from a family that didn't foster bonding with one another. I don't know. I only know that from my earliest memories, the times we didn't argue were far and few between. And we brought this pattern into our adult life, choosing to live our lives far away from each other.

But things have changed somewhat. We still don't speak frequently – but we speak. And in every conversation, you say, "I love you." And so do I. And we *mean it. And it was you who opened the dialogue some years ago. It was the day you called out of the blue and apologized for past transgressions. You told me you were sorry and wanted to be the big brother you had never been – to somehow make up for lost time, to stay in contact, to bridge the gap. I'll never forget it. I was on my bicycle and pulled over to the side of the road, sat on the curb and listened in disbelief.*

*You called when I had asked for a miracle. I had been depressed and asked God for a sign that things were going to be okay. I even remember saying, "And don't send me a seagull flying across the sky as I'm asking for this please. I need a concrete sign that you are here with me, God." And my cell phone rang. I almost had an accident reaching in my pocket with one hand on the handlebars, the other searching for the phone. And there you were. I felt your sincerity. We spoke for an hour. Years of pain were washed away by the tenderness in your voice. After we hung up, I thanked God for giving me the miracle I asked for...and one I would never have expected.*

*And there have been more conversations. We don't speak often and the old triggers still play out sometimes but the love is unquestionable.*

*You know, when we were at mom's hospital bed last year – just you and I – there was a quiet, unspoken love that permeated the room. I don't remember our conversation but I do remember the closeness. It was a gift we were given to be the only ones in the room – time alone with mom beside us. She would have been so happy to witness our peaceful, loving exchange. Perhaps she could sense it even in her coma. And I was so proud of you for coming when you had once been adamant that it would never happen. Your relationship was not a good one. But there you were. You came in spite of being very ill and weak yourself. I had never seen you so vulnerable. And as though you were with a beloved friend, you took mom's hand and held it tenderly in your own. You moved your face close to hers and whispered kind words into her ear. I couldn't hear what you were saying and I didn't need to. I felt the love pouring out of you. You said later that you didn't really feel what you were saying; you just wanted her to hear the words she needed to hear. I remember being startled by this remark as you were so gentle and tender. What I realized was even if you didn't fully feel the words you were saying at the time, it was a true act of love and kindness. And you stayed with her long into the night, not leaving her side until she breathed her last breath.*

*I know that your life has been challenging over these past few years with your illness and many losses. If my prayers were answered, you would never know another unhappy or unhealthy day. I want only the best for you. I know the pain you endured as a child and teenager. The judgments that were placed on you crippled your self-esteem. You were rarely supported or encouraged to bring your gifts into the world and you have many. I hope that you will recognize them now and find ways to bring joy to every day. I hope you are inspired to do the exercises in this book in order to re-write your own life by reflecting on the courage it has taken you to move through the challenges this life has presented you with. And then to acknowledge how far you've come. And don't forget to write the last chapter – the highest vision you have for yourself and I shall hold the vision with you in my heart.*

*Thank you for your birthday wishes last week. I was in a deep sleep. It was midnight. I answered my phone and heard the words, "Happy Birthday. I wanted to be the first one to say it." I don't know if you could hear the gratitude I felt inside. Probably not as I was groggy and disoriented. But I felt it and I still do. It is one more affirmation of the love you have for me. It fills a place inside me that sat empty for so many years.*

*I love you, Howard. And I give you back your words, the ones you have left on your answering machine for decades: "Have a lovely day and may your God go with you."*

*Love and only love,*
*June xoxo*

## From Grief and Sorrow to Relief and Liberation

by June Swadron

*May 17, 2007*
*My beautiful sister Barbara, how can it be? How is it possible! You should be here with us. You're not supposed to be dead. I can't even say the word and not shudder. I am staring at your photograph – the one from Bradley's wedding reception. He's standing beside you. You look so beautiful. You were always so beautiful. For years your beauty belied your inner-most truth. In recent years your pain caught up with you and settled on your face and body. I'll never forget how shocked I was when I saw you at Patricia's wedding. You came late. A family emergency. When I saw you walk into the room I wanted to weep. You were so haggard, exhausted. Your eyes were black and filled with unshed tears.*

*I wanted to take you home, comfort you, massage your body, say the right words and let you cry. I never heard you cry. Did anyone? Did you ever?*

*I read your emails the other day. Each one began the same way – with an apology for not answering my phone calls but that you loved me dearly – work* was exhausting and taking up all your time. The business was failing, the snow had slowed down the traffic, two of the drivers didn't show up, the accidents on the road brought everything to a halt, parcels were late. Your best clients quit and went elsewhere. Your best letters, the happiest, were when you described the joyful visits you had with Rachel and your grandchildren or when Bobby came by with Zion or the times David just dropped in unexpectedly. I was under the impression you saw your family fairly often but Rachel just told me the opposite. She was angry with you about it. She said you were married to your work. We all knew it to be true. It was your escape from the pain you lived with at home.

But in spite of all that, along with your full schedule, you managed to care and do for others. Especially Mom – constantly putting up with her impossible demands – like sending a driver to pick up and deliver cigarettes for her on your busiest days. You'd send her clothes and money and purses and food. But actually, she didn't want all that really – she wanted you. We all wanted you – not flowers to make up for the absences – but you. I received my fair share of flowers over the years. In all the years I lived in Toronto, I can't remember you ever coming over for tea and a conversation. At some point you closed yourself off from the rest of the world.

It wasn't always that way. You had friends and backyard pool parties – always elaborate and elegant with gourmet food that you'd prepare yourself – like the 40th birthday party you gave me. It was almost embarrassing because it was more like a wedding. You rented tables and chairs and placed them on the outside deck by the pool with rose coloured tablecloths and spring flower centerpieces on every table. You had napkins at each place setting embossed with "June's 40th". You even had the evening video taped. All of this because I casually mentioned my guest list was getting a bit too big for my 2-bedroom apartment and I decided to have the party in the park across the street. I loved the idea but you wouldn't hear of it. You insisted on giving me a party. But never in a million years would I have expected such...I can't even think of the word. It was overwhelming. And then it all got ruined. From a balmy but beautiful summer's night, the sky filled up with racing dark clouds, the thunder and lightening moved in and the rains came pelting down. All the work you put into my party was drenched with rain. Without skipping a beat and with infinite grace you simply moved the party inside and created a beautiful ambiance there.

You know Barb, I was thinking, I never saw you in blue jeans or sweat pants or even flat shoes. Designer clothes, purses and shoes were your style – always looking elegant even in your most distressing times. We are so different. With my hippy ways, I never dressed like you nor lived like you and yet we loved each other fiercely.

Among the so many amazing things you did for me, I shall never forget you coming to Vancouver to see my play. You planned it with Lucas and totally surprised me. I was speechless. You were terrified of planes and bridges but you came anyway. You can't escape bridges if you're in Vancouver, but there you were. You did that for me. You said you wouldn't miss it for the world. And you came with Rachel, my beloved niece, who was still nursing Jakie, only a few months old. I'll never forget that time. I felt so loved.

I wish life had been kinder to you. Sometimes it was. I remember your exquisite dried flower arrangements that gave you such joy and you were so proud of. They were a genuine work of art. Your home was a work of art – a masterpiece, filled with elegant furniture, classical and modern paintings and artifacts. Everything was stunning yet you managed to make it cozy and welcoming as well. No outsider would ever know how your heart ached inside this camouflage of comfort.

I wish you hadn't lacked the confidence to do what came so naturally to you. I could have easily envisioned you as a designer for the rich and famous. But instead you worked yourself to the bone running a courier company. I remember laughing when I called you one day and you said you were in the middle of writing up an R & R programme for your drivers. From my frame of reference, being a therapist, I thought, "How wonderful. Barbara is offering a rest and relaxation plan for her stressed employees." When I stated that out loud, you said, "No, silly – Rules and Regulations!"

And then one day, not that long ago, your business failed and the bank repossessed your home. You were left to move into a rented condominium where there wasn't even enough room to put a table and chairs. You ate off your lap in the living room. I'll never forget how you made your voice sound cheerful as you talked about the living room floor picnics on blankets with your grandchildren and how much fun you all had. But I knew losing your house was an unspeakable loss and sense of shame for you.

I wish I could have cradled you just enough so that you would feel safe. And I'd take you on a road trip across Canada and bring you here to the coast and we'd tell each other stories all the way and sing into the wind and laugh and dream. Dream Barbara. But we'll never get to live that dream.

You were diagnosed with cancer. Six weeks later you died and I didn't arrive in time to say goodbye.

Instead you came to me in the wee hours of the night and I woke with a start. I looked up and there you were at the foot of my bed. You were bathed in an aura of shimmering white light. And you were smiling. A full and glowing, radiant smile! I had never seen you that happy. I've never encountered anyone like that before. You had brilliant light all around you that cascaded throughout the room. Your eyes were dancing and the outpouring of love from you to me is beyond words.

*You didn't stay long, but long enough for me to experience something I had never experienced before – a flooding of pure unconditional love, grace and joy. I had always believed that we are pure spirit but if I needed proof to take me from believing to knowing, you gave it to me that miraculous night. And I know that you came to me because I could not yet get to you and you were about to die. And you came to reassure me that you are well. Beyond well. Blissful. Ecstatic. And I choose to see you that way now forever.*

*I have a gazillion birthday cards from you. I've kept them all, you know. And all the pictures we took at the party you gave me before I moved to Vancouver nine years ago. I remember our embrace in front of your house and then holding hands on my way to the car. You told me I was the bravest person you've ever known.*

*I treasure the little pillow you gave me before I went to Korea. Inscribed are the words: "Giggles, secrets, sometimes tears, sisters and friends throughout the years." I miss you Barbara. I want to pick up the phone and say hello and hear the joy in your voice when you know it's me. You can even put me on hold as you did a million times because the other lines were ringing. I promise to not even get annoyed this time. Yes, sisters and friends throughout the years. Death has not separated us. Our love keeps us connected now and beyond forever. God bless you.*

# *Let's Write*

As you settle at your writing table, stilling yourself by focusing on your breath, begin to bring to mind your family of origin – specifically your brothers and sisters. If you were an only child, you will have an opportunity to write from the experience of not having siblings.

If you have one or more brothers and sisters, where do you fit into your family – oldest, youngest, somewhere in the middle? How many siblings do you have? Picture them on the screen of your mind one at a time. With each sibling, see them and feel them. What would you like to say about them?

Are you close to your siblings? Are you close to some and not others? Describe what that's like for you. Has your relationship with them changed over the years? Was there a time you were closer or further apart? What caused the change?

Do you have a favourite sister or brother? What makes them special? How often do you get together? What do you do together? How do you feel when you meet? Do you get together generally as a family group or one-on-one? Which feels better for you? How would you describe that experience? Is it a celebration to be together or does it cause you anxiety, worry or fear?

Are you holding any old hurts or resentments toward any of your sisters or brothers or stepsisters or stepbrothers? What are you holding on to? Are you ready to let it go and move forward? If the answer is yes, now is the time to speak freely to them. The following is a healing exercise I encourage you to participate in.

Imagine telling each one individually what you've held back until now but what you want them to know. Speak from your highest truth – taking self-responsibility and doing your best to let go of anger, resentment and fear. Simply state the circumstances as you remember them. Tell them everything you have needed to say until now. Release it all. Release and let it go.

Now what would you like from them? What would you like them to say to you? In this exercise, imagine them saying it the way you would like to hear it. Imagine they have been listening intently to you with an open heart. They too have been hurt and have wanted to bridge the gap between you. They have heard you. You feel listened to. Begin to have a loving dialogue with each other. Do this with each sibling.

If you're ready, you can call your sisters or brothers to you one at a time and tell them you love them, forgive them, release them and let them go. Do this for each sister or brother that you are still carrying negative energy toward. And breathe. Now forgive yourself for holding on to angry energy and for perceiving yourself as bad or wrong.

Breathe in the love of your siblings. In your mind's eye, you may want to give them a hug. If it feels safe for you – as you have been lovingly and compassionately heard – see yourself in a healing embrace. Breathe this in.

Write the stories of your brothers and sisters and the gifts and lessons they have brought you.

If you are an only child, what was that like for you growing up? Did you feel left out and alone with no one to play with? Perhaps you were happy that you had your parents and your toys all for yourself.

How have you felt as an adult being an only child? Has there been a lot of responsibility? Are you caring for aging parents by yourself? Perhaps you married someone with siblings. What has this experience been for you, now having in-laws?

As an only child, write into what your life was like both as a child and currently as an adult. Write from the place of loneliness or contentment and everything in between. What have been the gifts for you being an only child?

# Chapter 12

## ABOUT CHILDREN

## Birthing Our Children, Birthing Ourselves

by Shoshana Litman

*When I was eight years old, I watched a film called "Man and His World" at EXPO '67 in Montreal. The film featured the live birth of a baby, a messy process which looked so painful for both mother and child I swore I would never do it myself. Not me. No thanks.*

*Nine years later I became even more convinced that it would be unwise and downright irresponsible to bring another being into this brutal, chaotic world. The Cold War and my concerns for the environment cinched the deal.*

*Then twelve years later, as the world prepared for the Berlin Wall's fall, I received a degree in environmental science that provided tools for positive change and began to work in the field of ecology. My anti-birth stance began to soften with these global and personal triumphs.*

*A tandem bicycle trip with my husband, Todd, up the Columbia River and through the Rocky Mountains convinced me that love could conquer even the greatest heights and made the messy business of birth look possible again. Birthing and raising our two boys is, in fact, the best thing I've ever done, no matter how illogical or painful.*

*First there's the tiny body: slippery, warm, complete. Totally in the moment, totally at one with all that is. We are divine to each other. Mother holding, child being held: moments of utter, indescribable peace.*

*Our first son, Graham, emerged with a wizened face, fists bared to the world, screaming. His happiest moments arrived later, when he held a book or crayon in his hand or better yet, when he could run free, exploring our wild garden under his own steam.*

*Our second son, Raviv, emerged smiling. He didn't cry or even request milk. For ten hours he basked in the joyful air until his need for nourishment kicked in and I could provide. Together we stepped into a new reality as integral parts of our growing family.*

*In between these two live births, there was a molar pregnancy: a strange occurrence where a placenta formed without a fetus. After three months, the nurse midwife noticed that there was no heartbeat.*

*Until then the pregnancy had progressed much like the one before, except I bled more. I couldn't pick up Graham when he cried. It was as if my insides had been let loose. So much blood. So much sickness.*

*Graham and Todd came to see me in the hospital before the surgical procedure, known as a dilation and curettage or D & C, removed the errant tissue.*

*I'd been throwing up most of the time but tried to smile for the sake of our two-year-old son who wondered why I wasn't coming home with him and his Dad that night.*

*The surgeon and anesthetist held my hands as I went under.*

*Later, the pathologist explained in more detail what he had found. He wasn't sure what caused the malfunction, but it occurred more often than most people realized.*

*I would need to be monitored for cancer. More blood tests. No more pregnancies for a while. My body still prepared itself for birth, though. Until the full nine months ended I felt incredible loss and confusion.*

*One day we travelled to Whistler Mountain where my sister and brother-in-law had a home. I walked alone through the snow and washed my hands in an ice-cold river, letting the urge to birth flow out of me so I could be more fully present again. I wrote poetry about my mother's kitchen swept clean, based on a post surgical dream.*

*In the midst of all this, one of the blood tests came back with a warning. My birth hormones were rising again. It was either cancer or pregnancy and I'd been told not to proceed with another birth yet.*

*I did the math, though, and felt sure it wasn't cancer or another molar pregnancy. It was a real, live baby. And it was. What a gift, our second son.*

*Raviv is a deeply thoughtful, caring person who writes and thinks with precision and humour. Both he and his brother, Graham, have taught me to embrace life's responsibilities with joy.*

*I had run all my life from difficulties before arriving at the Evergreen State College in Olympia, Washington to pursue a degree and marry my sweet, supportive husband.*

*Once our children arrived, I stood many times hanging out clothes in the verdant garden of our turquoise house realizing that our love had birthed two strong, brilliant souls.*

*Now, as Graham explores political science at McGill University in Montreal and Raviv explores Italy on a student exchange program dedicated to world peace, I am birthing myself anew along with them and am just as slippery about it.*

*Graham's studies have convinced him that if we want sustainable peace in the world it is essential that we educate women of all classes and races to realize their full potential and to raise wise, peaceful children if they choose to do so.*

*I continue to benefit from a marvelous education in school and out, thanks in large part to our creative sons who are, along with me, unfolding, holding and being held, becoming something new the world hasn't experienced yet.*

*God willing, there will be no rivers of blood as we birth ourselves anew. I hope for each of us that there will continue to be more moments of ecstasy, joy and a simple, scintillating sound; a brilliant, divine, high note here, within.*

# Child-Free

by Ella Brown

*Maybe if they arrived fully toilet trained and able to speak (with a full set of teeth), I'd have considered bearing a child. I get along best with kids between the ages of four and nine and have even been known to play 'Auntie' from time to time. Babies, however, scare me.*

*WAAAAH!*

*What do you want, baby, shall I warm your bottle?*

*WAAAAH!*

*Not hungry. Okay, let's check your diaper . . .*

*WAAAAH!*

*Pacifier? Teething Ring?*

*WAAAAH!*

*Hmm . . . rock-a-bye baby on the treetop*

*WAAAAH! (doesn't like my singing)*

*WAAAAH! (That last one is me!)*

*And tots – so cute! But wherever you don't want them to go, there they are! Ever notice how they look back at you while trying to stick the cat's tail into a socket? Ever tried to have a decent adult conversation with these screeching whirling dervishes underfoot? Worst of all: "Sleep? What's sleep?" a friend, the mother of two toddlers cried. "They never want to go to bed when they're supposed to and their idea of sleeping in is, like, 5 a.m.!"*

*Pardon me, if I sound negative, but it's not just me. Have you seen the Oprah show with all those young moms wailing, "Why didn't they tell us it was so hard?" Hey, I could have told them! When I was nine, the stork dropped off my baby sister; then a few years later, my brother. I got to see it all – live, three dimensional, with full sound effects. (Talk about surround sound!). Thanks but no thanks!*

*And what about 'the terrible teens'? Your loving children won't even want to be seen walking down the street with you. What parents? Hell, no! I sprang forth from nowhere with fuchsia hair, with the tattoos, piercings and rings through my nose!*

*And that's not the worst of it.*

*All my life people kept saying, "Oh, you'll change your mind." Now I'm 60 years old and they're still saying it! What I don't understand is why people seem to feel threatened by my decision to remain child-free. One Polish woman yelled at me on the bus, "YOU NO GOT KIDS BECAUSE YOU LAZY!" Others ask who will look after me when I'm old. A few look at me pityingly and tell me I'm missing out on one of life's most worthwhile experiences.*

*The 'lazy' I can certainly relate to. I love my peace and quiet, the lovely afternoon naps with my two cats. I enjoy being totally free to engage in whatever "meaningful experiences" I choose. It is up to me and no one else to provide the 'meaning' in my life. As for "old age", are kids born with a warranty promising to return the favour of changing diapers when parents reach their dotage? THIS is a reason to have children? I think not!*

*So now you know why I have this magnet sitting on my fridge door: IF I WANT TO HEAR THE PITTER PATTER OF LITTLE FEET, I'LL PUT SHOES ON MY CAT!*

# *Let's Write*

Are you a parent? How old are your children? How do you feel being a mom or a dad? Is it a fairly even mix between joyful experiences and challenges or do you lean to one side more than the other? If you don't have children, how does that feel?

Get in touch with your breath as you move back to the time when your children were born. Bring in the details. Some of the following memory prompts are focused on having one child. If there are more than one, you can come back and apply the prompts for each of your children.

What was the date your first child was born? How old were you? Was it a home birth or did it take place in hospital? If you were giving birth, was your partner with you? Perhaps you were facing the birth of your baby alone. How did you manage? Who were the supports in your life during this time?

Continue to remember the circumstances surrounding this birth. Was it planned? Were you happy and excited? Were you scared? Who was the first person you told that you were expecting a child? What was his or her response? Did you feel supported?

In what ways did having a baby change your day to day life? Did you go on maternity or paternity leave from work? Did you stay at home once your child was born? For how long? As a dad, how involved were you during the early years of your child's life? How did having a child or children affect you financially?

Were you happy to be a parent? What were some of the biggest changes that took place as a result of being a parent? How did it affect your relationship with your partner?

What is the gender of your children? What are their names? How did you choose them? Were your children born healthy or were there health challenges? If so, what were they and how did you deal with them?

Perhaps you adopted a child or children. Describe that experience. What was the adoption process like? Did you travel to another country to find your child?

Consider the birth of each child. Were there any that you gave up for adoption? What were the circumstances surrounding this experience? How did you feel? What did you do? Who were the supports in your life? How do you feel about that today? Have you since reconnected with this child? If so, describe how that came about and what it is like for you now. If not, are you hoping to reconnect or is this part of your past that feels complete?

Are you or were you a foster parent? Describe how that experience has affected your life.

Now allow all the sacred memories of the times you have spent with your children to surface. Birthdays, summer holidays, vacations, graduations, sporting events, picnics, whatever. Bring these memories into the forefront of your mind.

Now, remember the trying, challenging times – even heartbreaking times such as if you were separated from your children through divorce. Think of the times of stress, worry, frustration and pain. Perhaps there were times you would have liked to walk away from it all if you could have.

Breathe. Think about the quality of the relationships you have with your children today. What are their ages? Are there some children you are closer to than others?

What are the most significant ways that your life has changed as a result of having children? Was there ever a time that you felt regretful or even resentful because you were unable to live out some of your own personal dreams or ambitions? Instead you were too busy raising and educating your kids and there wasn't time or money to pursue something that you deeply desired. Write into the truth of this.

Now consider the things you have learned from being a parent. What are some of the most precious gifts they have given you whether they were born from hardship or joy? Is there anything that you would do differently if you could? This is simply for awareness and growth and not to beat yourself up in any way.

Perhaps you didn't have children. Perhaps you wanted them but it never worked out that way. How has that affected your life? Perhaps it was a conscious choice not to have them. Are you happy with your decision or did you ever regret it? Was your choice respected or was there family pressure? How did you handle that? Perhaps there are other significant children in your life – nieces, nephews, friends' children. What are their names? How have they impacted your life?

Now, take an overview of your life and the spirits who came in as your children or someone else's children for you to love.

Gather your memories now, move to your writing table and begin to cluster or write your personal story on children.

# *Chapter 13*

## ON FORGIVENESS

## The Key

by Judy McIlmoyl

*I have contemplated the theme of forgiveness all week. While sitting at the keyboard now, I am listening to one of my favourite music discs, "The Healing Garden". That visualization is one that I have thought of several times during the past few days and it is how I have decided to impart the balm of forgiveness to myself and others.*

*I picture a garden, now still and quiet after a tumultuous storm and heavy rains. Puddles lie everywhere, allowing for a different perspective on the familiar. All is dripping with droplets, remnants from the clouds just passed. Never has the green of the mosses and ferns looked so verdant, dipped as it were in liquid greenness. The flowers of the garden are bent over, heavy with moisture, bowing their heads as if in silent prayer. A vigil of hopefulness that all will be well, complete and whole.*

*Stepping through the old wooden gate, I brush past an ancient wisteria, its pendulous flowers releasing a heavenly scent as if an angel has just flown by. I pause at the simple copper water basin just inside the gate, to wash the soil of the outer world from my hands as I enter the realm of the garden. Delighting at the sound of the water falling from the ladle I let it run gently through my fingers. The sound of birdsong returned reaches my ears. They, too, know the storm is gone and are rejoicing in kind.*

*I follow a winding pathway scented with cedar to a well-worn wooden bench waiting under a canopy of yellow-green leaves. All about are trees in varying stages of their lives, each with a distinct personality. In many ways, trees are very much like people. Each with its own way of interacting with the world. Each with its own beauty. Each marked by storms weathered. Scars endured.*

*Sitting on the bench, I close my eyes, allowing all the sounds of this sanctuary to fill me. Joining the sparrows and finches is the delicate, sweet tinkling of wind chimes hung from an overhanging bough. Further along the path glass and bamboo chimes partake in the chorus orchestrated by what is now the softest of breezes.*

*It is written that time stands still in a garden. While I understand the sentiments of the writer of those words, I think it is more that we have a different awareness of time when we are in a garden. At least I know I do. It is a time kept with the falling of the leaves, the changing of the seasons, the passing of the old to the new. I can become achingly aware of the transience of life, and just how precious it is, when I am alone with nature. For hers is a world lived eternally in the present.*

*And I remember those I have loved who are no longer with me. I think of my mother, with whom I was very close. She is one of the people I believe I have forgiven, but wish to do so now in a more meaningful way. I think of our relationship as my eyes view a small evergreen growing under the reaching arms of a much older fir. Unbeknownst to the older tree, whose progeny the little evergreen is, the reach and density of the parent's branches keep the nurturing sun and rain from reaching the seedling. That is why it reminds me of the forgiveness I need for my mother. I never knew, until the last year, that I had been emotionally abused. I know my mother loved me very much. But what I never really understood was that she had halted my growth in meaningful ways. By teaching me to suppress my fears, I did not learn how to confront them. By curtailing my self-expression throughout my teenaged years, she affected my growth emotionally, sexually and spiritually. And I remember how she would withhold her love if I did something she did not like...and how I would do anything for her not to be upset with me. I do not think she meant to do this. At least not all of it. I know she told me I was smart and attractive and special to her and my dad. But, because I had never been allowed to express my fears, my unique scars, my growing pains, I could not truly accept her words. With this awareness I momentarily leave the garden, returning with a few gardening tools. Reaching for a large branch overhanging the little fir, I say a prayer of thankfulness for my mother's love as I carefully remove the old limb. Looking down I see a new ray of sunlight gracing the little tree and I sense its wonderment and joy.*

*Returning to the bench, I notice that the storm has knocked over a tender, newly rooted sumac. The winds must have knocked over the bamboo stake I* had used to help it along in the world. This makes me sad, so sad. Because it reminds me of my father. When I was little, my dad and I had spent a lot of wonderful times together exploring the world. Even though, emotionally, I was strongly bound to my mother, it was "Daddy" that I called for in the night. Then the day came when an event in our family made me see my father in a very different way. I saw him not being there for my mother. That is when I became her confidante, her protector. Things my father should have been for her. I was there for her for many, many years until my mom passed away. All that long time I stayed emotionally distant from my father. Finally, just before his own death, I forgave him – my daddy – and I have always hoped that he knew that. I send a prayer aloft to the heavens here, in this moment, straight to his soul, as I lovingly straighten the collapsed sumac. I know how much I missed my dad those lost years, even though I was hurt by his actions. Perhaps, like the bamboo stake whose absence hurt the young sumac, it wasn't all his fault that he wasn't there for my mom. And me. Maybe the winds were just too strong for him. Sensing that all is whole again in the world of the sumac, I move along the path toward a freshly turned patch of earth.

This small section has been empty for a while now. I don't know why, really, but I sense a hesitation, a soul-deep aching beyond words when I view this open soil. In the past I have instinctively known what I have wanted to plant, to sow and reap in my little garden. But not now. Thinking of my parents, of all the joys and the hurts we shared and the scars that run deep within me still, I kneel on the moistness of the ground and weep. My tears fall freely as the rains had earlier that day. When my sobbing ceases, I realize that I am kneeling at the end of the path that meanders through my garden. Then, with a knowing beyond human doubt, I understand what I have been meant to place here, in this secluded corner. On the pathway of forgiveness I have walked this day...at its end, I will place a piece of myrtle wood brought home from Cannon Beach, my mother's favourite place on earth, in remembrance of her. In my dad's memory, there will be a collection of rocks from Shoal Bay, where he and I spent so many carefree hours beachcombing in my childhood years. And for me...as a reminder always to forgive myself for being so afraid, for caring so much what other people thought that I lost myself in the process, for negating my spirit as though it did not matter, I will place an old key from the truest friend I have ever had, my brother...because no heart that knows forgiveness is ever lost.

# Yellow Bird

excerpt from *Born Into a Late November Sky*
by Nathalie Vaschon

*The angry sky is split in two and*
*I tiptoe through the raindrops*
*As you taught me on*
*Annual summer visits*
*Bringing a suitcase full of warm bagels*
*You would ask for company*
*On that winding path to purchase your paper*
*And, well, I came along for the candy*
*On this muggy July, the sky split in two*
*You taught me how to*
*Tip toe through those raindrops*
*Your belly stretched tight*
*A firm full Buddha*
*Not even the biggest buckle could*
*Keep that full moon covered*
*And you kept hoisting up those pants*
*An orchestra of dimes in your pockets*
*Activated when you danced*
*And tip toed through those raindrops singing*
*Yellow bird*
*Up high in the banana tree*
*Yellow bird, you sit all alone like me*

*Now I'm alone and the angry sky outside is split in two*
*And I think of you*
*By my side as we slide, back and forth*
*Metal rocking on concrete, back and forth*
*As the July night sky*
*Clings to our bodies*
*There's no use tip toeing our way through these drops you'd say*

*So we'd stay*
*And rock our worries into the ground*
*Gazing through sheets of rain*
*Eyes glued to the blackness, hearts pounding*
*Waiting for that blinding vein to signal the counting*
*One alligator, two alligator*
*Thunder pounds and shakes the sky*
*And jolts me from my rocking rhythm*
*And we know the storm is moving closer*
*The next one's sure to split that angry sky in two*
*"Sure to be a biggie!" you'd say*
*So we'd stay...*

*But I know you also had an angry streak that could split that sky in two*
*I saw you forcing and plowing your way through those raindrops*
*And as summers passed*
*Those suitcases filled with warm bagels*
*Were also filled with knives that cut*
*It's been five years since the doctors said, "be rid of that full moon*
*A simple in and out procedure if you lose that Buddha belly"*
*But with those meager meals*
*Did you also lose your spirit?*

*Five years and I've been only once to your grave*
*But today, I sit alone as the angry sky is split in two*
*And I think of you, yellow bird*
*Up high in that banana tree*
*And I wonder, yellow bird*
*Do you sit all alone like me?*

After my grandfather's death, I realized that I was holding onto anger toward him because of his sometimes angry/stormy personality and because of the way he could treat my grandmother. Writing this piece helped me to come to terms with both the light and the dark side of my grandfather, to balance both and find peace for myself.

# Perpetually Pissed and Beyond

by Michele Hibbins

*It is surprisingly easy for me to write this assignment on forgiveness; I believe the time is right, as I have been aware of needing to forgive Mom for a long time. It started about four years ago when I caught a part of a lecture that Dr. Christiane Northrup was giving on women's health. She spoke of her book Mother Daughter Wisdom and the importance of forgiving our mothers in order to create healing; on a physical level, as well as emotional. What? I thought. I had a wave of energy rush through me as many conflicting emotions and reactions were provoked. A part of me observed the strength of the response I was experiencing and realized there was something powerful for me to learn. So I started thinking about it a bit more calmly and decided to try and practice saying the words. I could barely even think them, much less get a sound out that resembled the idea. "I….." "I for….." "I fffff……..". Hmmm. Clearly this needed some time and attention.*

*So I ran out and got the book, and there it sat…for months. Back into denial and familiar patterns of thinking. Perhaps I was reluctant as this realization came hot on the heels of Mom's visit to BC before our wedding to ostensibly help with ideas and planning. In typical fashion, there were moments that degraded into hysterics on her part, and while I am proud of the boundaries and healthy way I dealt with her in the moment, I was still pissed. I suppose having a part of me that is "Perpetually Pissed" at Mom has become a way of thinking of her, a framework if you will, even though I have done tons of work (read, therapy, thinking, journaling, art, processing with friends, changing ways, growing, making realizations) to bring peace to this relationship. It is still a relatively new concept to not be trying to change her, to not NEED her to change, but to change myself and my perceptions to bring on the healing. So, here is the next layer of that old onion; Forgiveness.*

*I never did read the book in its entirety; partly because I believe I got the lesson from the beginning, and I knew it as Truth: I needed to forgive Mom. I had been talking to a friend about whether it is necessary to tell a person that you are forgiving them; I had imagined many scenarios, from writing her a letter to having a lunch, to springing it on her spontaneously and as though it* were no big deal. But perhaps this wasn't important at all, and my friend and I talked about this; do we really need to tell the people we are forgiving that we are forgiving them? Truly, the forgiveness at this point was about me, not her. And why risk another disappointment, depending on how she handled the revelation? That shouldn't affect the act of forgiving her, but it sure could color the situation, and add insult to the injuries I'd rather stop re-living.

I did manage to broach the subject with Mom last year during a visit to Michigan; we were talking about a client of hers who had died (or was dying, I can't remember) and the importance of making peace before you go. I asked Mom what she would need to do, and she said, "Nothing, Uncle Paul and I have made up and that has been the most important thing for me". She and Uncle Paul had essentially not spoken for 15 years, so his return to the family was a big deal. I admit being mildly hurt that there was no mention of needing to acknowledge past hurts to me or my stepfather, but was used to this myopicness by now. Without her prompting, I mumbled into my shoelaces that I think I would need to forgive her for the rough times we had had. I was very aware that my heart was racing, I couldn't look her in the eye, and that I was forcing myself to say something I wasn't quite ready for...almost like a practice run. Either she didn't listen (regardless of whether she heard it or not), or chose to ignore it, another fine skill of hers. I was relieved, feeling I had opened a can of worms I was not ready to set free in the garden yet, and mildly reproachful with myself for bringing it up in the first place. What I have learned from that is that not all opportunities need be jumped on; timing can be just as important.

So there is where my "background" thinking has been: you know when you sit with something unconsciously (or perhaps procrastinating-ly?) and when the right time to address it again presents, you go deeper? Well, here we are. June announces our next writing assignment is on forgiveness, and I groan. But I realize in hindsight I groan out of habit; that upon more reflection, I am actually perfectly ready to confidently say these words: I FORGIVE YOU. Wow, that was easy. Really? Try again. I FORGIVE YOU. Hmmm, a strangely neutral feeling is upon me. But I go with it; the ease with which I can articulate this phrase compared to my absolute lack of ability to utter it when I first realized the need is astounding, and the surest sign of some deep healing.

Still amazed, I spent the rest of the afternoon writing these words over and over: I forgive you. I forgive you. I forgive you...filling 3 pages until my hand was tired. It was strangely un-cathartic; a statement made, with no strong feelings around it one way or another. However, I am not interested in analyzing this as some sort of indicator of not being fully resolved; what I have learned is that no matter what the pain, my perspective and relationship to it is always changing; while there are major milestones along the way that bring peace, there will be more learning along the way. I trust that now; perhaps in a little *while there will be another level of awareness to this statement: I forgive you. But for now, I'll take it as truth.*

## Screaming through the Silence

by June Swadron

*I have been working on forgiving this situation for a very long time. It has come in stages. I have done work on it, but every now and again the anger surfaces. So the time is now. I am ready to finally release the pain of the past – to let go of my anger, resentment, sense of loss and grief. Perhaps by telling the story from a more loving stance, I can fully live my word – not just put a bunch of pretty words on the page.*

A few years ago I was making my plans to leave Vancouver and join my partner in Korea. It was a big move and my life was in disarray and chaos. I was missing Lucas immensely. The year passed slowly but I closed in on the final details for my departure a month or two hence. I worked as a mental health worker at a men's shelter in a dangerous part of Vancouver – an area highly populated with people who were drug addicted and homeless. Crime was often a daily occurrence. Although I loved my work and the people I cared for, there was a lot of stress attached to it. Added to this I was taking a fast-track course in teaching English as a Second Language at the local community college. The course was intense with many tests and written papers. There was also a practicum at an ESL school for which I had to prepare well-thought-out lessons. On top of all of this I facilitated writing groups and saw private clients. My life was stretched to the limit. I looked forward to being with Lucas and getting off the North American treadmill.

The biggest dilemma in all of this was trying to find someone to foster care my beloved cats, Caesar and Buddy, while I was away for the year. These were my friends whom I had brought with me from Toronto four years earlier and I loved them beyond measure. Whoever it was would have to adore cats and give them consistent tender, loving care. They were gentle cats and used to a lot of love.

After putting out the word for several weeks, finally, my friend Susan came forth. Her six-year-old son, Brandon used to have sleepovers at our house and loved my cats. Susan said she discussed it with her husband, Russ as well *as Brandon and everyone agreed it would be a good idea. I was so relieved. Leaving my beloved animals behind was the hardest part of my whole departure. I considered taking them with me but was afraid to because of what I had learned about how they treat some dogs and cats in Korea. What if they were to run out of the house? Would I see them again? What would happen to them? Taking them with me was out of the question. At the same time that Susan offered to take Caesar and Buddy, she also offered her basement as a place we could leave our household belongings for the year. She said there was a large room down there that wasn't being used and there was no point in paying for storage costs when it wasn't necessary.*

*I spoke to Lucas about it and he was reluctant about them keeping his things – especially the art work. These were people he didn't know. I met them after his departure for Korea. I convinced him it was okay. And why wouldn't I have? I was convincing myself at the same time. I was almost frantic with my daily schedule and all that was going on. I asked Susan if it was okay if I moved in with her for the last six weeks of my time in Vancouver so that I could transition with my cats. That way I wasn't just dropping them off and running away. This would give them a chance to get comfortable in their new home with me in it. That was agreeable to her and her family and this is when I truly began to realize things weren't as good as they appeared.*

*Susan and Russ were having marital problems. I didn't know him very well but the tension in the house was sky high.*

*They lived by a ravine and most mornings before heading off to work or school, Susan and I would take long walks. We spoke at length about her unhappiness and confusion. I was as compassionate as I could be and I was also troubled for my own sake. One day I said to her very clearly, "Susan, you must promise me something. If things don't work out in your marriage and you and Russ separate and leave this house, you must swear that you will look after my cats until I return." I also added, "Please put our things in a storage locker. I will send you the money immediately." She agreed without question. We left it at that.*

*I wasn't home very much but when I was, it was rarely pleasant. I stayed in my room downstairs with my cats and soaked up the love that was so readily available from them. I pushed down the voices that were practically screaming at me from my gut to not leave them there. I'd drown them out by rationalizing that it was because of my crazy busyness that I was worrying and there was nothing to worry about. After all, I had Susan's word and she was my very close friend.*

*Well, fast forward to about four months later. I received an email from Susan while I was in Korea, telling me her marriage was over and she had to leave the house in a hurry because of violence. She grabbed her son and ran to her sister's home. She said she left everything including my cats and Lucas's and my belongings with Russ. And she couldn't go back there. I was frantic. Within a short time I also learned that Caesar and Buddy were put in a cat shelter and all of our things tossed into a locker. But the emails from Susan stopped. And I didn't have a phone number. I didn't know what to expect when I came back. And finally, I did come back. And this is what I found: I found Buddy had died from questionable causes and Caesar had such bad asthma that every time he wheezed and coughed, I didn't know if he would live.*

*I also learned that Russ became a cocaine addict and almost everything we owned was sold, broken or stolen. There was hardly anything in that locker at all – nothing but odds and sods. We were art collectors and all the paintings were gone. Even dishes, pots and pans were gone, as were the bed, sofa, lamps and treasures that fill up a household. The stereo and fax machine were broken. The racing bike was stripped naked. There was nothing. My beloved Buddy was dead and Caesar very, very ill. Susan didn't want to speak to me. She said, "Too much drama" and her husband only threw me insults and curses.*

*My illness kicked in again. It took me a long time to recover. But I have now. Years have passed and it's time that I let go of this story. And so I shall.*

*I forgive you Susan for how I perceived you treated me when I trusted you. I forgive you for the sense of betrayal and abandonment I perceived. I imagine you must have been very afraid, needing to take safe shelter and not knowing how to deal with the pain of a broken marriage, the chaos of your world collapsing and on top of that, having to deal with all of my stuff as well. I can only guess how stressful that time must have been for you. But I am proud of both of us for our willingness to come back into our hearts some months later. You are remarried now and I understand you are very happy. It fills my heart with joy to know that is true.*

*And Russ, I forgive you for what I perceive was your intolerance, disrespect and rage toward me. I can only imagine that you must have been very desperate to do the things you were doing in order to survive. Life for you must have been very threatening and painful to destroy, sell and defile our possessions and worse, to abuse animals. My prayer is this: that you are living well now, that you have recovered and found your way back to health and balance. That your life reflects kindness, creativity, beauty and love. If I were to see you on the street today, I can safely say that I would want to look you in the eyes, give you a hug and let the years of hurt, resentment and unforgiveness drain off both of us.*

*I choose to take 100% responsibility for my part in all of this. I too was living in survival mode. I was on a crazy treadmill and ignored the prompts from my Higher Self. My intuition was telling me things and I wasn't listening. I was too busy. So busy that I put my precious animals in peril, disrespected my partner's wishes and didn't tell my full truth to Susan. I didn't want to hurt her feelings after she agreed to take care of everything. I didn't want to bail out and give her reason to think I doubted her word. Not listening to my inner voice brought about chaos and destruction, unnecessary pain and anguish for all of us.*

*So I not only forgive Susan and Russ for my perception of their actions, but I also ask for their forgiveness for having held them as the enemy for so long, instead of with compassionate understanding. I am also ready to fully forgive myself for not acting from a deeper knowing and for judging myself as a bad person. Gratefully, Lucas and I also came to a peaceful place together after I acknowledged my part in creating this drama. And I know I have asked Buddy and Caesar's forgiveness hundreds of times throughout these years and trust that it has been given.*

*I now ask that all negativity that I have regarding this story is cleared one hundred percent and that there is no lingering residue. After all, it is only a story. Another one I am letting go of. What remains? Simply the love.*

*What have I learned? I am learning to be gentler and more compassionate with myself and others. I have also been learning that when my intuition speaks to me, I listen carefully as I recognize it as a voice of Higher Wisdom. And perhaps more than anything else, this story has given me another opportunity to learn the gift of unconditional forgiveness.*

*I love you. I'm sorry. Please forgive me. Thank you.*

Addendum

I want to add something here. I want to be clear that what I have written is my own perception as to what happened and I own it completely. The people mentioned in this story (their names have been changed) will have their own perceptions as to what happened. I wish to respect that and state that this story in no way is meant as anything other than a vehicle to work through my own process of forgiveness. I have struggled as to whether to include this story in the book at all because when you forgive fully, you let go of the story so ultimately there is no story and therefore, nothing to forgive. I feel that way right now. We are all innocent. Still, this book is about writing and healing the stories of our lives. Wishing to stay true to that, it is my participation in this process that I wish to share with you, the reader. And it is my wish that this story will inspire you to also pick up your pen and offer forgiveness in your life to whomever you perceive has hurt you in any way.

The following will help you to move gently through this process.

# *Let's Write*

Before using the following memory prompts and writing this story on forgiveness, I recommend that you first read the Centering Exercise found in Book 1, Part C, and the Invocation found in Book 1, Part D. After the memory prompts you will be guided into an experience that will help you let go of any anger, guilt and resentment you may be carrying with respect to someone in your life. This process offers you an opportunity to transform your negativity as you fully let go of the past and move unencumbered into present time.

To begin, start to focus on your breath. Let your own natural rhythm of your breath help you to slow down and relax. Embrace this moment. Know that you are safe in this moment. Whatever happened before is part of the past and cannot hurt you now unless you give it power. Do not give it any. Remember this as you begin to focus on someone you need to forgive and allow the memories and image of this person to come to you now on the screen of your mind. See his or her face. Breathe. Describe this person. Who is she or he to you? A parent? A sibling? A friend? An acquaintance? An ex-lover or spouse – a present lover or spouse? Perhaps it's even you. Perhaps you are the person you most need to forgive in order to let go and carry on. Get a good look at this person or imagine him or her in front of you and breathe.

Now bring forth onto the screen the memories about this person that have upset you. You do not embody this memory. Remember you are watching it from a safe distance. Allow yourself to simply be an objective observer without emotional attachment to what you are about to witness. Breathe. You and that person are now on the screen of your mind. Where are you? What are you doing? What is happening? How old are you? Do you recall what year it is? Are there words being spoken? A conversation? An argument? What is the other person doing? Are there other people involved? Watch this movie from a safe distance until you are aware of all the details – the sights, sounds, smells – remember it as though it were occurring now. Continue to breathe. Are you aware of anything different as you look at it today from this perspective? Is there anything new that you see? Take your time. Be open to the possibility of a different perspective.

What did you do when whatever happened was over? Have you been in touch with this person? Did you ever express your anger, frustration, disappointment, sense of betrayal or whatever you felt toward this person? Did you ever tell that person how you feel? If not, why not? If so, what was the response?

Call up that person again in your mind's eye and look directly into his or her eyes. Tell him or her what you've been wanting to say for perhaps a long, long time. Say it all. Hold nothing back. In this visualization, I want you to also imagine this person listening to you quietly – not interrupting, not defending, explaining or arguing but listening to you with understanding and compassion. Imagine this person hearing you perhaps for the first time. Continue to tell him or her what has hurt you for so long and why it's taken you so long to forgive. Let this person know now that you are ready to forgive him or her. Know inside that you are doing this for your own freedom and release. So that you can go on. You are about to call your power back – so much of your energy, your personal power, has been invested in this person, this situation – and you are, through the act of forgiveness, about to finally let go.

Move now into your heart. Focus on the truth that love is Divine Power and is the only true power that makes any difference in our human experience. While here, ask yourself whether you care enough about yourself to protect yourself from anger, resentments and other stressful situations that could be handled instead with love and compassion. This is your opportunity to let go of all negative energy toward this person as well as free up the life force energy that is available to you. Through the act of forgiveness, you let go of the pain, anger, grudges and resentments that have taken away your power – your vital life force. Your energy has been invested in your past events with this person and perhaps others too or other situations. Remembering to breathe, move into present time where you are safe. As you begin to forgive this person, forgive yourself and allow the pain of the past to dissipate and melt away, you will be calling your energy back.

See the person you need to forgive clearly in your mind and silently say, "I forgive you. I willingly release you and I release myself from the shackles of pain, anger and resentment that have bound us together in the past. I let go with love." Breathe this in.

Now let go of that image. Let the screen go blank and breathe deeply. Imagine yourself in a beautiful place in nature where your spirit feels at home. There is a path leading to a natural spring with a glorious waterfall. Go there now with all your senses awake and alive ready to experience the beauty here. The sun is shining and you are feeling wonderful. You have just undergone an essential process of forgiveness. Begin to fully take in the sights, smells and sounds as you walk toward this sparkling natural spring. You are alone. You are safe. Begin to remove your clothing as you skip toward the water, step in and notice how refreshing it feels. The temperature of the water is absolutely perfect. Begin to splash around feeling liberated, happier than you've felt in such a long time. Now swim to that luxurious waterfall just a few yards away. Find the perfect spot to stand under it and allow its pure essence to wash over you. As it does you feel yourself becoming even more alive and free. The sparkling water cleanses and purifies and you know now in your heart that you have indeed let go. You have let go years of old pain. You have taken your power back and feel totally liberated. Enjoy this moment. And now, with this new vitality in your body and spirit, swim back to the shore where a towel is waiting for you. As you dry yourself off in the sun, begin to reflect on this situation and the person you have just forgiven. From this perspective, what do you notice? What new awareness comes to mind? What have you learned about yourself? What lesson or lessons do you think this person came into your life to teach you? How do you feel right now?

As you feel inspired, begin to write into this story. Express it all, the beginning, middle and end. Be certain to include what this process has come to teach you. Be gentle with yourself. And finally, congratulate yourself for taking these courageous steps toward liberation, freedom and fresh new beginnings.

Addendum: Ho'oponopono

Recently I have become aware of another forgiveness process called Ho'oponopono. The premise is that we take 100% responsibility for everything that comes into our life. Everything. So even when a friend tells you that he is upset about something, it is now part of your life and the part of him that is in you is ready to be healed. Even when you read something terrible in the newspaper and it triggers you and you get angry, frightened, frustrated or sad, herein lies another opportunity for self-love and healing. The practice is very simple. You say to the Universe, "*I love you. Please forgive me. I'm sorry. Thank you.*" That simple process can foster amazing results in every area of your life. It can bring about a deep sense of peace within you.

Dr. Ihaleakala Hew Len, a Hawaiian psychologist healed an entire hospital of criminally insane people using this prayer. He never even saw the patients as a therapist! He simply read their files, identified their pain as his own and said these words over and over. Within a few short years they closed down the hospital because everyone went home healed! These were people who were violent, in restraints and highly medicated. I strongly recommend reading Joe Vitale's book *Zero Limits* for the whole story about this extraordinary transformative practice in compassion and forgiveness.

If you choose to use this practice, it would be a good idea to keep a journal on the 'before' and 'after.' Record what you notice when you first offer the prayer and the tangible results that come afterwards.

Here are a few of my own: A few weeks ago while I was in the middle of a painful medical procedure, I said inside to the pain and the Universe, "I Love you. I'm sorry. Please forgive me. Thank you." Within seconds the pain diminished and a sense of peace washed over me.

I was thinking about a friend who I hadn't heard about in a couple of months. I knew he was annoyed with me and I also heard he wasn't doing very well. With deep sincerity, I said the same words inside me as I thought about him. That evening he called and was incredibly loving and kind.

A third example is what happened with a young child who used to be in my life but I hardly see any more. We used to do fun things together including having sleepovers at my house. I have photographs that come up as part of my screen saver on my computer. His photo appeared and I felt a sadness come over me because I missed him tremendously. I said "I love you. I'm sorry. Please forgive me. Thank you." Within a few hours my phone rang. It was his mom asking me if I would like to baby-sit on Saturday night and would it be okay if he had a sleepover! You can imagine my excitement!

More than anything else that I can sensibly understand (our small minds can't understand these concepts) – I have been experiencing a sense of well-being and peace amidst a current situation that in the past would have left me feeling potentially depressed and devastated. I believe there are many paths to love and healing and one of the most vital one I know of is that of forgiveness. It is a gift we give ourselves and the person we are forgiving. It brings us back into present time where the gift of inspired living awaits us.

# Chapter 14

## TRANSITIONS & CROSSROADS

## Trust in Me

by Melba Burns

*From a distance I saw my darling 18 year-old nephew, Grant, gleefully zooming on his dirt bike across the pavement of a parking lot. But then he skidded on a patch of slick oil. I watched in horror as his bike fell but his body kept on going, skidding all across that pavement, skinning bloody skin off his left leg and arm and back. He was screaming. I wanted to help him but all I could do was tense up like a scared child, adrenaline rushing, heart pounding, hearing those loud screams.*

*Then, I awoke, drenched in sweat, my mouth still open and raw from screaming those screams. Oh God, this process of leaving was eking into my dreams. No reality was safe anymore.*

*Ever since I'd made the decision to go, the universe had thrown me into a cauldron of terrors – forcing me to reconsider. After all, I did have a choice here; at 49 years of age any person in their right mind would think that I'd know what was best for me. Well, part of me did know. But the ego-part of me wasn't sure about the voice of my higher-Self whispering, "Venture out into the unknown and I will be with you every step of the way." Oh sure.*

*I'd bought an old Dodge Ram van. I'd put the contents of my lovely little one-bedroom apartment into shoe boxes which I would store under the gaucho bed (a couch, used for everything); at night, I'd pull it out and sleep on it.*

That winter the van was going to carry me through the States. I could stay in trailer parks, interview people and write their stories; Okay, I could do that. I'd moved several times and I knew how to adapt. However, I'd never lived in a van and I usually had some sense of where I was headed. This time I had no idea. Hysteria was mounting.

Not only the nightmares, but the hot flashes and night sweats were killing me. Sometimes at 4 a.m. I'd stumble into my bathroom for a pee, glance in the mirror and say out loud: "You know, your little home is going to be just this size. Can you do it?"

I'd return to bed, try to sleep, toss and turn – then flounder through another day. I wasn't sure what I was doing. But my apartment needed to be packed up within a week so the woman subletting it could move in. I had a lot to do and there was no point in thinking about it. Just do it.

The day after that serious nightmare, the pain in my own left leg was so bad that I ended up crawling across the beige carpet of my living room, packing up boxes of stuff – china, books, records, junk – but a sharp knife was cutting a definite line down from the buttock and all through the thigh. "Sciatica," a friend said, "Don't worry, it'll go away." Oh, but not that day, or the next or even the next. Nope, my leg was dragging its tail and telling me to "Stay put."

I couldn't. I had to be out of there by the end of September. So, while I tried massage, hot baths with Epsom salts and even more meditation, the pain persisted. I guess it was crying out for the whole me. The terror was mounting with this crazy idea to leave Los Angeles, "City of Angels", a place I'd called home for the past 8 years, leaving dear friends and my 25-year-old daughter, Donna.

But I had to go.

Why? Because I'd been advised by my Higher Self to leave Los Angeles. Sound a little crazy? Yes, most of my friends thought so. Donna did, too. We walked across the beach one evening, just as the sun was setting, and she asked me again, "Mom, why are you doing this?"

"Honey, I have to go. It's hard to explain, but you know all that meditation I've been doing, well, I've really been guided to leave here." She already knew that, through the meditation, a lump in my breast had disappeared and I'd gotten in touch with my Higher Self.

She strode ahead of me with her long legs planting her sure feet angrily in the sand. Neither of us spoke for a while, but silence was okay with us, too. After a little while, we linked arms, then ate chocolate ice cream and laughed while it dripped down our chins and onto our tee shirts. "But what am I going to do without you, Mom?"

I shook my head and looked away so she wouldn't notice the tears welling up in my eyes. I wasn't sure how I would get along without her either, but I knew we would see each other again. It would work out. Somehow.

To create funding for the trip, I sold off most of my furniture. This included two very beautiful pink velvet Ladies' and Gentlemen's chairs, circa 1600, plus an antique French inlaid cherry wood table, which I still miss. As I was trying to shed the old skin of this former self, I had to let most things go. Yes, I cried, but not as often as I could have. Not even when I sold my diamond engagement ring to a pawnshop. Well, maybe then.

I needed the money, didn't I?

I finally got out of my apartment. However, the van had to have some major repairs and I was forced to stay with Donna. That was challenging. We had already said goodbye, really, and when the work on my van dragged on and on for three weeks, and when my boxes were littering up her kitchen and some of her bedroom, it was too much. But the day she said, "It's time for you to leave Mother", my heart got all squished in my chest and then the tears came.

That weekend, I had already planned to attend a workshop with Lucas Cole Whittaker in Anaheim, so I drove the van there from Santa Monica; not a long trip. When I found the steering loose, that it wobbled even in clear, blue-sky weather and I couldn't really control it, I got scared. How the heck was I going to live in this and drive it in a blustery rain?

It was then I experienced a strange miracle.

While parked in a lot in Anaheim, all the lights in the van went out. Was the electrical system malfunctioning? On the way back to Santa Monica, still with no interior or exterior lights, I shakily pulled off the freeway in rush hour traffic, lay down on the couch and prayed for an answer. Prayed hard. A half an hour later, the answer was clear: "Take the van back."

The next day when I drove into the van dealership, I announced that I wanted out of my contract and explained why. The salesman flashed his widest capped-tooth smile and nodded in agreement. Then, he said, "Okay, I can release you from the contract, but you'll have to forfeit your deposit." –$1000! I hardly had that kind of money to my name. But as I stood there in that L.A. sunshine, I became very clear: No ruddy van was going to own me!

I nodded, "Okay then," and we shook hands. I was so relieved I hugged him. He probably shook his head as I walked away. But I'd never felt so free.

The next day, I replaced the van-storage shoe boxes and packed all my stuff up into a couple of suitcases, which I loaded into my little green Datsun 280Z, which, for some wonderful reason had never sold; I'd worried about what I was going to do with that car. I hugged my daughter farewell and drove off. Destination unknown. All I knew was that I was tuning in to a deep part of myself and I had to listen to that voice.

*As I ventured up #1 Freeway, now the third week in October, I headed into cold weather; so I'd bed down in inexpensive motels. Often, as I awakened with night sweats, listening to the rumbles of the tractor trailers roaring by like prehistoric monsters, I'd bolt up in terror. Where was I? In the dark, all I could see was the flashing red sign of the motel "Vacancy, vacancy, vacancy." But I then breathed in deeply and heard the sweet voice of my Higher Self, whispering to me, "Trust in me and you will never be alone."*

*I trusted – and it got me safely to Vancouver, where I am now.*

## Nothing but Acceptance

by Janet Lawson

*They say a cat has nine lives. Leo, born in the Year of the Cat. Am I still counting lives? Living on borrowed time? Or just gearing up? Like most people who dig deep I am impelled by the search for meaning. Even as a child I would look at things, on purpose, from many angles, to find that the most interesting explanation was the one that encompassed the most question marks, holding the possibility for their resolution while respecting that the deeper mystery would forever remain intact. Is it truthful to say that this search is what motivated my journey into the drug world? Or simply the curiosity of a cat looking for fun? More likely both and lots in-between. And it must be said – the cowardice of one who doubts her ability to face the challenges of life. So the crossroads that emerge in my 'defining moments' are in one way or another the choice between life and death.*

*Fifteen years old. Having ingested formaldehyde and seventy-seven (count 'em) aspirins, then swum, clothed, far into September's dark night lake, I perceived the choice from within and without and all around and through me and the dictum – sentence? – that There Is No Way Out Of Here. Your Choice. Do It Now Or Do It Later. Live Now Or Next. We Strongly Urge You To Swim To Shore. As I recall, that was the first turning. I shed the sopping clothing and climbed into my bed, not knowing if I would awaken.*

*After the event, I chose to forget the black and white karmic insight presented to me, or at least to gray it out. My brain at that time was relatively clear of physical pollutants. Excluding the evening's poisons, a bit of pot and a few occasions of alcohol spewing were all I had experienced. The great mystery continued to woo me, but now was compounded by the darker deeper waters of post puberty perspective. I rejected the known paths, the tried and true safe passages through. Oblivion was irresistible. I wrote and sang about it, Velvet Underground's Sweet Nuthin' became my theme song and guidance. I sought and courted those who seemed to me to rise above or below meaning. Meaning Less Ness. Nothing. The mathematical mystery of Zero. Writers like Huxley who had ventured into madness, or Watts who wrote beyond duality. I rejected the choice of All Or Nothing. I wanted All And Nothing together. Give me the Big Bang! Mystery! So yes, it was both – fervour for the unfathomable and a haughty distaste for the regular rules of human travel. I did not at the time recognize that courage lay in the acceptance of the human condition. Or that cowardice is simply the refusal to Be in the moment. I was so unbrave. The chronology is a little crazy here. There were years after that choice in the lake where I tried to muster. Pulled my willpower stockings. Study. Marriage. Travel. But I left it all, gradually, eventually and finally willingly surrendered to Sweet Nuthin'. I remember well that moment when the drug of the day coursed stronger than my mindpower. That instant was indescribable, irresistible. Take me out and away we go! Away I went for four years. Flailing around in a big city, my main entertainment being to watch and see what she would do next. She became lost. Toyed with people. Came to enjoy the flaunting of her sexual power. My sweet Sweet Nuthin' she had reduced to Nuthin' Much. Then one night she/I took something that was not what it had said it was. Some weird trip. Farther out than I had ever been. Until there I was indeed in oblivion. The splendour of the cosmos, cold wide open firmament. Nothing But Acceptance. Paradox in para-dise, yes I see that. I will never know the bottom of the meaning of those three words Nothing But Acceptance. Anyway, for three days I travelled those outer limits. What is that old Dylan song... Love Minus Zero/No Limit. Anyway. There I was, rocking my skinny body and writing myself down to keep body connected to soul. Once again I had arrived at the crossroads of Life and Death. Do What You Will. There was no urging, this time to turn back. All was absolute and pure. Nothing But Acceptance. We can fan your tiny flame or swallow you whole. Do what you will. All And Nothing – available to me. Certainly it was a tempting offer.*

*I chose small. I tried to retreat into my body. Strand by strand I pulled loose thought onto the page, into the bloodstream. Eventually phoned a lover to hold and contain me as I collected. Asked him to drive me to the local looney bin, where with luck I landed upon a wise woman. She had me write lists of what to do – next fifteen minutes, next hour, next meal (what – me eat?!), next day. In short, she had me define what I must do in order to remain sane, then cloaked me with her faith in my ability to do it as she sent me on my way. I did not quit drugs, or beat an addiction, or give them up even. I simply came to the cross-*

roads and turned. I won't say it was easy. Far from it. But the choice was truly made, for there was no question of ever un-making it.

When I look back now at the years following that choice I see a tentative young woman. But she was armed with the invaluable certainty that "Do What You Will" is actually a universal law. Anything goes. Spent a couple of years in a trio of spots in Europe to heal and regroup. Several months in a cave in the Canaries. Cueva en las canarias. And the canary in the cave? Well, she learned that, as long as we are human, living in the material and temporal world, that every moment is precisely as important as the next, because they connect, all, one to the next. Each involves a Choice. All moments are cross-roads, especially this one. Now. Because Now is the only moment a human can affect. There is still great mystery.... As above, so below and all that. This could easily segue into my spiritual beliefs, the next topic in our course. And it may. But this writing and remembering has left my body cold and shaky. I must make hot tea and prepare sustenance for this body. The inherent humility of being human, finally embraced.

# *Let's Write*

This life story is about a time in your life when you stood at the fork in the road and had to make a choice. Read each of the following memory prompts slowly. Be gentle with yourself. Remember to give yourself ample time between each prompt. Listen with your heart and begin to remember:

Where were you? How old were you? Do you remember what year it was?

Where were you living? Were you going to be moving from that location? What was going on in your life at this time? What were the circumstances? Were you leaving a job, marriage or other relationship? Were there other people involved other than you? Who else was involved? How would your decision impact them? Begin to see the images on the screen of your mind.

What was it like for you to be at the edge of change? Were you frightened? Perhaps you were excited. Both? What do you recall? Did you feel that your sense of security was threatened in some way? How were you weighing your choices? Were others helping you decide or influencing your decision? If so, who and how? What did that feel like? Were you feeling alone even though others were around? Did it seem like a long time before you made a choice? Did you, in fact, consciously make it or did life's circumstances (fate) make it for you? i.e. a sudden accident or your husband coming home and saying, "I'm leaving you." *(keep in mind that everything that occurs in our lives, we brought to ourselves on some level, even if we were not consciously aware of it at the time)*

What finally occurred? Which road did you walk down? Was there a sense of relief when you finally said yes to one possibility and no to the other? What new circumstances did you move into? What was the period of transition like for you? Did you adjust easily or was this a particularly vulnerable time?

Were there children involved? How were they affected by your decision? Who were the supports in your life at that time? In what ways were they there for you? In what ways were you there for yourself? In other words, what were the strengths you relied on? Recall them now. Once you made the decision and followed through on it, did you notice new doors opening to confirm you had made the right choice?

Perhaps you never looked back because you were operating in survival mode. You hurried quickly into your new life and buried what went before. You very likely were not aware of any other option. You just needed to move on. And so you did.

As you look back now, is there anything left over from that time that you need to own or acknowledge or heal? Is there anything you need to let go of? Is there something you want to say to someone that was never said? If so, you will have an opportunity to write it in your story today. What is your body telling you now? Let yourself feel whatever it is. Take another deep breath.

Perhaps your situation was more akin to this: you have looked back and realize you haven't really ever let go of that time even though you made a decision to take a different route. Perhaps you have been living a brand new life or many new lives since then, but part of your energy is still invested in that old life – before you made the decision to move from it. You're still asking yourself all the "what ifs".

Are you still holding onto something or someone from your past? Who or what is it? Is there still a place in you that harbours hurt, confusion, regret, anger or disappointment about that time and circumstance? Are you still wondering what the outcome would have been if you had stayed where you were, or if you had made another choice,? Are you still holding on? Notice what you are feeling in your body. Breathe. Know your truth. Let whatever is there simply present itself. You are safe. And now, acknowledge yourself for making the choice you did. Perhaps it was difficult for you afterwards but what have you learned about yourself? How has your life changed as a result of that decision? To what new paths did the road you chose lead? Could you possibly be where you are today in terms of self-awareness and growth without living the life you've lived? How have you grown because of this decision? Conversely, how have you stayed stuck?

Perhaps you are incredibly grateful for this particular transition because of ultimate success when you crossed that threshold. Embody that success, enjoy the feelings once again.

Remember there are no accidents. And this is about acceptance. Acceptance of yourself, the choices you made and the courage it has taken to live these choices. Be willing to see the gifts and growth these choices have brought you even if they have caused some hurt or suffering.

Once again, take a deep breath – breathing in self-appreciation, self-acceptance and self-love. Now gather your pen and paper and begin to write into your truth about a significant crossroad – a time of transition and choice.

# Chapter 15

# A HEALTH SETBACK:
# AN ILLNESS, AN ACCIDENT

## An Almost Fatal Car Crash that
## Changed My Life Forever

by Teya Danel

*I'm floating in space and all of a sudden find myself in a restaurant where I worked. Everything is twilight and surreal. I step into the restaurant and see one of my former co-workers. There is a sudden understanding that I cannot possibly be there physically. I see lots of flashes of bright light and they seem to swirl and twirl around me moving in and out of consciousness. Where am I? What is this place? I drift back into unconsciousness.*

*My eyes are closed and I start to stir slowly.....Again, where am I? Everything is hazy and I can't move my body. A sudden paralyzing fear hits me.... Oh my GOD, I think to myself, where's Daved? What's happened to him? Is he alive? My heart is aching and beating hard. I become full of apprehension. I vaguely remember him being with me but cannot place my finger on it. The realization that something really terrible has happened slowly enters my mind. As I open my eyes the first thing I see is a railing on the side of my bed with a photo of my eight-year-old boy taped onto it. He is sitting in a hospital bed surrounded by my relatives and I see a big smile on his face. Huge relief flows through my body. He's okay. He made it. I take a deep breath and I start* to cry with relief and gratefulness – he's okay, we're okay. I'm still here. Where exactly is here? Where am I? I look down my body and I see these contraptions on my legs. My whole body feels numb and I recognize that I'm in a hospital and I'm sensing I had a car accident. I wonder how long I've been here. I can hardly believe the state I'm in.

It's August 6, 2004 and I'm trying to make sense of my condition. All I know is that I'm lying in a hospital bed just about broken to pieces and very high on morphine. I'm in very rough shape and my face is all swollen and I look like death warmed over. Thank God for modern technology and pain relieving drugs. I can't imagine what kind of pain I would be in if I could feel my body.

I learn that I've had a very close call and in fact, it is a miracle that I'm still here. I've just been through a 14-hour tandem operation with surgeons working on saving both my legs and my left arm. There is so much damage that they can't deal with it all at once. More surgery is scheduled. I'm in ICU and fade in and out of consciousness. It turns out that there are multiple breakages in both my legs. They went through the floorboards of my car and my right leg is off by 10 degrees. My left elbow has splintered like chicken bones, a number of ribs on my right side have been broken and the right side of my face, which hit the steering wheel, is caved in and black and blue. I'm lucky that I still have my eye. I find out later that on my way to Nanaimo to pick up my older son, I went through an intersection, up and over an island and straight into a post that scrunched my car on the driver's side. Much later when I get to see the pictures, I can hardly believe that I've come out of there alive. I'll never really know what happened that afternoon; I have no memory of it whatsoever. In fact all I can remember is leaving the house. The rest is blank.

But there I was sprawled over the steering wheel in deep shock and not even conscious. However, the mothering bond is so incredibly powerful that even in the midst of such incredible trauma, I manage to somehow inform the police that I have a 14 yr. old son arriving at the ferry terminal. Don't ask me how I do that. I ask him a year later about his experience that day and he tells me that when he heard his name on the speaker at the ferry he intuitively knew something was terribly wrong. The policewoman takes him to the hospital in Nanaimo where he sees me and his brother in pretty bad shape. I'm screaming and have not stopped since they pulled me out of the car. I can imagine how horrifying it is for a young 14 year old to witness his mother and brother in such an unbelievable condition. He ends up being taken under the wings of a woman who runs a volunteer organization called Victims Services, which I've never even heard of. When I hear the story of his journey I say a prayer of thanks to that woman who took my son home with her, gave him a bed that night and money the next morning so he could board the ferry back to his father who is here in Canada to enjoy a holiday on the Sunshine Coast.

*Meanwhile, back in the hospital, my sister Mona comes to visit every single day. She takes good care of me. She makes sure I'm comfortable and washes my hair every few days in a special little basin that sits snuggly under my head. Having lived in Vancouver, I still have a good number of friends there and they start to file in and offer support in whatever ways they can. My adopted mom, luckily lives only a few blocks from the hospital and she visits me almost daily. Having my friends and family around me offers me much comfort, courage and hope that I'll make it through all this.*

*Will I ever lead a normal life again? Will I ever walk? I cannot even bend the middle finger of my left hand and am unable to feed myself easily as my one hand does not reach my face. I was born a left handed person and learned, with my grandmother's prompting to write with my right hand in the days when it was not proper to use the left hand. Anyway, I'm grateful for my ambidextrous skills now, because I'm going to need them to feed myself. It's about the only thing I can do for myself at this time. Being unable to take care of my basic needs is quite humbling, to say the least.*

*I feel a very strong sense of determination and commitment to do whatever I need to get back my life and heal my body. I believe that I can and I hold on to that thought with all my heart and soul, even though a small part of me has huge doubts given the nature and extent of my injuries. The mere thought of spending the rest of my life in a wheelchair is completely overwhelming. I begin the long journey of rehabilitation and healing and there are no guarantees being offered as to what the outcome will be.*

*I end up spending a month in Vancouver General Hospital and when I am well enough to make the journey I ask to be transferred back to Victoria where the Royal Jubilee Hospital will be my home for the next two months. The surgeon who is taking over my case, a fine man by the name of Michael O'Neill, informs me upon arrival that I'm a very lucky woman. He says to me "not that long ago, you wouldn't have made it" and I know in my heart that that is the truth. As I lie in my bed, day in and day out I am astounded at how strong and grounded I feel. I can barely move and yet I feel totally powerful instead of powerless, which one would kind of expect, given my circumstances. My spirit is strong and my will to live and heal is just as strong. I make peace with my situation, totally surrender to it and accept what is.*

*Every day I get better and better. Even the pain and the long sleepless nights seem somehow manageable. As I start to get stronger I learn to shuffle my butt slowly as I inch my way across my bed and into my electric wheelchair, which offers me mobility and a change of scenery.*

*Every day I am working out in the rehab section of the ward named RP2. I remember being taken into the rehab section one day and with the help of three therapists I was able to grab onto a pole and stand up on my good leg. My right leg was damaged the most and I've been told that I cannot put any weight on* it for at least three months. So here I am standing on one leg, holding onto the pole and having a realization that there is yet some hope for me to walk. Before too long I graduate to a walker and make great progress, one day at a time. I come to realize how much of my daily life I'd taken for granted and in my present state, I truly begin to appreciate every small thing that I can accomplish on my own. You have no idea how humbling it is to have to have your bum wiped for six weeks – to not even be able to take care of the basics.

I've learned that out of so much adversity, so many gifts have come. The biggest one being a deepening of the bond between my sister and I. I learned, big time, not to sweat the small stuff and to be grateful every day for my life and my healing abilities. I know now that I'm going to be okay. I can see that I am an inspiration to many of my friends and acquaintances. They tell me they feel strengthened by my courage. I acknowledge myself for having reclaimed my life and my body. Now, three and a half years later, I'm waiting for my last small surgery, which is an implant in my face and after that, it's clear sailing. I am astounded by the progress I've made and pretty soon you won't even be able to tell that I had a broken body. I will never look at a disabled person in a wheelchair or scooter ever again in the same way. I've been there, done that and my compassion and love for people has taken on a whole new dimension. I am free and standing tall and so very thankful for who I am. I know in my heart that sharing my experience will help a lot of people. I really believe there are no accidents in life. I was meant to have this experience, to get through it and learn so much from it. It has been a huge gift, the importance of which I am only now able to even fathom. I see life very differently now and have learned to never, ever again take anything in my life for granted. I am excited and await all the new adventures that are coming my way with great anticipation and joy. I have a new appreciation for life and intend on living it to the fullest from now on.

## This Is Who I Am

by Warren Bailey

*In 1993 I was given the results of a blood test for H.I.V. Even though I had the suspicion of it being positive after being with someone with H.I.V. it felt like a freight train hitting me when I was told that I was positive too. The doc-*

tor informed me that I had a good ten years left to live. "How do I tell my parents?" was the main thought running through my mind at the time.

As the years went on, I felt fine, healthy and vibrant. In 1994 I entered into a relationship with a man who also was H.I.V positive. Our difference was that when he was diagnosed, he needed the medications immediately. My doctor felt since my counts were so good, drugs were not needed at that time.

In December, 2000 I contracted pneumonia and was hospitalized for a week. My body seemed to have this ability of bouncing right back very quickly. Medications were still not needed.

In April, 2001 I left my partner to move to Victoria from Vancouver. I was an alcoholic and my alcoholism took a turn for the worse. I went from one job to another and was never given the real reason why I was being let go. I knew. I couldn't stop drinking. So I moved through life a lost soul and I ached to not be here anymore.

In the summer of 2005, I couldn't explain what was happening in my body. I became very unstable with periodic bouts of dizziness. As the months moved on, standing in one spot for more than a couple of seconds was next to impossible without my legs giving out on me. The only thing I knew to help me cope was alcohol.

My mind got foggier, I was completely unstable and very confused. I had no job and lived in my parents' basement suite at the time. I had mentioned to my mother one day that I had a doctor's appointment the next day. It was decided that she would go with me. I don't remember much about that time. The alcohol didn't make it any easier for me or anyone around me. When I woke up the next morning, I wasn't sure where I was let alone what day it was. There was a knock at my door. It was Mother wanting to see if I was almost ready to go. I tried to tell her there was no appointment for that day. She didn't buy it. I'm not too sure how I made it into the shower and back out again, but I do remember taking one. By this time, I couldn't stand on my own. Mother gave me a cane to use but I had no coordination to handle it. I hung on to her arm. It's very unclear as to how I was able to manage getting into the doctor's office but I do remember him telling my mother to get me to the emergency right away. I have no recollection of being admitted or lying in the bed waiting for something to happen. I now see that I was hallucinating all through that first night. I was in and out of consciousness.

I'm not clear on when I came to, but when I did I learned that I was in a different hospital and had undergone a major operation. I was battling cryptococcal meningitis. I had been in great need of a shunt to replace the clogged passages from my head down into my stomach. The severity of this was told to me by my doctors. It really hadn't sunk in until my mother told me that the doctor had called her after the operation. He said they did everything they could but maybe it was time to prepare for the worst. My poor mother!

*During my stay in the hospital my parents saw evidence of how serious my alcoholism was when they stumbled upon empty bottle after empty bottle in their basement. How could I deny the truth? I could no longer fool either them or myself.*

*Over time the doctors and nurses worked with me to regain my strength and restore my cognitive functioning. During this stay, I learned that my H.I.V. status had changed. I now had AIDS. Anti-viral drugs were prescribed for me and the medication whirlwind began. Yet it didn't seem to faze me. Considering I didn't want to be on the planet anyway, this wasn't bad news.*

*A month after the operation, I was free to go. While waiting for my father to pick me up, I learned, from a phone call with my mother, that a dear friend of my parents died that morning from a heart attack. As my father and I drove away from the hospital, gratitude was the farthest thing from my mind. Why am I still here? A good man, like Dr. Pazder was taken from us and I'm left here, for what reason? I didn't understand. As the days turned into weeks, I maintained one thought, "There has to be a reason why I'm still here!"*

*The alcoholism took off again and try as I might, I couldn't end my life. I stopped my medications with one outcome in mind. I was done. Or was I? I needed to know what it was that was keeping me here and why a good man was taken from us that day.*

*The day I entered into my first AA room, I felt a connection like I've never felt before. These people all think the same way I do. Their beliefs were on a spiritual level in the same way I always believed for myself but thought I was alone. This for me was the first stepping stone to a whole new world of hope. Soon, however, I came to see that AA was not providing me with the help that I knew I needed.*

*As time went on, I still couldn't stop relapsing. I couldn't understand at the time why this was. I ended up at Alcohol and Drug Services. I found the anger that was building up inside of me unbearable. Over time I was able to find the ability to forgive and let go. I was open and willing to accept what was being offered to me. I felt more determined to find the answers.*

*In a desperate attempt to help me, my parents asked me if I would be interested in trying out a church they had attended once before. It was called Unity. I discovered that here was a place where I could expand on my own thoughts and ideas that I had lived with all my life but thought I was alone. Then on July 11th, 2007, I woke up after a drinking binge with a new sense of life. I had a feeling inside me that made me realize for the first time I truly wasn't alone. Everything seemed brighter and everyone I encountered had some message for me that I understood.*

*On July 11th, 2008, I celebrated my first year of being sober. In June of that year I turned 40 and decided to have a big party. I needed to have all the people around me who stood by me before, during and after my world changed to a new awareness and light. It gave me a chance to say "Thank You" to all my friends and family. I will never forget that day.*

*Today the craving to drink has gone and my will to live has taken over. I understand my purpose in life. It is something I have adopted from my minister, Doris Trinh Lewis. It is to live the life I love and make a positive difference in the world.*

*In everything I do today, I see that this is who I am. I'm excited about sharing my journey about where I came from, what inspires me today and about my dreams of tomorrow.*

# One September Morning

by Deborah Hawkey

*It was a rainy Vancouver evening in September 1959, about the time of year when the leaves start to change color. I was five.*

*At about 6:00 p.m. the phone rang.*

*My dad, who was sitting at the green and chrome kitchen table smoking homemade cigarettes, continued rolling his stash of cigarettes and flicking the ashes into the rolled up cuffs of his green work pants. They served as an ashtray. I guess that's why my mom always complained about him never having a shower or changing his clothes. They always argued because he never changed out of his work clothes and smelled like soot and oil from working in the boilers for the school board.*

*"Get the milk and put it away", he said, in his gruff voice.*

*"I'll get it," I said and I rushed to the phone and lifted the black handle from the hook on the wall.*

*"Hello, hello." I said*

*"Hello," he said "is your dad there?"*

*It was a man's voice I knew to be Joe's.*

*And immediately, without warning, a firecracker went off in my head. KAPOW!!!!!*

*"Hello, hello." I said, but no one answered.*

*"Who's on the phone, bring it here" my dad said angrily.*

*And he talked to Joe.*

*The next thing I remember I was wearing headphones and dropping colored marbles into a pint milk bottle at the hospital.*

*The nurse said I was supposed to drop a marble into the glass bottle each time I heard a sound.*

*This is how they discovered I had become deaf due to having developed mumps twice.*

*"Unheard of!" the doctors proclaimed but coupled with everything else they weren't surprised.*

*The mumps caused such intense pressure in my head it blew out the eardrum in my right ear.*

*I soon learned coping skills. I learned to read lips and feel vibrations penetrate the wood desk at school in grade 1. At times when it was difficult to understand what the teachers were saying I would place the side of my face on the desk and as if by magic, the sound would resonate in the bones in my face and I could understand what they were saying.*

*My dad constantly claimed in his sarcastic tone of voice that I could hear what I wanted to hear, but he was wrong. I could hear sounds but words were garbled.*

*I became an observer of life. I learned to read people's lips and not interrupt when people spoke. In order to understand what others were saying I learned to be quiet and pay attention, because people surely do speak in a variety of ways. I learned to observe people's facial expressions and developed an intuitive knowing that only comes through observation. I learned that people also speak and express themselves with gestures, using their hands, for example. I developed a keen eye and patience.*

*I developed a love for classical music and jazz. With no lyrics to figure out, it made listening to music truly enjoyable. The yelling and screaming of rock music and heavy metal, for me, made it impossible to comprehend and only reinforced the trauma of living with a mad man.*

*While everyone was into 60's rock and Beatles, I was feasting on sumptuous Latin rhythms, Brazilian sambas and cool jazz.*

*I've had the distinct honor of meeting with jazz icons, Ella Fitzgerald, Tony Bennett, Oscar Peterson and many more. One day, when I was 16, my dad handed me a piece of paper. It had Portland Hilton in blue as the heading and on it was written in black felt pen, "to Debbie" and the signature of the jazz great, Duke Ellington. My dad had him as a customer in his taxi the night before and thought to ask for his autograph. To this day, I'm not sure what is more amazing, that he had "the Duke" in his taxi or that he would think of me in that time. I consider that autograph as one of my most cherished possessions.*

*What I am most profoundly grateful for is, along the way, I learned to be still and hear the inner voice. To this day, the inner voice is my guide and my salvation, my comfort, my trusted advisor, my constant companion and my most cherished friend.*

# *Let's Write*

Begin to remember a time when you had a serious accident or health setback that significantly impacted your life. As you begin to remember the details of this particular time, do not embody the memory. Instead simply witness it as you would a movie on a movie screen and remember to consciously breathe as you begin to bring in the details.

Looking back – where were you? What year did the illness begin or the accident take place? How old were you? What happened? If it was an illness, what symptoms were you having? How were you treating them? How did you feel when your doctor first told you what was wrong? Was anyone with you when you learned the news? Or after an accident, were you taken to hospital? Did you learn right away what was wrong with you? Were you conscious? Was there anyone else in the accident with you? What were some of your first thoughts, impressions and feelings?

Think about the circumstances whether it be an illness or an accident – how, when, where and what happened, and what followed immediately afterwards?

What was the prognosis that you were given? How did you feel about it? What did you do?

Who comforted and supported you during this time of crisis, if it was a crisis? Did the level of comfort you received help you get through this stressful time? What was the quality of the medical treatment you received?

Were there new people you met during your recovery that you became close to? Have they remained in your life? How have these new friendships impacted you?

How did the circumstances of your life change as a result of your illness or accident? Who else was affected by what happened to you? Did it impact a spouse, children and/or colleagues? Were you in a job that you couldn't return to right away? Did it severely affect your income? How did you manage?

What did you do to help yourself through your healing process? What strengths did you employ? Were you able to stay positive or were you frustrated or afraid? What were some of your greatest fears? Was there someone or something that helped you stay positive and have hope?

How did having this illness or accident change you? Are you different as a result of it? Do you have new insights or a new appreciation for life?

Perhaps you are still burdened by the effects of this illness or accident. Perhaps it isn't a burden at all but seen and experienced in a totally different way. What is your experience now? Reflect on all the ways your illness or accident impacted your life and where you are today as a result of it.

Get a glass of water, approach your writing table and begin to cluster or write your story.

# Chapter 16

## DEATH OF A LOVED ONE

### I Love You
### I Love You More

by June Swadron

*Mom, Mommy, Minnie, Minnie-Mouse, Moth–er! Mimi, Memes, Mindle, Ma, Minerva, Mama.*

*She was all of the above. Each a different personality. Still, she was my mother. Minnie Swadron. Born in 1919 in the miniscule town of Shaunavan, Saskatchewan; first born child of Romanian immigrants, Joseph and Lily Lazarus.*

*I remember being at the hospital and holding Mom's hand. She didn't know I was holding it. Or perhaps she did. Who's to say what a person in a coma knows or feels or perceives. Sometimes I would hold her hand a few inches above the sheets and then let go of it – let it fall. It was an eerie feeling but I did it hoping the sudden drop would wake her up. I wanted so much for her to wake up and smile up at me with her beautiful green eyes.*

*And yes, there was that day – the day that you did open them Mom and you recognized me right away. And you held your hands out to me and I bent down and you kissed my face. You kissed my cheeks, my forehead, my chin, my eyes. There was a desperation to it – an aching, a pleading, a hanging on. A memorizing of every feature: the shape of my eyes, the smell of my hair, the feel of my breath upon your face as you drew me into you. Soul to soul. And I* loved you more than ever knowing how much you loved me. No holding back. In those kisses, you gave it all. You kissed me with an aching need to hold on which caused my heart to split open but I understood. I needed to hold on then too. It was a moment of truth. Just us and the love – no one else in the room. No one to criticize your love for me. Like T. who was embarrassed by your displays of affection.

I used to be embarrassed too. I hated it when I was in my teens or twenties and even thirties and we would go to the Lawrence Plaza or for walks anywhere and you insisted on holding my hand. I guess it reminded me too much of being a child sitting next to you on the couch watching TV and you would want me to scratch your legs. It used to repulse me. But the queasy feeling left once I moved West and went back for visits. Of course I was middle-aged by then. And last October when I stayed with you after your surgery and you seemed so little and vulnerable, I would have done anything to make you feel better. So I actually heard myself offering to massage your back. I did and as much as you cooed expressions of delight, it was me, I know, who benefited the most.

And now you're gone and I remember those Toronto days traveling the T.T.C. There was snow piled high on the ground when I took the bus from your apartment on Chaplin Crescent to The Scarborough General Hospital. Sometimes there were blizzards as I walked and waited for the bus. I hate being cold but I loved the snow. It held me. It supported me. It reminded me of so many other Toronto winters. And the times you and I spoke with glee on the phone from our respective homes after the first snowfall, loving the beauty, the stillness, the freshness in the winter sky. We loved so many things like that. Standing on your balcony or mine midsummer when the thunder storms crashed through the sky and the rain came down in torrents and splashed heavily onto the pavement below. We loved the drama. We even loved the humidity. And I remember when I was a little girl living on Neptune Drive when you took me outside during the rain showers to wash our hair or catch the drops in our mouths. And we'd giggle and dance in the puddles. Those were on the good days. And those are the ones I care to remember for now.

Last night in my writing group I wrote:

I'm here with you again Mom. Sometimes I think I've forgotten you because my days get full and I don't remember to miss you and I've gotten used to not calling you every day. Used to it? I don't know. Buried it is more like it. Sometimes lately when I've spoken about you, I talk about how crazy you were when I was a child. I don't talk about the summer sun shower dances or my teenage years when I'd walk in the door after school and Dick Clarke's American Bandstand would be blaring from the television set. I'd breathe in the comforting smells of dinner cooking on the stove and then be greeted by a happy you in your hot-pink summer short-shorts and freshly ironed white cotton blouse. I'd toss my books on the table and in two seconds we'd be jiving to *Elvis Presley* or twisting to *Chubby Checkers*. And I wouldn't talk about the numerous times my teen-age friends gathered in our living room to be with you even when I wasn't home. They came because you offered wisdom or encouragement or simply because you were fun to be with.

No, I haven't been mentioning those times at all. And then it struck me the other day why not. It became as plain as day. Simply put, I don't have to miss you. I don't have to yearn for you. For your gentle words. For the unconditional love you have had for me whenever my illness struck. Without fail you'd rally round no matter if we were face to face or oceans apart. Your tenderness caressed me through the phone lines, comforting me with loving words, reminding me how courageous I am, how I've beat this time and time again, and how I will this time, too. And you'd remind me how many other obstacles I've faced and how I fought and won. And you'd talk about the beautiful life I made for myself and my successful therapy practice – how I helped others when I couldn't see that I was helping or when none of it had any meaning for me. And you'd remind me of the constant flow of friends I've always had who love me to pieces. And you'd talk to me and talk to me and even when I couldn't imagine there could be any more words left you'd find more to convince me not to give up. You were my champion mom and possibly the reason I'm still on the planet. But the irony was you also passed this hideous illness down to me. Even though you were never formally diagnosed, it was blatantly obvious. But you fought too, Mom. You fought, too. Differently than me. You locked your doors. You judged and blamed and eventually scared everyone away.

But I don't want to go there now. Because in my heart, I know you were hurting. And perhaps that was the bond between us from the early days on – well, that and the laughter too. All of it. Perhaps in some strange way it's what kept our hearts intact – beyond the madness when you got too crazy to be around. Or I did. Funny, how we held each other on a pedestal which of course, never lasted. Before long, we were side by side on the floor scraping to help each other up again. And we always did. We did it with laughter, we did it with tears. In the end, we always did it with love.

I still carry you in my heart wherever I go and on some days I miss you fiercely. Whenever I see something beautiful or funny, touching or strange, I imagine you beside me, laughing your infectious laugh or smiling your beautiful smile or making a witty comment or a judgmental one. No doubt if it's judgmental I'll give you my ridiculous self-righteous lecture. Inevitably, you'd take a deep drag on your cigarette, look me directly in the eyes and say, "Junie, don't use that therapy voice on me." and we'd both burst out laughing.

I still have messages from you on my answering machine, Mom. In one you say: "I miss you, Junie. I miss you honey. That's what I do, I miss you." And I feel your lonely, aching heart. And now it's my turn. Such irony. But as I type *this now, a peace has washed over me. Perhaps it's because you're here with me. Yes, I feel you here and yet ironically I sense you telling me that it's time to let go. Like the vivid dream I had only weeks after you died where you came to me and said, "It's time to let go of me now." And I fought with you. I said it was too soon. And I didn't know if you meant it for my sake or yours or for both of us.*

> *And I am ready to do that. It's been almost a year since Lorraine called me with the news. It was 8:30 in the morning. I was awake waiting for the call. I knew you had died. Still, I got off the phone and started wailing. Wailing! And when I stopped, all I could remember were the parting words we used in our daily telephone conversations.*
> *"Bye, Mom. I love you." And you would always answer back. "I love you more."*
> *So goodbye, Mom. I love you. And you know what? It's my turn to say it now:*
> *I love you even more.*

My beautiful nephew Robert, son of my late sister Barbara, has been battling a drug addiction for many years. He had a very special relationship with my mother, his grandmother, and I emailed him the above story with a request. The request was to write about his new abstinence. I didn't know if he would or if he even could. Within 20 minutes I received a reply with the following story attached to it.

## Hi Memes, Bobby Here

by Robert J. Saffer

> *To continue fighting with the legacy of your moods might be the single greatest gift the universe could have ever presented to us. You taught in thundering simplicity how one can follow through with their own plans and even how to stand up for the eagles who willingly forget they fly higher than the rest.*
> *I wasn't with you for very long towards the end of your life as my drug addiction got the better of me; yet in some way, I'm glad because losing both you and my mom in the same year or so, well, it would have killed me if the*

*drugs didn't. I'm sure of it. Some things happen and I find myself giving myself advice in the way you might have told it to me. 'Stop your crying. Are you a man or a mouse?' It was never that sweet, but always busting through was the truth. So really, not that I am making excuses – as you would say in that friendly yelling voice of yours – 'Bobby, stop making excuses!' Or something of that nature. The point is in my heart you remain sketched, forever changing into similar tunes of tolerance; a clever and powerful, distinct beat pumping my attitude back into life.*

*I pray for you every night. It's a new thing. I remember how you would always pray for me and how much I appreciated it, knowing I really needed your prayers, but not completely understanding why. Perhaps it was because you saw things before they happened. You saw the ups and downs with both their motives and memories attached to them. YOU SAW THE EYES OF ALL. Now that the needle no longer bleeds me away from the burning sun or the wishing-well snow; out of jail, back in touch, every day I am perplexed by my lack of living when you needed me most. 'Bobby, get your head out of the clouds!' Both you, Memes, and Papa and my mom, your beautiful daughter, reside somewhere close to that place now. Funny how things work out. Since I never said it to you, I will say it to the world instead. Your touch, your way has led me past my imbued hurt and sometimes considerable disgust for a life gone wrong. The life of how I think you would want me to live it is ingrained deep within my travels; woven within my sobriety – an arrangement of vivid designs as much a part of me as I could ever hope to be.*

*I miss you and honour you.*

*The face you gave me when I reluctantly showed you my veins bleeding from death, perhaps because I needed a reality check and no one else had the power to give it to me quite the way you could – remains the quantum light on my road to recovery. You injected me with some type of imaginary thiopental when you looked at me and cried and simply remarked, 'how could you...you're smarter than that.'*

*Today in honouring your contribution to my ever changing character, indeed I am smarter than that.*

*My latest addiction is not having one.*

*Well, if you don't consider cigarettes and coffee, two of your favourite hobbies, too much of a stretch.*

# Goodbye Papa

An Excerpt from *On Her Way Home*
by June Swadron

*We sat there watching to see if he was still breathing. Day after day. Sometimes we spoke. Other times we were lost in our own worlds, unconnected in almost every way except for the blood tie that brought us here. He'd been in a coma only two or three days but the doctors were talking about taking him off life support, pulling the plug. After the shock wore off, it seemed the reasonable, even compassionate thing to do for everyone except my mother. Dad had been slowly dying for two years. We understood her resistance, her terror of him leaving her after 49 years of marriage. But he had already left her. She couldn't acknowledge that. "Don't you bring those funeral faces to my door," she started demanding months and months ago. That was even before he was in this state but already looking feeble and gaunt and the cancer had eaten up two thirds of his body. "Where there's life, there's hope!" she'd declare over and over again as if to convince herself of a truth even she could hardly believe. But we had already started to grieve. I remember walking around with a permanent lump in my chest that just wouldn't go away.*

*Now, here in this hospital room we spoke lovingly before him. Some of us were with him all day long. Howard, for instance, never left. He held his hand from morning to night. His only son. The one with whom he rarely saw eye to eye. He came faithfully. Others came after work – his other children, grandchildren, sisters, his one remaining brother. We'd tell each other the stories of our days. Sometimes we laughed and joked; then as if it were wrong, we'd retreat into silence and be separate again. But our being together in this love-filled room with a dying man seemed to dissolve any of the distance we felt between us. The anger, the resentments didn't matter here. They were gone. I basked in the love because I knew that all too soon it would end and we'd go back to our other lives and our unhealed hearts.*

*I don't know how much love Mom was able to let in from any of us during this time. It seemed to be fear, pain and anger that fuelled the pump that kept her going. She was adamant for him to live no matter what his condition. Gently, and away from his room, we tried to dissuade her. "Think of Dad,*

Mom. He's in pain. He's got little fight left and is so tired. Try to let him go," was how we put it.

Ten minutes before my father took his final breath and after 36 hours of an uninterrupted coma my father opened his eyes. They were as clear as stars and filled with love. It was beautiful and remarkable. Mom was sitting beside him. This time, when she took Dad's hand, she tenderly spoke, "I love you, Jimmy. I love you so much. What are you trying to tell me? That you love me too? I know you do darling. Your children are all here. I'm going to be fine sweetheart. Truly I am. You do what you must and know that our love will always be with you." Tears fell softly from my father's eyes. He could not speak. He could not move. But the love expressed in his eyes said more than words could ever hope to do. I wasn't sure if I believed in miracles before this. No one has to convince me now. My father awoke from a coma to say goodbye.

# The Day My Father Died

by Steve Silvers

The day my father died I had come into town with my partner, Beth, to visit him. He had had a very long bout with cancer and had fallen into a coma for the last six months of his life. My father had been an uncommonly vital and passionate man, so it was difficult to see him in his unresponsive state, knowing it was the last thing he would have wanted.

I spent many hours in his room at the nursing home with my mother, my sister and Beth, waiting endlessly, not knowing what to say, not knowing what to do. Finally, I decided it was time to take a break, not only from my own weariness with the process, but out of concern for Beth, who I had dragged with me into all of this.

When my father retired, he and my mother moved to Catalina Island. Catalina is a stunning place, a sun-splashed, semi-arid jewel floating in unbelievably clear green seas, twenty-six miles off the coast of Southern California. For countless weekends, over many summers, my father, a boater, had taken our family there. Whenever we would arrive, as soon as our boat was secured to its mooring, my father would put on a bathing suit and bound off the stern of the boat into the cool, crisp water, then float on his back past the many boats in the harbour, singing, stopping at times for random conversations with other boaters as he floated past. In my youth, I often found my father embarrassing.

Several years after they had retired to Catalina, my father's cancer had begun to demand care that was hard for my mother to manage alone, and medical interventions were not available there. She moved them both off the island, taking an apartment in Los Angeles near one of my sisters and her husband. It was to this apartment that I now headed with Beth. When we got there, we quickly changed into bathing suits and went down to the pool. It was a hot Southern California summer day and there were many people in and around the pool. Beth and I dove in and I began to propel myself through the water, lap after lap after lap. It was during one of these laps that I was overtaken by a sense of unease. I knew that I needed to return to the nursing home and Beth and I headed there hastily.

When we arrived, my father was no longer in his room and the looks on the faces of my sister and mother told me unmistakably what had happened. They said my father had died about twenty minutes earlier and a feeling of despair came over me. My mother and sister had dutifully stayed by his side, sensing that the end was close, while I, apparently oblivious to what was coming, had gone for a swim.

I went into the room where my father lay. I looked at the absolute stillness of him, and suddenly I was struck by his sense of serenity. I touched his hand and it was still warm. I could feel him leaving. Suddenly, this thing called dying seemed like the most natural thing in the world, just an extension of life, not something to be feared. My father, who in life had been in many ways a fearless man, was now teaching me not to fear death. I suppose that is what it always means to be fearless. I sat with him there as his life, his spirit, seemed to be gently departing from his body and transitioning peacefully to someplace else.

Before I said goodbye to my father, I told him things that I had never said to him in life. In this moment, we had a kind of intimacy that I had never known with him before. I wanted him to know that despite our many differences, despite my years of wandering, of drifting through life, I would make something of myself, even though, in that moment, I knew that it really didn't matter to him at all, that he loved me simply for who I am. In the end, I chose to tell him this in his own language. My father was a big, brawling man who had grown up in the mean streets of Hell's Kitchen in New York. "Dad," I said, "You'll see. I'm going to knock 'em dead."

As I was about to leave, I looked at my hand holding his. We have the same hands. Suddenly, I thought of my hands swimming through the water at the very moment my father was dying. I thought of the muscles of my young, strong body powering through the water, the hot sun warming my flesh. And I knew that whatever part of my father that lived on in me would have wanted, at the moment of his death, exactly that.

*Today, as I write this, I am on a small, tucked-away beach on Southern Vancouver Island, where I now live. It is another hot summer day. The water beckons. I dive in and swim toward a float that is anchored a hundred meters offshore. There is another man in the water, a large white-haired man, somewhat older than me. Like me, he is enjoying the delicious cold of the sea, and the view from the water of the sun-bleached shore framed by a forest of green. He looks sideways at me. I am not a gregarious man like my father was. I would prefer to swim silently toward the float, enjoying my solitude, my own company. But this time I stop, look at him, and say, "Hello." "Isn't this beautiful," he says. "Yes," I say, "It couldn't be nicer." We chat briefly, then I swim on.*

*I climb onto the float and dry in the sun. Small waves rock the float and I am transported back to my youth and my father and the waves gently rocking our boat moored at Catalina Island. As I lie on my back remembering my father, I look up as an eagle makes slow circles in my direction, its white head and tail feathers gleaming in the sun. I know, instinctively, that it is coming to me, and then it breaks its circular pattern and flies directly overhead. I look to my right and I see a perfect half-moon looming in the bright azure sky. I know that I am in the presence of my father, that he is with me.*

*I dive into the sea and swim back to my spot on the beach. I look out over the water. There is no one floating on their back, singing. It has been more than twenty years since his death, and I have never once seen another person float on their back and sing. Nor, for that matter, have I yet "knocked 'em dead." But, who knows, perhaps someday that person floating on his back, singing, will be me. There's still time.*

# *Let's Write*

This topic is about remembering some of the deaths that have been part of our lives – deaths of people we have known and loved.

I encourage you to use the same method as we've used before – seeing the events unfold upon a movie screen so that you are not embodied in them. Instead you are an impartial witness, watching them unfold from a safe distance with the clarity, safety and wisdom of today. You can enhance your experience by imagining there is a lever at the side of your chair allowing you to make the pictures bigger or smaller, turn the volume up or down, zoom in on particular details or use a telephoto lens to see the entire landscape.

You may want to begin this story with the Centering Exercise found in Book 1, Part C and/or the Invocation found in Book 1, Part D.

There may be several people close to you who have passed. For now, please choose one. Feel free to come back and write about the others, if you are moved to, at another time.

Breathe deeply and travel back in time to the death of someone important to you. Perhaps it was someone you loved dearly. Let the pictures come up on the screen now of this particular time and this particular person.

Where are you? Who is there with you? How long ago was it? How old were you? What is happening? Are you in a hospital? A funeral perhaps? Someone's home? What is going on? Is someone sick? Perhaps there's been an accident. Bring in the details with clarity upon the screen of your mind. How are you feeling? Let the pictures reveal themselves. Remember to consciously breathe as you bring back these memories. Let any questions you have had about this person or the circumstances of his or her death unfold. Allow whatever memories or information you need to appear in order to release any pain you may still be carrying from this time.

Whose death are you reflecting on right now? What was your relationship with that person? Was there time to talk to this person before he or she died? Did you have an opportunity to tell them how you felt about them? If so, did you? Did you tell them? If you did, how did it feel to tell them the truth? Where were you when you had your conversation? Were you alone? What was their response? Were they able to respond? Perhaps you didn't have the opportunity to speak to them before they died. Maybe it was a sudden death or other circumstances made it impossible. Perhaps you were afraid to tell them what you were feeling. Perhaps you didn't know how. Are you at peace concerning this person's death or are there still things you would like to say that you've been holding on to? If so, what would you like to say? Breathe and say it to them now. Say it silently to yourself – speak from your heart and tell them what you have always wanted to say. Do you miss having that person in your life today? If the answer is yes, tell them. Do you love them? Tell the person you love him or her.

It has been written that nothing, not even the death of those we have loved can separate us from the love we shared with them, for love is far stronger than death. In the end the greatest gifts of love will be received again and again far more than we can imagine. We have been changed by those who have loved us, altered in every direction, so that at the centre of our souls, they now inhabit us and we inhabit them.

Breathe that in. There is no separation. Love moves through all barriers. Know this.

Is there anything else you need to say to give closure to yourself and this person? If so, say it now and feel the love in your heart expand as you can imagine this person receiving the love you have just offered him or her through your truth. Bless and release her or him now and let the screen go blank. Breathe.

Now go to your writing table and write a letter to this person. Be sure to say everything you wanted to say but never did. Empty your heart onto the pages. Imagine this person receiving your words with love and appreciation. Or you can write about the time surrounding his or her death and your experience with it and how you are still feeling today. This is an opportunity to let go of any negative or guilty feelings you may be carrying. Or perhaps it was a very peaceful passing and your experience was a beautiful one that you want to capture upon these pages. Whatever your experience, begin to write it now.

## *Chapter 17*

# ANOTHER KIND OF DEATH: THE DEATH OF YOUR SPIRIT

## See Me

by Nan Campbell

*There is an invisible wall*
*behind which I dwell*
*the wall is solidly constructed*
*fear, shame, anxiety*
*tears, joy*
*laughter*
*dreams*
*up and down she goes*
*cascading chaotic cacophony*
*the burn of the rope*
*the thundering racing of my heart*
*exploding in orgasmic release*
*only to be built again*
*of invisible bricks and mortar*
*I climb out of the toxic tailing pond*
*hoping that today the cosmos will be kind*
*how many meditations does it take to reach sanity?*

*many of our brightest walked in madness*
*Virginia and Ernest died in madness*
*a seemingly simple solution perhaps*
*but not this time*
*trudging along, one foot in front of the other*
*just keep moving*
*maybe no one will notice*
*there is beauty behind the wall*
*the certainty of the change of seasons*
*morning's mist on the pond*
*tall grasses swaying on purpose*
*the burnt sweet life of lilies wafting in the breeze*
*the allness of being sweeping through like a pacific wind storm*
*torrential clearing of wounded wood*
*fresh start*
*I climb out of the toxic tailing pond*
*hoping to leave the past behind*
*how many little pink pills does it take to reach sanity?*
*the time for psychotropic altering is over*
*could this be crazy masquerading as knowing?*
*perhaps if I dismantle the wall*
*chipping away at the mortar*
*removing each invisible brick, one day*
*they will be able to see me*
*hold my hand*
*walk with me*
*calm my racing heart*
*sing songs of serenity to my heart of sorrows*

## Cats Know

by June Swadron

*D. and I played scrabble tonight. It's been a long time since we did that. It felt so normal again. But when it was over, I just wanted to go upstairs to my apartment, back to my loving and furry companions, Shadow and Georgie and tuck myself safely in. And not think. The panic is choking me again. I remember the time a long time ago after we played scrabble and I was wearing my pink sponge rollers. For some reason, I wasn't feeling safe to go up the three flights of stairs to my floor so I asked her to accompany me. She looked at me straight-faced and said, "June, you needn't worry. You are singularly unattractive!" Well, we both broke up laughing and it was that spark of laughter that led me up the stairwell without a care in the world.*

*But that was another world ago. I am no longer in that apartment and Georgie has since died and Shadow is just barely making it in her 19th year. Still, I thought about how well I've taken this last move considering what I had to contend with. I thought I'd go crazy with Shadow screaming in the middle of the night almost every night on Burnside Drive. Cats are sensitive. She ingested the vibes there and if I was a cat I would have just screamed all night too. As it was, it's what I wanted to do. Instead I pounded my fists into the pillow and muffled my screams so no one would hear me and confirm that I had gone crazy.*

## Bi-Polar Blues

by June Swadron
Performed in *"Madness, Masks and Miracles"*

*I've got revolving door bipolar blues*
*Today I'm a winner, tomorrow I lose*
*Hey Momma did you get the news*
*I've got the bipolar blues*

*Spent all yesterday lyin' in bed*
*Today's I'm shoppin' way over my head*
*Get down Momma, get down I say*
*We're gonna have a party in the ward today*

*Uppers, downers, prescribed by my MD*
*Must be okay ta take 'em cause he gave 'em all to me*
*Some make me nauseous, others make me cry*
*Others make me fidgety, weepy, creepy and sleepy,*

*They can't determine why*

*Crushed by depression, ain't got no self-expression*
*Did ya hear my confession – I'm calling to you.*

*Really sorry honey*
*That we ain't got money*
*Spent it all shoppin' at the corner store*
*Bought you a gift. It sure gave me a lift*
*If I hadn't spent it all, I'd buy you more.*

*And I ain't got no libido no more*
*Sex is a total bore*
*Am I a woman or just a machine*
*Can't figure who I am or who I've been*

*My man, I just know he's really scared*
*I'm sure he was not prepared*
*That I wouldn't want him like I used to do*
*Mak'n love all day and all night through*

*These pills have dead-ended the woman in me*
*I want my man but I want to be happy*
*Isn't there something that can just set me free?*

*I don't want a dry mouth so I can't even talk*
*I don't want to be sleepy when I want to take a walk*
*I don't want trembling hands that everyone can see*
*I don't want to pretend that all is well with me*

*I just want to feel safe to tell you who I am*
*And not be afraid that you won't understand*
*I don't always know myself what will come tomorrow*
*But if we work together, perhaps we'll ease the sorrow*

*I'm just the same as you are*
*I laugh. I cry. I feel.*
*It's just that I have removed the masks*
*So that what you see is real.*

*And I'm learning now who I am*
*Under everything that was pretend*

*And even though I'm not steady yet*
*I'd rather be this, lest I forget:*
*I may have bipolar blues*
*But here's the latest of the news*
*I'm setting down the label now*
*Can you just call me by my name?*

*Not stupid or dizzy or crazy or lazy*
*Or coo-coo, nuts, weirdo or sick.*
*Just call me by my name.*
*And I will do the same.*

*Cause I'm not always in the dumps*
*And I'm not always high*
*But I can't control it all the time*
*But my God, I sure do try*

*I've got the bi-polar blues*
*And I don't want to lose*
*If you could understand*
*It's not what I choose.*
*I'll work with you if you work with me*
*Let's make an effort to live in harmony*
*I am you and you are me and we are all the same*
*Let's just drop the label*
*And call me by my name.*

*Please, just drop the label*
*And call me by my name.*

# When Will I...?

by Nikki Menard

*When will I love myself?*

*When will the struggle stop? I've worked at integrating myself, accepting my shadow-self, accepting the pain-self, all of the selves.*

*I've work-shopped them, read about them, meditated upon them, intentioned them, embraced them, experienced them, allowed, disallowed, controlled, released control, witnessed them, dreamed them, painted them, sculpted them, journalized and wrote poetry about them, sang, drummed, danced, swam them, gardened them, movied them, telephoned them, brainstormed, self-pitied them, abused, drugged, threatened, sat, Spirit/God/Creator/Grand-mother/Mother Earthed them, medicine wheeled them, coloured them, therapied them, stressed, distressed, thoughts of suicide and leaving the planet...*

*When will I...?*

# A Higher Purpose

by June Swadron

*I have lost count of the times when I couldn't feel my heart – neither to love myself or another, or especially to receive love. I also couldn't understand how someone could love me when I felt like I was giving nothing back – those times when despair and hopelessness crippled my days and nights. Such is the peril of bi-polar affective disorder. Sometimes that's what frightens me the most. The fact that even when I'm well and I believe the anxiety and debilitating depressions won't return, they still do. I used to be smug because years could go by without an episode and I would think I'm out of the woods. But then, seemingly without warning, the old foreboding would show up. I'd wake up with it.*

*I'd talk to myself incessantly trying to think positive thoughts but sometimes in vain. Both my ego and my brain chemistry have their own force and often win out. During those times I even forget that my soul has chosen this experience before I incarnated in order to assist me in my spiritual evolution. Instead, at best I am grasping at the tools I have honed just to get me through another day, minute by minute.*

*Right now I'm in one of my good places. A place where optimism reigns. I am loving my work, my friends, my choir, my writing, my pets, my just-about-everything. For the majority of this calendar year I have felt grounded, relaxed, happy, motivated, confident and in good spirits. My groups and therapy clients help to ground me and keep me honest and sane. I love what I do. I believe I am living my life's purpose. I'm in one of those places where I am filled with gratitude for being so abundantly blessed. It's during times like this that I take myself less seriously and can relate to a poem I wrote years ago. I wrote it to help me through one of those dark times and it became a song that was performed in* Madness, Masks and Miracles. *I thought about all the phobias and fears that we all seem to have – me, my clients – the world! As much as I honour and respect the feelings that come up for me and others when the fear and panic takes over, from this perspective, you just have to laugh!*

## Phobia Song

*Fear of dying and afraid of life*
*Fear of flying and afraid of strife*
*Fear of losing and afraid to win*
*Goodness-gracious where does one begin!*

*Claustrophobia, agoraphobia and phobias we can't spell*
*Pathophobia, xenophobia, hydrophobia, zoophobia*
*We know 'em well.*
*Now what would Freud or Jung say*
*If they were in this room*
*Their likely fear would be to get out of here*
*In case they caught the gloom!*

*Are we crazy; no we're not,*
*We're simply concerned by what we've got*
*Fear of hunger, afraid of fat*
*Fear of wars, chores and doors*
*Can you imagine that!*

*Fear of Satan and afraid of God*
*Is there anything here we're not afraid of?*
*Between our birth and dying,*
*We have so much to fear*
*Was God, do you think, in His right mind*
*To ever have put us here!*

*Fear of cats and afraid of snakes*
*Fear of laughter for goodness sakes*
*Fear of aging or growing too tall*
*Face it. If it's not worth fearing, is it worth it at all?*

*Afraid of getting out of bed, a fear of eternal sin*
*Afraid of germs, afraid of worms, afraid of your own kin!*
*Afraid of black, afraid of white, afraid of in-between*
*Afraid of going out alone, afraid of being seen.*

*Are we crazy, well maybe yes*
*You decide. It's anyone's guess*
*Are we crazy, well maybe not*
*Isn't it something that everyone's got?*
*La la la la la la la*
*La la la la la la la*
*Crazy, crazy, crazy?*
*Who us!!*

# *Let's Write*

Another type of death is the death of the spirit. You may recall times in your life when you were walking around like a mechanical pulse machine – going through the motions but with no life energy, depressed and hopeless. This is also akin to a death. Many of us have experienced such times.

If this is true for you, go to a time in your life when you felt like your spirit had died. A time when getting out of bed in the morning seemed like an insurmountable task. It was almost impossible because you felt so unmotivated, so lacking in life energy. Possibly you were terrified. You felt you had nothing to look forward to. Maybe your body was wracked with anxiety. Perhaps you felt like a burden to others. Perhaps you felt hopeless and that life was meaningless. Depression was part of every breathing moment. Maybe you were furious about it all but too tired to fight. Once again, I encourage you to use the Centering Exercise found in Book 1, Part C and/or the Invocation found in Book 1, Part D, before venturing into this story.

What do you remember about that time? What stands out for you the most? What were the circumstances that preceded your feeling this way? Did something in particular happen? A crisis? A series of painful events? What happened? See it on the screen. Do not embody this image. Remember, you are a safe distance from it. Simply witness it from the safety of your chair in the movie theatre in your mind. Who was in your life at that time? Do you need to use your lever to make the picture smaller, larger – turn the volume up or down? Who were your supports? Friends, family, strangers? Did this time bring you closer to your own sense of spirituality – your trust in the Universe, in God or did you feel abandoned?

Sometimes, for me, my inner life was abundantly rich, but I had no frame of reference for it in my outer life...the life that was asking for performance and making sense. I had no words to articulate the invisible paralysis that engulfed my body and mind when I tried to relate to the outer world – the one with all the comings and goings. It was all but impossible but somehow I would relentlessly fake it. Yes, fake it until the final showdown when even faking it was impossible. How was it for you? Look at yourself in this picture frame, at the gut wrenching pain at having to pretend all was well to a world that lacked understanding or maybe it didn't but you felt too much shame to test the waters. A time when you felt hopeless or had a total lack of energy. I want you now to please insert onto the screen a different picture. Imagine and feel your loving adult-self embracing the younger you – it may be years younger or maybe only months – but you are holding your hand or rocking yourself gently with unconditional love and compassion for the despair and anguish that you carried. Breathe in the comfort of this.

Now, on the screen, allow the images to unfold of the ways you came through this time. What did you do? What happened? Who were the supports you had in your life? Perhaps strangers showed up as your special angel guides. Perhaps old friends and relatives or new ones were there for you. How did they make a difference? Maybe it was you relying solely on yourself or your Higher Self. And as you look back from today's perspective, what special strengths did you harness at that time that perhaps you didn't think you could? Breathe. Now on the screen imagine and feel yourself as strong, vibrant and alive. In fact, sit in your chair right now as if you were feeling excited and passionate about life. Imagine yourself being passionate about writing your life stories. About setting yourself free by speaking your truth on the pages. The very act of doing this creates a physiological "being-ness" – a shift whereby you raise your vibration and experience feelings of well-being. Breathe in from this place of strength. In what ways are you stronger than you thought? How did you become the phoenix rising from your very own ashes? Are there things you learned about yourself that you can recognize now that you are on the other side of this soul-wrenching experience? Are there tools and resources that you have that will prevent you from going into long bouts of despair again? Do you reach out? Are there people you can call? Are you eating and sleeping well? Do you find yourself uplifted while in nature? In what ways do you take care of your precious self? Once again, see yourself as strong, vibrant and alive. Breathe in the miracle of the moment and enjoy this poem. I wrote it when, after another bout of depression, I learned to breathe in another reality – the reality of the Wonder of Now.

# Now Is All There Is

*You can talk about yesterday or talk about tomorrow*
*You can talk about the falling dollar, talk about your sorrow*
*You can talk about chemicals and how they're poisoning the earth*
*You can talk about how bad it is and how it's getting worse*

*Or you can take this moment and softly close your eyes*
*Breathe a breath from deep within and do not compromise*
*Take another and then another and in the stillness feel*
*The wonder of this moment – can this too be real?*

*Stay within the silence and notice what you hear*
*Listen with your heart and watch your fears all disappear*
*For in this very moment, a miracle is due*
*If you listen with your heart there will be a message just for you.*

*A child is being born right now; can you hear the sound of life*
*In a little church just down the way vows are being made as husband and wife*
*Somewhere on a hilltop a traveler has found her way*
*And the dew upon the morning grass has welcomed a brand new day.*

*Stay within this moment for the miracle is here*
*There's nothing that you need to do, nothing but be sincere*
*Life is bursting forth in every breath and in the stillness find*
*A place to love, a place to join with every heart and mind.*

*Rejoice for in this moment you can send blessings near and far*
*Rejoice for in this moment you are a living star*
*And every time you feel afraid and wonder what to do*
*Come back to this one moment and know the miracle is you.*

What surfaces for you from this chapter? Are you ready to describe the times you felt hopeless as well as the times that saw you through to the other side?

Once again, go to your writing table and begin to write into the feelings that are with you now. Be open to any new insights that might reveal themselves.

# Chapter 18

## LETTING GO

## Resist or Accept– Always a Choice

by June Swadron

*Letting go used to be one of the hardest challenges of my life. Some people would say, "How can that be when you move around so often? You have had many relationships, many homes, lived in so many cities, countries. How can letting go be a challenge for you?"*

*Perhaps it's because it's my Cancerian nature. It's noted that Cancers are tenacious. That's about holding on – the opposite of letting go. Welcome to the paradox of my life.*

*A friend commented to me the other evening, "June, how is it that people can fall in love again and again? I was so shy in high school. I married the first man I dated and that wasn't until I was twenty seven. When that ended I had a brief relationship with another man for a couple of years and nothing since for 13. I've known you only a year and yet you've just left a relationship with Stephan. There was Lucas who you were living with in Korea before that. And there were others. How do people do that?"*

*That got me thinking. What causes me to move as often as I do? What is that sense of completion of where I am that draws me to move outward and away from someone or somewhere and begin all over again? My oldest sister has lived with her same husband of forty-nine years in the same house they bought at least thirty years ago. Mind you, before I moved West, I was in the same home for 16 years. Since then I've moved more times than I can count.*

*How many times have I yearned to know home? One home. And yet something causes me to move, change. And when that feeling comes upon me it seems impossible to stop it. Besides, everything lines up as though an invisible conspirator, or angel perhaps, is dancing outside in the wings, manipulating all events to bring me effortlessly, and with much enthusiasm I might add, to my next destination.*

*Once there, and somewhat settled from the unpacking, making it all look like home again, the unrest of "what next" eventually sets in and I'm out again collecting boxes.*

*I never used to think of myself as a rebel but I suppose in some ways I have been. I did not do what society had expected of me years ago. I did not marry out of high school like my sisters did. My best friend and I spoke for years about travelling together long before it was popular for girls to do such things. We were barely 19 and we did it. We flew to New York from Toronto in the early fall of 1970. Then we walked aboard a student ship that sailed 10 days across the Atlantic to Le Havre, France and on to Southampton, England where we docked, got off and stepped into a future that neither of us could have predicted. We intended to be away for a year. It didn't happen. At least not together.*

*This was where the biggest letting go of my young life happened...and it took me years and endless tears to finally let go of the pain.*

*Lisa and I met in grade 2. I don't remember what it was that initially made me follow her until she finally agreed to be my friend. She did and we became inseparable. We walked to school together every day, did our homework together at night and in those long, hot, Toronto summers we hung out with each other in the park behind the apartment buildings where we lived. One summer when I was twelve I was sent to camp and we cried bitter tears in the parting. We wrote to each other every day. We grew into teenagers and double dated.*

*At 18 Lisa got engaged and so did I. Within a year both of our engagements ended and we decided to make our childhood dream come true. Set out on a travel adventure. It didn't unfold the way we envisioned it.*

*Once aboard the ship Lisa stopped talking to me. For 10 unbearable days she ignored me. None of my pleading brought her any closer to telling me what was wrong.*

*In desperation I pretended to have fun with the new friends I was meeting but inside me was an agonizing loneliness. Not until the day we sighted land and were to disembark did Lisa finally let me know what was going on. She was carrying a horrific burden, a dreadful secret that she only felt safe enough to tell me when we got to the other side of the world. (It's her secret so I'm choosing not to share it.) As she spoke she wept and I held her. We wept together. It was beyond what either of us had any experience with or were pre-pared for. It was totally outside our comfort zone and neither of us had the tools to know how to handle it.*

*Within a very short time it brought about the end of our friendship. I re-turned home from Europe a year later with my first experience of clinical de-pression. There were many things that preceded and contributed to that crisis, but none that held the weight of despair like losing Lisa's love.*

*Letting go of her was among the hardest things I ever had to do. Somewhere in the letting go process I wrote this:*

> *"She enters my thoughts out of nowhere and suddenly I'm con-sumed by that familiar longing again – a crippling emptiness that has all the scars of a motherless child – vainly searching shadowed street corners for the one who's never, ever coming back. I suppose I'll go to my grave with this. Therapy and the years have played their bit in assisting to dull the ache but it comes back anyway. It comes back in torrents and floods and then ebbs away again leaving me like the dark-ened streets, desolate and bare.*
>
> *And again someday when I least expect to remember – when I'm doing something menial like ironing a shirt or crossing a street or thinking about buying myself flowers – she'll return in full life-size form and dimensions, equipped with sounds and tastes and smells and the movie projector is running on automatic and we're children again, running in the park and giggling over some silly joke or about one of the teachers at school. The secrets. We told each other all our secrets and shared all of our dreams for what we wanted when we grew up. We shared it all. Teenage tears and fears and the excitement over a new boy. And we sang. How we loved to sing! We knew all the words to every song. Nat King Cole's 'Smile' was ours. And we did everything together. Best friends. We were best friends. Blood sisters. Didn't we cut our index fingers until they bled when we were eight, then rubbed them together and swore an oath to never, ever part. It worked. She lives inside my veins. It's only in the other world she ceases to exist – the one that shows its face to the others. But the woman-child who lives inside me and peeks out only now and again is the one who re-members and she's the one who misses you, Lisa. She's the one who wishes more than anything else in this entire life that you would come back and love her again."*

*It has been 2 decades since I wrote that and the pain has long since sub-sided. I have a flood of loving tenderness when I think of her. Wherever she is, I hope she is happy and fulfilled in her life. As with all experiences, I know they happen to heal and bring us into deeper understanding of ourselves and the world around us. I understand that if we had had the tools, we would have surpassed the crisis that separated us forever. For many years I blamed her for rejecting me but in truth I did that to myself. I locked myself into a coffin of guilt and hopelessness so it was no wonder I became clinically depressed.*

*Letting go has been much easier of late. I've had the death of both my mother and sister in the past year and a half to help me practice. A spiritual tenet that seems to work for me is to accept what is. To fight against what is only creates suffering and unnecessary drama. I can try to hold on but in this temporal world, nothing stays the same. So it helps to remember I have the conscious choice of how to respond to situations. Do I want peace and contentment or do I want to suffer? If I want to suffer I hold on and fight. If I want peace I can accept what is and see the beauty and perfection in all situations. It doesn't mean I don't feel pain or sadness. I do. And then I embrace it and hold compassion for the part of me that is hurting. In the honouring of the pain it dissipates and the letting go process is organic. I don't make it go away, it just does and I move into a state of well-being.*

*When I remember Lisa today, she is like a very long ago dream but one that had a tremendous impact on my life. I learned early about the bitterness of separation and betrayal. I learned of guilt and anguish. It took years to stop re-enacting the same patterns. Hopefully I have learned enough to pass on what I have learned in a way that can assist in lessening someone else's pain.*

*Wherever you are Lisa, know you are loved. I am grateful for the gift of remembering us all those years ago and acknowledging where I am today. I am at peace. I pray that you are, too.*

# My Mother's Love

by R.L. Spiro

*My mom is dead. I was at her funeral. I saw her in her hospital bed. Lifeless. Gone. And yet my mom is alive to me. It's in all the eerie, cosmic moments when, just as I am wishing my mom were here with me, her favourite song comes on the radio and there she is. My mom is with me when I hear something funny and the image of she and I sharing the laugher comes to me in a tangible and real way. My mom is just with me. I carry her in my heart. This feeling is what keeps me from drowning in sorrow and regret. It is not denial because the feeling of loss is also real. But somehow I feel that I am being protected from the absolute pain of my mother being dead, by somehow feeling that she is here with me right now. And in some ways, my mom is more unburdened and free now. So much more so than she had been in so many years – years of constant work and stress and disappointment. The mom that is always with me now is filled with light and laughter and flies on the wings of angels and dreams. Somehow, I feel that my mom is protecting me from feeling the total devastating blow of her death. Now how can that make sense to anyone else? Maybe this is a delusional way for me to keep the truth of my mother's tragic death at bay. Maybe as long as I keep up the pretense that she is with me still, then I can continue to avoid thinking about how much she must have suffered those last few weeks of her life. I can also keep myself from thinking about the pain and embarrassment I must have caused her by not rushing home to see her in the hospital until it was too late. By continuing to keep my mother alive in my mind, I can avoid dealing with the anger I feel at everyone for not making me realize that my mother was dying and needed me by her side. It is just easier to not talk to anyone who was actually by my mother's side because they will be the witness to my shame and truth. And so I will continue to keep my mom alive in my heart and in my dreams. I will see her as beautiful and free instead of dying alone in a cold and ineffective hospital room surrounded by strangers – people she would never want to have seen her in that condition and feeling betrayed by the one child she thought she could depend upon. I say these words but I won't allow myself to feel the consequences of their meaning because in my heart my mom knows I am still here for her, loving her with all my heart, breathing everlasting life into her legacy of decency and kindness. This is the magical way I have found for keeping the demons of guilt and regret lurking in the shadows. And if I keep my mom's memory alive through acts of love, then maybe the shadows of pain and remorse will eventually be diminished by the light of truth which is that I love my mom and she loves me and love is eternal.*

# *Let's Write*

Buddha said the cause of all human suffering is attachment. To help the human condition and reduce our suffering, we are often asked and sometimes forced to let go – let go of things, of people, of places where we've lived, of anger, of sorrow, of regret, of our once youthful bodies or our once comfortable socioeconomic status. Sometimes the letting go seems impossible. Sometimes it is as easy as the out breath. Often it comes in stages over time. When I find myself holding onto something I am often reminded that what is, simply is. Resisting what is brings about unnecessary suffering while the acceptance of it ultimately leads to inner peace.

Consider a situation, a time, a person or a place that you had to let go of. Perhaps you are at an age where you are having a hard time letting go of your youth. In our North American culture where so much emphasis is put on being young and that only young is beautiful, especially in advertising, getting older and letting go of one's youthful appearance can be disturbing, even traumatic for some.

There are other reasons to let go. Perhaps when you were a child or teenager you were forced grow up in a hurry. Maybe you had a sick parent and you were required to look after him or her as well as younger siblings. You had to let go of your youth.

Perhaps your letting go was of a dream – a walk down the aisle that didn't happen, or travel plans that went awry. Maybe your letting go had something to do with an educational achievement you hoped to accomplish but other things got in the way. Or perhaps it was a promotion that someone else got instead of you. Maybe it was letting go of an ideal or a particular belief. Did you ever have someone close to you move away and you had to let go of relying on him or her being there for you? Or did you have a friendship that ended in tears and regrets? And of course, when a precious pet or someone we dearly love passes away, that is the ultimate letting go.

As you recall a particular time in your life when you had to let go of someone or something, portray what the process was like for you. Describe if you were able to turn the page easily or if it took you a long time to move on. If so, what was it that helped you to finally let go. Perhaps you're still holding on to something today that no longer serves you. Are you ready to take a step toward letting it go? Write deeply into the heart of your situation. Find the courage to stay with the truth and let it carry you as far as you need to go for you to set yourself free. What story comes to mind? Breathe deeply. Bring a glass of water to your writing table and gently begin to write.

# *Chapter 19*

# HOLIDAYS

## Children Are Our Best Teachers

by R.L. Spiro

*This is a story of how I learned not to stress the small stuff especially when it feels like big stuff.*

*For the past few months, we have been witnessing a historic low in the stock market and high unemployment rates. Even though I religiously live within my means, the unsettling feeling that accompanies economic woe seems to be contagious. Or could it be the simple fact that with four growing children and the Holiday season upon us, I am feeling the stress of the financial responsibilities of my blessed life? Or could it be that we don't have insurance and I have spent the last month taking my kids and their inherited cavity prone teeth to the dentist?*

*(Considering the fact that I deny my kids most of the sugar that they seem to inherently crave, it seems like a cruel joke of the universe that our healthy diet doesn't pay off in cavity free living. But I digress.) In fact, I had just spent two and a half hours under the drill of the dentist, the harsh light seeming to illuminate my anxieties and stresses, as I spent the hours making mental lists of the gifts and items I needed to purchase for the upcoming holiday party at our home.*

*The noise of the drill still hadn't faded from my ears, but I could not block out the shock I felt when they told me how much my precious teeth were about* to cost me. Now I know why they call it a crown, because you have to be royalty to afford such things! After an afternoon of stress, I was grateful that my husband was home making dinner and taking care of the kids.

This day seemed to be all about facing up to my dreaded responsibilities, first my teeth and now the pre-Christmas Department store. But after the dental experience, shopping didn't seem so scary.

From the look of things at the store, you'd never know that we were in a recession, but I spent a painful amount of time talking myself out of items, searching for the best deals and taking things out of my cart when a better deal was seized. The sound of the drill had been replaced with the sound of department store noises and my nerves were still frayed. As my list grew shorter and my shopping cart began to overflow I began to feel the thrill of the hunt. And then I saw the checkout lines. Feeling the need for speed, I rushed to take my place in the smallest line and took my first break of the day. I grabbed the juiciest looking gossip magazine while waiting to pay for my purchases.

After helping the frazzled cashier pile all my consumer goods into my cloth bags, I noticed the huge line behind me and was grateful that the lady behind me seemed to be the most patient person on this planet. And then it happened – every shopper's nightmare!

My VISA that I religiously pay in full each month was declined. The betrayal was brutal but I was not without means. The Aeroplan points would have to wait. I reached for my old reliable friend, the debit card. A quick swipe of the card and I would be on my way home to my happy household. Or so I thought, until the nervous looking cashier informed me that my debit card was also declined.

This could not be happening! I stole a quick glance at the growing line behind me and proceeded to call my husband for help. He went on line to our internet banking and reminded me that I had already exceeded my daily limit due to the enormous dental costs. He also let me know that for some reason VISA had not yet acknowledged my payment.

I felt the tears forming along with perspiration as the manager was called to the checkout. I was told that there was absolutely no lay-away and my only option was to unpack my environmentally friendly bags and get the heck out of there as soon as possible. I turned to apologize to the lady in line behind me who had by now finished reading every magazine on the rack. She looked at me with kindness and said: "Tomorrow is a new day; your daily spending can start again tomorrow."

I told her that any other person would be yelling at me to get going and how grateful I was for her kindness. I still felt like crying as I unpacked my huge cart of what I thought were my belongings. Oh the time I had wasted. It seemed so unfair, to think that I would have to start all over again tomorrow. The feeling of shame and embarrassment felt like more than I could handle. I *took my empty bags back to the comfort and privacy of my car and had a good cry.*

*Now, I would like to say that I was a grounded person who knew how not to sweat the small stuff but I could feel the sweat of my shame against the cold winter night. In my mind this was no small catastrophe. You might think that I would have had the perspective to count my blessings and realize that it was no big deal. After all, I am one of the lucky people who had the warmth of my automobile and the financial savings to try again tomorrow. In fact, any sane person would have laughed at the silliness of this situation, but it took me a little longer to gain my perspective. It took the reaction of my three year old for me to regain my sense of humour.*

*As I pulled the car up into our driveway, I was met by my children waiting for me at the living room window. My three-year-old's blessed little ballerina soul was doing the happiest "Mommy's home" dance I had ever seen!*

*My thirteen year old came out into cold night without any coat, just to help me in with my bags. I told her briefly what happened. She turned to me, gave me the biggest, warmest hug and said, "Mom, its o.k. We're just glad that you're home."*

*And so there it was, my moment of truth, when I realized that nothing in that department store could give me what my children had just shared with me for free. For the icing on the cake, the house had the wonderful aroma of a home cooked meal made by my devoted husband.*

*Now my perspective was restored. My humour was restored as well when my three year old took the time to look inside each empty cloth bag for goodies and, when she found nothing, started putting her toys into the bags instead.*

*I realized that all we really needed, we already had in each others' love. And that is how I learned not to sweat the small stuff.*

*p.s. I did go back to the department store the next day and purchased their gifts. When my bank card was approved, I sighed a breath of relief, counted my blessings and smiled as I headed home.*

*Life with children is the best opportunity to learn the meaning of love and love the meaning of life.*

## Six Months 'Til Christmas

by June Swadron

*December 16, 1992*
*I remember on June 25th, my father would say "Six month's 'til Christmas."*
*On September 25th he'd say, "Only 3 months 'til Christmas." He was always*
*using Christmas as this pivotal point for something. The beginning of some-*
*thing. End of something. Something. I used to laugh because being Jewish,*
*Christmas meant nothing in our home. But neither did Hanukah. Well, not*
*since I was very young – seven or eight. Christmas lights and cut out snow-*
*flakes adorned the windows of neighbours' houses, not ours. But I stopped*
*the lonely pattern. I started decorating trees with my Christian friends. My*
*boyfriend's Christian. Protestant, I think. We have a tree in the living room.*
*It stands next to the Chanukah menorah. Both are symbols of happiness and*
*light. Our home is not happy. I wish it wasn't December and I didn't have to*
*pretend.*

# *Let's Write*

More than any other holiday, Christmas is the one that is celebrated the most in hundreds of countries around the world. In the country where I live, Canada, December 25th is a mixed bag. On one hand, it is the time of remembering the birth of Christ and all that stands for – peace, love, forgiveness, doing unto others as you would have them do unto you, good tidings, family gatherings, turkey dinners, gift giving, Midnight Mass, caroling, decorating trees and putting up Christmas lights to herald in the season.

But far more often than not, this is not the case. I just heard on the radio the other day that in Bethlehem pilgrims are gathering (It is December 11th , 2008 as I write this) but on every street corner and on top of buildings are armed soldiers to ensure the peace. Local people do not go out at this time. The streets are too dangerous.

And here on the North American continent Christmas is a time of madness, stress, depression and a yearning for what it symbolizes. This is especially true when money is scarce and it's difficult to buy gifts for the people you love, or when family gatherings are something that 'other people' do but not you. Perhaps your family members are far away from each other and haven't been under one roof for years. Or perhaps they live in close proximity but are totally dysfunctional or estranged. Christmas time may mean putting on a lot of false smiles and wishing in your heart that it were different.

Also the darkness at this time of year is a huge factor contributing to S.A.D. (Seasonal Affective Disorder).

Depression and loneliness reign at this time of year.

If this is true for you, I highly suggest you reach out to at least one person. Please do not isolate yourself. Why not volunteer at one of the food banks or dinners that are put on for the homeless by the Salvation Army or other agencies? Sometimes there is nothing that will lift our spirits higher than when we are lifting them higher for others.

Last year I had a wonderful gift at Christmas. I live in a small apartment on a peaceful street and the building I live in is filled with many friendly people. On Christmas Eve I heard loud voices outside my door. This was quite startling as it was the first time I ever encountered that. I opened my door and saw an open door to the apartment directly across the hall. The young man and woman who lived there, who I had not met as they had only recently moved in, were shouting and throwing things. Then they punched one another. It was serious. I immediately ran to the property manager's apartment and told her what was going on. In the meantime my neighbours slammed their door shut. We knocked and they wouldn't answer. The shouting continued. We knocked louder. They finally opened the door and the manager said, "Stop this immediately or I will call the police."

At that moment I was inspired to go into my apartment and get a candle. I found a beautiful white candle and lit it and walked into their living room. In the middle of the chaos, I said, "Hey guys, this is Christmas Eve and this is a candle of peace. How 'bout a time out?" They seemed stunned. In the pause, I offered the man the candle. I caught him off guard and he took it. He held it awkwardly. Then I said, "Would you like a hug?" Again he looked stunned but quietly, in almost a whisper he said, "Yes." I immediately hugged him and he began to cry. He simply wept as I, a total stranger, held him. At the same time, my manager was hugging the woman. An aura of love and peace enveloped their living room. After a few moments, the man left my embrace and walked over to his partner and took her in his arms. We quietly left.

Now this is what I call a Christmas story. The kind I trust and believe in. (And we don't have to wait for Christmas). I believe in the indomitable human spirit – the one that seeks out kindness. I was inspired to get the candle. If I had to think about it, I probably wouldn't have done what I did. I don't think I'd go into the middle of a physical fight and try to break it up. I didn't "try" to do anything. I just acted as I felt directed to in the moment and a miracle took place. It was Divine Inspiration that led me to take that action which melted the fury that was taking place between two people. A little amount of love goes a long, long way.

What does Christmas or the holiday season mean to you? Write about some of your favourite memories. Write into your truth – either the joy or the sadness or both.

Here is another exercise you may want to consider. Write what you envision a peaceful, joyful holiday would look like. Write about it in first person, present tense as though it were happening right now. See it on the screen of your mind bringing in all the details of how you would like it to be. See it, feel it, smell, taste and touch it. Get excited about it. This is a method of intentioning something in order to make it real in your mind. Remember this is about "Re-Writing Your Life". You can Re-Write your script for the holidays by focusing on your highest vision. At the end of this exercise, surrender it and let it go.

# Chapter 20

## RE-WRITE YOUR LIFE:
## THE HIGHEST VISION YOU HOLD FOR
## YOURSELF

NOW THAT you have gone through the exercises in this book and written your life stories, you have probably noticed a common theme. That theme is to see the fuller meaning of the many stories that have made up your life, impacting how you experience the present moment.

Those stories have also impacted the story you have been telling yourself about your future.

Now you can consciously and deliberately choose how you want the next stories of your life to be. You can consider the qualities that have the greatest meaning for you – things such as caring, kindness, love, joy, good health, abundance, generosity of spirit, meaningful work, harmonious community, devoted friendships and a loving primary relationship.

Everything we see in the physical world has been in someone's imagination first. In our imagination, the sky's the limit. This final chapter is about writing the highest vision you hold for your life – your life without fear, without limits. I will ask you to be playful – to have fun with your imaginings. Put on your designer hat and go first class. See, feel and believe you will create a happier life. Know that whatever arises in your life you will have a tool to get through it all – you can Re-Write the story.

Everyone has hard times but it's what we do with the feelings they invoke in us that makes the difference. We can fight what is happening and stay a victim to our feelings and circumstances or we can embrace life by saying YES to whatever shows up. All of it. Imagine that no matter what shows up you are not burdened by it because it just is. Not good. Not bad. Not right. Not wrong. It just is. Can you feel the freedom in this?

In this exercise you will write down your heart's desires. And here is the key – write them down as though they are happening right now. Not in the future, but now. Write in first person, present tense. Bring it fully into the Now. Make it real. Get excited about it. Passionate about it. Experience your dream in every living cell of your being.

Twelve years ago I attended an eight-day intensive personal growth retreat. Every day they asked us to write down the vision for our life in the same fashion – first person, present tense. At the time I was living in Toronto. I had a successful psychotherapy practice and was facilitating three groups a week. I was settled in my life but I also knew I had an underlying dream to move to the West Coast. It had been with me for many years but I never really thought I'd actually move there – especially after I had established a healthy career where I was. During those eight days I was writing from a deeper place within me. I was paying attention to the details of what my life really could look like if I followed that long ago dream. By the eighth day I was writing that I was living and working in Vancouver and living and thriving in a like-minded community of people on a spiritual path of creativity and growth. It felt so real I could almost taste it.

One year later, almost to the day I was living that dream and am still living it 11 years later. Every day I wake up and walk along the ocean and am surrounded by mountains. On some of my walks I see herons, hummingbirds, eagles, seals and sea otters. I am also blessed with a community of wonderful friends just as I imagined it.

Writing down our dreams brings clarity and with clarity we know in which direction we want to move. Often the Universe will support us in our efforts when we align ourselves in our hearts and minds for the greatest good of all concerned. We live in a benevolent universe that wants us to be happy and live our full potential.

# *Let's Write*

Once again, this is the story of your life that you have yet to live, although you will be visualizing it as though you are living it right now.

The Law of Attraction states that the Universe responds to that which we focus on. In other words, whatever we focus on grows. Our thoughts will create our reality. Be passionate about the life you are intending and imagine it all as if you are living it now.

An important thing to remember is once you focus on your happy dream, let it go. Surrender it to the Universe. Don't worry about how it's going to happen.

You are about to play a movie on the screen of your mind where you are the main character. You are also the writer and the director. This is a movie of The Highest Vision You Hold For Yourself. If you choose to say YES to this experience, don't be surprised when synchronicities start showing up. You are planting the seeds that will create your life the way you've always dreamed it could be. For now suspend disbelief and put any suspicions or pessimistic thoughts on hold. Dare to dream your highest dream to live the life you truly would love to live. Okay, let's begin!

On the screen, see yourself waking up in the morning feeling rested, at peace and happy to begin a brand new day. Notice you have excited anticipation for what the day will bring. You are like an innocent child, waking with enthusiasm for what you will discover today. You don't know what will happen, but are willing to live in the mystery – with an open heart.

Envision your health. What is it like? How are you living to support the level of health that you desire? Are you eating delicious, nutritious food? Are you participating in a fun fitness program? Are you getting restful sleep, taking time to pamper yourself? See this on the screen and feel the experience fully.

Look at the supports in your life – your friends. Who are they? What are you experiencing with them? Are you laughing with friends, having heart to heart conversations, enjoying favourite activities together, honouring each other with your love, compassion, humour, and thoughtfulness? See this on the screen.

Now focus on your family: parents, siblings, children, grandchildren. Are you enjoying one another and feeling comfortable together? Are you communicating in loving ways in spite of what worldly differences you may carry? Remember this is your highest vision. In this realm all things are possible. Allow the Universe to provide you with all you have dreamed of for yourself.

What about a loving relationship? Describe your true love. What are the special qualities about this person that you would love or already do love the most? Do you see or sense the two of you on the screen cherishing each other, devoted to one another, feeling safe, relaxed, happy? Perhaps you don't want a partner. That's okay too. Just fill in the screen the way you want it.

Next on the screen, if appropriate, place yourself in a work or career environment – a place where your work is your pleasure, your passion. See yourself enjoying the service you are providing and being highly valued for it. Are you earning top dollars and fully appreciated for what you give? Perhaps you are doing volunteer work – see yourself uplifting those around you.

What is your relationship with nature? Is relaxing in nature a joyful part of your lifestyle? If so, see yourself in the ideal spot, the place in nature where your spirit feels at home. It may be somewhere you've been before, or somewhere your imagination takes you to for the first time. Embrace the vision. Feel the wonder and glory of this majestic place. Let it fill you up with tranquility, inspiration and wonder.

What about your relationship with The Creator, God, your Higher Power or whatever name you use? Do you see yourself quietly meditating or connecting with this Divine Energy in another way? Do you feel yourself being uplifted, supported and tranquil?

And how do you make yourself happy? What things do you like to do on your own that bring joy to your life? See yourself doing them. Continue to project onto the screen all the pictures that will fulfill your life in the best way possible.

Open yourself now to the unexpected. Live in the mystery patiently. Allow for Divine Timing as well as Divine Intervention where everything is orchestrated to bring you to your highest good.

And most importantly, knowing that our lives are made up of circumstances that can bring us joy as well as circumstances that have the potential to make us feel sad, frightened, angry or disappointed; in this vision, imagine yourself handling whatever circumstances may come your way with ease and equanimity. You have the tools, the support, the balance, the foresight and wisdom to move through events with confidence. In fact you are a role model for others when it comes to moving through tricky and difficult situations. You are at peace with yourself. You are the eye of the storm. You live your life in the rainbow of promise. You see all challenges as opportunities for growth. No matter what shows up you are not burdened by it because it just is.

Now take a deep breath and get ready to write your Happy Dream. You may cluster the different categories if you choose. What is important here, when you begin to write your story, is to remember to do so in first person, present tense as though you are living it right now. Be passionate about it. Then give it over. Let go, knowing the Universe is supporting you in every way. Begin.

# In Conclusion

ONGRATULATIONS! You did it! You have written your stories. What a stunning accomplishment! I truly acknowledge you for your willingness to go back into your past, to visit old circumstances and events – pleasant and unpleasant – and to give yourself the gift of honouring your life.

It is through this journey of self-reflection that we come to see the full meaning of our lives and the growth that we have achieved over the years. We can look at all the people who have come into our lives who brought us love, comfort and encouragement. And we can also see with increased clarity all the people who entered our lives presenting challenges thus giving us an opportunity to heal our hearts and move forward.

And congratulations for Re-Writing Your Life into the highest vision you hold for yourself. For writing your happy dream – the life you wish for.

As we come to the conclusion of this rich, rewarding experience, I offer this final exercise. Take some time to re-read the stories you have written. Be with them awhile and acknowledge how far you have come. Acknowledge your strengths and how courageous you have been to move through some very difficult times. As you read through your stories, bless your life, all of the experiences in it and all the people who have walked this journey with you.

Take time to write down what you consider to be some of the most important lessons you have learned along the way. In what way can the wisdom you have gained from these life events assist you as you go into the future? What would you like to remember the next time you have a challenging experience?

Thank you for taking this courageous walk with me. May all your future stories be blessed with love, harmony and joy beyond measure.

Love,
June

We shall not cease from exploration
And the end of all our exploring
Will be to arrive where we started
And know the place for the first time.

T.S. Eliot

# Appendix A

# Contributing Writers

**Warren Bailey**: *This is Who I am* – Chapter 15
bailey2668@yahoo.ca

**Ella Brown**: *Child Free* – Chapter 12

**Melba Burns**: *Trust In Me* – Chapter 14
soulwrites@telus.net
www.wooyourwriterwithin.com

**Nancy Campbell**: *Time to Tell* – Chapter 3,
*Birth Days* – Chapter 8
*See Me* – Chapter 17
nancampbell@shaw.ca

**Teya Danel**: *An Almost Fatal Car Crash that Changed My Life Forever* –
Chapter 15
Book Cover Layout & Design
teyad@shaw.ca

**Carol Jean**: *Dear Sister* – Chapter 11

**Joy Emmanuel**: *A Little Rock and an Unfinished Poem* – Chapter 7
joye@telus.net

**Christie Eng**: *No Going Back* – Chapter 5

**Ange Frymire**: *Jesse* – Chapter 4
ange-frymire@shaw.ca

**Pearl Graham**: *I Honour My Mother* – Chapter 10
www.pearlgraham.com

**Esther Hart**: *Hitting the Brick Wall* – Chapter 6
          *It's Okay to Love Your Father* – Chapter 9
Heart Solutions
esther@estherhart.com
www.heartsolutions.com; www.heartsolutionsblog.blogspot.com

**Deborah Hawkey**: *One September Morning* – Chapter 15
writeitright@shaw.ca

**Eric Hellman**: *Glimpses on a Spiritual Journey* – Chapter 7
EricHellman@shaw.ca
www.EricHellman.com

**Michele Hibbins**: *Perpetually Pissed and Beyond* –
Chapter 13
msantosha@gmail.com

**Azim Jamal**: *Accounting For Business to Accounting For Life* – Chapter 6
www.azimjamal.com

**Julia Jirik:** *Cherished* – *Chapter 4*
juliajirik444@hotmail.com

**Debbi Jones**: *One Step at a Time* – Chapter 3

**Rebecca Kennel**: *Welcome Little* One – Chapter 8
rebecca@rkc.ca
www.rkc.ca

**Annie Lavack**: *Blessings Along the Way* – Chapter 1
 *It's Never Too Late to Be Born* – Chapter 8
www.TheSpiritualArtOfLiving.com
annielavack@gmail.com

**Janet Lawson**: *Recuerdos De La Alhambra* – Chapter 3
    *Nothing But Acceptance* – Chapter 14
**Doris Trinh Lewis**: *The Metal Beast* – Chapter 5
revdoris@unityvictoria.ca

**Shoshana Litman**: *Birthing Our Children, Birthing Ourselves* – Chapter 12
info@maggidah.com
www.maggidah.com

**Tom Little**: *Now I Lay You Down to Sleep* – Chapter 10
(Excerpt from a short story of the same name) copyright Thomas James Little 1998 & 2009, Vancouver, BC.
atomik@shaw.ca

**Michael MacGowan**: *The Architects Dream* – Chapter 7
michael.macgowan@yahoo.com

**Judy McIlmoyl**: *The Key* – Chapter 13
    *The Legacy* – Chapter 10

**Nikki Menard**: *When Will I* – Chapter 17
Book Cover – Original Artwork, Layout & Design
nikkimenard@hotmail.com

**Marya Nijland**: *These Hands* – Chapter 1

**Sharon Pocock**: *The Key* – Chapter 2
    *Counting Down the Years* – Chapter 9
    *Masks* – Chapter 10
sjpocock1@gmail.com

**Robert J. Saffer**: *Hi Memes, Bobby Here* – Chapter 16
Author of the novel, *Crazy Pants*
www.livedproductions.com

**Steve Silvers**: *The Day My Father Died* – Chapter 16
stevesilvers1@aol.com

**R.L. Spiro**: *My Mother's Love* – Chapter 18
     *Children Are Our Best Teachers – Chapter 19*

**Anne Sture Tucker**: *The Pain and the Relief* – Chapter 5
www.annesturetucker.com
**Nathalie Vachon**: *Bring Me All of Your Dreams* – Chapter 4
*Yellow Bird* – Chapter 13
info@nathalievachon.com
www.nathalievachon.com

**June Swadron:** *Silent Prayer* – vii
     *Opening to Grace* – Book 1, Part A – Chapter 2
     *Finding the Gift* – Book 1, Part A – Chapter 3
     *Rejoicing in the Union of Love* – Book 2, Chapter 1
     *Mr. Logan, an Angel of Kindness* – Chapter 2
     *The Creation of* Madness, Masks and Miracles – Chapter 3
     *Seoul, Korea* – Chapter 5
     *Two Love Letters* – Chapter 11
     *From Grief and Sorrow to Relief and Liberation* – Chapter 11
     *Screaming Through the Silence* – Chapter 13
     *I Love You, I Love You More* – Chapter 16
     *Goodbye Papa* – Chapter 16
     *Cats Know* – Chapter 17
     *Bi-polar Blues* – Chapter 17
     *A Higher Purpose* – Chapter 17
     *Phobia Song* – Chapter 17
     *Now Is All There Is* – Chapter 17
     *Resist or Accept – Always a Choice* – Chapter 18
     *Six Months 'Til Christmas* – Chapter 19

# Appendix B

# Re-Write Your Life
# Writing Workshops

R

E-WRITE YOUR *Life* has been born out of the hundreds of hours June spent with students guiding them in writing and sharing their life stories. It offers a deep and powerful process that acknowledges one's life journey. As well as celebrating the good times, this unique writing experience empowers you, the reader and the writer, to make peace with your past so you can rejoice in your life today. The themes and memory prompts found throughout this book are the same as those used in June's workshops *Sacred Stories, Celebrating Your Life Journey. Re-Write Your Life* is based on these hugely successful workshops. Read the testimonials in Appendix B.

This book has been written so that June's powerful tools can reach an unlimited number of people.

If you can't get to one of June's workshops in beautiful Victoria, BC you may be able to participate in a workshop with June in one of two ways:

> ➤ By presenting a *Re-Write Your Life* workshop in your area. To do so please send an email to june@juneswadron.com including your contact name and phone number as well as any other relevant information.
> ➤ By attending her workshop teleseminars. Go to www.juneswadron.com to learn more and to register.

# TESTIMONIALS

The following are testimonials given by participants who attended June Swadron's "Sacred Stories, Celebrating Your Life Journey" writing workshops. The testimonials reflect the participants' responses to June's loving guidance and the results achieved from writing their life stories as well as from sharing them out loud in a group setting.

"Sacred Stories was such an amazing experience for me. To write my stories was transforming and afterwards to have the opportunity to share the stories with the group as my benevolent witnesses was a powerful and incredible experience. It is such a gentle and respectful way to work with the painful parts and a wonderful way to celebrate all of what life is. June is a fabulous facilitator, warm, gentle and wise. I am going to give the stories to my children when they are older. It is absolutely the best gift I have given myself in years!"

**Anne Tucker**

"I had no idea that writing my life stories would allow me to sift through the contents of my life to find all that is truly precious about this journey. I have moved from a place of not valuing my own life's experiences to understanding that I am on a wonderful and sacred path. Writing has brought me to a place of peace and joy."

**Nan Campbell**

"I had been blocked for years. My stories have needed to be told...to be unburdened. I am living with so much more vitality and truth. I am celebrating my life. All of it. My God, I thank you!"

**Catherine Friedberg-Val004ederes**

"Hi June, I have to tell you about the most amazing things that are happening. When I heard my inner voice last summer say, "This is stress," that was all I needed to know. My doctors are dealing with my Parkinson's disease, I'm dealing with stress. After that, I looked on the internet for Post Traumatic Stress Disorder and found many of the symptoms were the same as Parkinson's. I am attributing a lot of the improvement I am feeling these days to your class. Reading and writing my stories, addressing the pain from my past, is getting it out of my system and I am feeling so much better. Your class is having a significant impact on my physical and emotional health. Thank you."

**Deborah Hawkey**

"The opportunity for closure of long-held grievances and unresolved issues is invaluable. You have a truly wondrous gift for establishing intimate, spirit nurturing environments. I felt the presence of the angels and sages about us at each meeting of our circle."

**Judy Anderson**

"Thank you for the peacefulness, safety and nurturing you provided. Also the memory prompts were meditations that brought me deep into my own stories. You were always uplifting and inspiring. I would highly recommend your class to people who are ready to move forward in their lives and truly let go and make peace with their past."

**Teya Danel**

"Our class is one of the highlights of my week...'writing ourselves/ myself home' is a very apt description. Thank you for listening to your soul and bringing this experience to life. There is magic here and I am grateful to share it with you and the others."

**Annie Lavack**

"Wow! Truly it has been divine order that I am in this writing class. I appreciate the process you guide us through to come 'home' to ourselves. Your encouragement, gentle caring and acceptance provide the guide rail along the path. Thank you for being that presence of realness and healing for me. Thank you for your gift. I praise God for you."

**Rev. Doris Trinh Lewis**

"Thank you so much for creating this class. It's been an incredible journey charting our sacred stories this way. You guide us all with so much warmth, sincerity and wisdom. I feel blessed to be on this path with you. This group provides a safe haven for exploring the wonders that emerge out of chaos. Together we are bringing forth something new in a creative way not yet explored. What a gift."

**Shoshana Litman**

"Supporting. Encouraging. Attentive. You know how to create the safe place we need to open up and share our words and stories. This is your gift."

**Rebecca Kennel**

"You offer a wonderful balance of kindness and sensitivity. Thank you for helping me silence my critic and to simply write. I am stronger because of you. You had the courage to show your fears and your struggles. You proved to us that we need not fear our challenges but embrace them. I honour the spirit within you that gently urges us on to places we do not go to alone – making us feel safe and special and loved."

**Debbi Jones**

"June, I appreciate your keen and penetrating insights as well as wit – responding to us always with deep sensitivity. Also your big heart and kindness has encouraged my own heart to open time and again. Thank you for creating an environment where we all may grow and blossom."

**Paul Monfette**

"Thanks again for a wonderful writing course. This is my third and I've loved every minute of it. Your encouragement pepped me up and even when I did not like my own writing as much, you would find something positive to say about it. I treasured that and felt safe. Whenever I write in my journal I'll be thinking of you!"

**Marya Nihland**

"The gift you have given me, and each of us gathered here, June, is that of community. Spirit, creativity, awareness, reflection, silence, love – for each of these, and your guiding star presence, June, I give thanks."

**Judy McIlmoyl**

"It was really good for me to have a place to express myself in writing – to do the actual writing itself and sharing it with the others. You are right, writing has the ability to heal."

**Dre Lavack**

"It truly has been a sacred circle, to be able to go so deep within myself to places that often hurt, to clear the pain and move further into my healing and also to go deep within to revel in my blessings. Then to be witnessed and to witness the others. What a privilege!"

**Rae Bilash**

"One of the great things about your workshop, June, is that it has given me a safe place to open some mental boxes that I'd been sitting on for years and allowed me to give everything a good tidy. The act of writing things out was liberating and illuminating."

**Sharon Pocock**

"I deeply appreciate the way June encourages her students to be comfortable and fearless at the same time. I found that I could go further than I'd expected in my writing, and this course inspired me to continue to work at this craft. I hope to take more courses with June in the future!"

**Melanie Cook**

"This course has given me the opportunity to revisit experiences of joy and pain and to eventually and gradually realize the deep sacred gift of each person and of each experience in my life. And also to take responsibility for all of the reflections of myself these people and experiences have been. Thank you for providing such a healing, safe space to reveal what has been so difficult to express even in private before."

**Rosemary Anderson**

"I wasn't prepared for what happened in your writing class. I wasn't prepared for you. Somehow, through your gentleness, caring and warmth, together with your knowledge and skills, you have created a space where I can feel safe and begin to tell my story in ways not before available to me. Your commitment and total belief in the process, little by little, removed my blocks and barriers to new awareness. Writing, once my survival tool, has now become a gift to be honoured and cherished."

**Anna Danylchuk**

"Thank you for your wonderful writing workshop. It truly helped me to see just how much writing has the ability to clarify, to heal and to comfort. I have loved your wit, your gentle nature, your subtle probing and loving guidance."

**Sasha Collins**

"Who knew that when I embarked on this part of my healing journey ten weeks ago that I would actually be grateful to dredge up the past – but I am. I finally feel freer than I have in a long time. I thank you from the bottom of my heart. God bless you."

**Michelle Lamb**

"Your course, "Sacred Stories", was a real healing time for me. I have to say that it wasn't all that easy for me and I felt like quitting a few times when I was remembering some of my painful past. But I didn't quit. Your gentle encouragement helped me stay with it and I am so grateful I did. I can see the gifts in the stories and also how much I have grown. Thank you."

**Julie Watier**

"At first I was not really sure about this workshop but in the end I am happy to have been a part of it. Thank you for opening your home and heart to us. You provided a safe environment and encouraged us –

no judgments, but truths. You helped me to believe that I have a story and that it is worth writing down – especially because of the healing that it has brought me. In your sharing it shows how courageous and strong you have been on your journey and that overflowed during our time together. Blessings to you."

**Wendy Kenny**

"Each week you set the tone for healing and loving work. I showed up like a drenched cat, desperate for hope in the latter weeks. And you were there – with kind eyes, with thoughtful words and hope that is real with listening that I have rarely seen in any setting. I hear the Creator and your soul speaking to me and I am so filled with gratitude. You held in there beyond our fears, beyond our resistance, beyond our wanting to hide out. Your determination to be there and not give up on us, on me – is so honourable and loving. You didn't have to do this. You chose to and I am so lucky."

**Laura Lane**

"June Swadron changed my life. Her course, "Sacred Stories, Celebrating Your Life Journey" offered me the opportunity to look at my life compassionately. June is a wonderful, caring Being and Teacher."

**Jaia Friesen**

"I believe June Swadron has the rare gift of originality, both in her work, her teaching methods and her way of life. In her classes, I was able to dust off my cobwebbed imagination and confidence, oil my rusted brain and actually share ALOUD what I had written! An almost otherworldly depth arose for me – high quality fertilizer for my parched mind, heart and soul. I thank you, June, for being a kind and determined angel of art, supporting the best in us all."

**Julia Jirik**

"June, I can't even begin to tell you how much my life has been enriched by taking your two courses. I didn't think that you could improve on "The Artist's Way" but somehow you did it. Doing "The Stories of Our Lives", helped me to see my life from a whole new perspective. Who says I don't have an interesting life!"

**Taylore Co**

"I was especially struck by the events that followed the imagery focused on 'forgiveness'. Not only did I receive a special inspiration during our session, but also I was able to carry that over in my daily life. I feel that an important event has happened to me while participating in your class, and that the effect isn't limited to that space, but like a seed, has started to take root and grow."

**Fiesta de Vries**

"June gave me permission, skills and encouragement to take feelings to thoughts and thoughts to words. My life stories were eddying about. Writing them has opened new spaces inside me and opened the doors and windows on my creativity."

**Christie Eng**

"Taking June Swadron's writing workshop was one of the greatest gifts I've ever given myself. She tapped into my persona by recognizing and nurturing my insecurities as a writer. She was the mid-wife who birthed my writing voice through skill, guidance and inspiration. June was the inkwell who fed my inner pen. My stories blossomed and matured under her expert eye. I am grateful for such commitment, honesty and integrity...and for helping me to find my voice on paper."

**Ange Frymire**